an exciting new world of MICROWAVE COOKING from LITTON

Contents

Pictured on cover: Rolled Rib Roast, page 80, Honey Glazed Carrots, page 122, Hot Dinner Rolls, page 127, and Snow-Capped Custard, page 143.

Pictured: Dinner Menu, pages 28-29 — Ham Slice in Orange Sauce, Simple Scalloped Potatoes, Fresh Broccoli and Fresh Apple Pie which uses combination of microwave and conventional cooking.

Litton

Dear Homemaker:

Convenience, Quality, and Versatility . . . all in the completely new and truly exciting world of microwave cooking from Litton. Our new cookbook will help you to enjoy all of these benefits in addition to appearance and flavor of foods never before possible.

All of the foods illustrated have been prepared in a Litton microwave oven. The recipes have been thoroughly tested and have been tried in homemakers' kitchens.

This cookbook contains every category of cooking that you would expect to find in a family-type cookbook. The versatility of the Litton microwave oven is apparent by just scanning the Table of Contents.

Microwave cooking will make your life easier whether you're cooking for one or a family of six or more. The recipes in this book give you the flexibility to cook for small or large numbers of people at any time of the day.

After carefully reading pages 4-9, choose your first recipes from the Beginning to Cook section. As you become familiar with the oven, begin selecting recipes and planning meals from the balance of the book.

The recipes will satisfy a wide variety of tastes and family styles and be useful for more elaborate occasions as well. You will want to make use of your Litton oven for every meal of the day, particularly those special occasions when entertaining guests.

The cooperation of The Pillsbury Company helped make this book a reality. With the invaluable help of their consumer research, we have developed this book around foods you are now buying and recipes you are presently preparing and we have introduced many exciting new dishes.

We at Litton wish you many delightful experiences in your new world of microwave cookery.

Verna Ludvigson

**Verna Ludvigson
Litton Microwave Cooking Center
Atherton Division
400 Shelard Plaza South
Minneapolis, Minnesota 55426**

WELCOME TO THE WORLD OF MICROWAVE COOKING. Soon it will become as familiar to you as your present cooking routine . . . but what a difference! No long hours of cooking unless you're in the mood; no over-heated kitchen in warm weather; no worries of what to serve unexpected company. Your microwave oven gives you the chance to go simple or fancy in your meals, exactly *when* you want. *You* decide. A new flexibility in your life and the lives of your family.

We have organized the book with the new owner in mind. It is especially important that you read the introductory section (pages 4-9) to become acquainted with your microwave oven and how it works. You didn't learn conventional cooking all in a day so take a little time to learn a few fundamentals and principles of microwave cooking. Try some of the beginning recipes (pages 10-36)— you'll be on your way to carefree cooking.

Use the oven however and whenever it best suits you. This book will give you a good idea just how wide the world of microwave cooking really is. You can use your oven for all three of its functions: for defrosting foods, for primary cooking (using the great variety of recipes in this book) and also for reheating foods . . . all in incredibly short times and achieving a fresh taste in foods. Obviously, your microwave oven won't do all your cooking . . . no single appliance will do that. You will use it to heat rolls in just seconds but you'll still use your toaster for making toast. Your cakes will rise higher and fluffier in your microwave oven but you'll need the slow cooking of a conventional oven for foods such as soufflés that depend on air as a leavening agent. You can cook a beautiful, browned beef roast in only about 20 minutes but you'll probably still prefer your broiler or grill to prepare steaks.

You probably have eaten food prepared in a microwave oven in a restaurant, perhaps without your realizing it. They are a different type of oven, designed to meet the special needs of a restaurant, just as your oven is designed to meet the special cooking requirements of your home.

COOKING WITH MICROWAVES

Remember . . . it is TIME and not temperature that will vary with your microwave oven. Instead of setting an oven at both a temperature and a time, you only set a timer with your new oven. The amount of time needed to cook a particular food is directly related to the food's STARTING TEMPERATURE, VOLUME and DENSITY.

Starting Temperature: The colder the food, the longer it takes to cook. You may want to try the following experiment: fill one cup with cool tap water and another with warm tap water. Heat both cups of water for 1 minute and then remove from oven. Notice the cup that had warm water in it is hot already but the other one will need 30-45 seconds more to reach the same stage.

Volume: As the volume of food increases, the cooking time increases. For example, to make a single serving of instant coffee, heat one cup of water for about 2 minutes, 30 seconds or until hot. Then add desired amount of instant coffee and stir. For two cups of coffee, heat two cups of water for 3 minutes, 30 seconds. You have increased the cooking time about 1 minute to allow for the second cup of water.

Density: The more dense a food item, the longer it takes to cook or defrost. A 1½ lb. piece of meat takes longer to cook than a 1½ lb. loaf of bread because the meat is more dense than the relatively porous bread.

Many of the techniques of cooking with microwaves are similar to conventional cooking. However, because of the increased speed when cooking with microwave energy, they become especially important to remember. *Microwaves first contact the outer section of food, creating heat that is then conducted toward the center of the food.*

This fact of cooking from outside toward the center (similar to conventional cooking) is the reason behind several of the techniques of cooking with microwaves. It affects your defrosting and stirring of food, your allowing a standing time for food before serving and your arranging food in the oven.

Defrosting: *Always alternate cooking times and standing times when defrosting.* The standing time allows heat to be conducted toward the center for a more evenly defrosted product. If you defrost with just one longer, continuous cooking time, you obtain food with a cooked exterior and a still frozen interior. For example, a frozen pound of ground beef is defrosted in four stages: cooking periods of 2 minutes, 1 minute, 30 seconds, 30 seconds, with a standing or rest time of a couple minutes between each cooking period. The first cooking time is longer because the meat is still solidly frozen; as it begins to thaw, the cooking time eventually decreases to 30 seconds.

Standing Time Before Serving: *Because food continues to cook after being removed from the oven, a standing time is needed before serving.* This standing time to allow heat to be conducted toward the center varies, depending on the volume and density of the food. The time is most often as short a period as it takes to put the food on the table, but larger and more dense foods take more time. The recipes note the standing time when it is necessary. The temperature of the food rises during the standing time because of the continued heat transfer, so food is removed from the oven before it reaches a serving temperature. For example, cook a medium size baking potato for about 4 minutes. Notice that the potato is still quite firm to the touch when you remove it from the oven, but after it stands for a few minutes it will be ready to eat.

Stirring: *Because the outside edges of food tend to cook first, stir some food mixtures during the cooking period.* This stirring of mixtures such as scrambled eggs or pudding keeps the cooking even by bringing the outside cooked portion toward the center and bringing the less cooked center portion toward the outside.

Arrangement of Food: *Think of the shape of a ring when arranging food in the oven.* Because microwaves first cook the outer section of food, the center takes the longest to cook. The hole in a ring creates more outside edges and does away with the more difficult to cook center. If you place several items, such as baking potatoes, in the oven, it is best to leave spaces between each of them so there are more separate outside edges. If they are all grouped together, you create a dense center that would be difficult to cook.

When arranging food on a plate or cooking dish, place the larger and thicker part of the food toward the outside edge of the dish and the thinner and smaller part of the food toward the center so it will not overcook.

MICROWAVES: AN ENERGY SOURCE

All food products are cooked by the addition of energy which causes an increase in molecular activity. The energy required must come from some source such as a gas flame, burning charcoal or electricity. When electricity is used for cooking, it must be converted into heat energy.

When you turn on a light bulb, you are seeing electrical energy being converted to light energy. When you turn on your microwave oven, electrical energy is being converted to electromagnetic energy by means of an electron tube, called a magnetron, that is contained inside the oven. When microwaves enter food, they simply cause the liquid or moisture molecules in the food to vibrate at a fantastic rate . . . friction created by this vibration produces heat energy and this heat is conducted throughout the food. If you rapidly rub the palms of your hands together you will feel another example of heat that is created by friction. Microwaves are electromagnetic waves that are classified as being of a "non-ionizing" frequency which means they do *not* cause a chemical change (as do "ionizing" rays such as x-rays).

Microwaves allow food to cook *itself* rather than being surrounded by an outside source of high heat such as 400° inside your conventional oven.

Because the energy necessary to heat food is so direct in your microwave oven, the food is cooked faster and more efficiently than conventional cooking.

Microwaves act differently with different substances. According to the substance, microwaves can be either ABSORBED, TRANSFERRED or REFLECTED.

Food will *absorb* microwaves because food contains moisture molecules.

Glass, paper and some *plastics* are *transparent* to microwaves so they transfer microwaves without absorbing them because glass, paper and some plastics do not contain moisture molecules. This is the reason you can cook food right on a napkin or a glass or ceramic plate — microwaves will go through them and cause the food to cook but not the paper or plate.

Metal objects *reflect* microwaves. The walls and top of the oven are made of metal so that the microwaves will bounce off them and into the food placed in the oven. Because metal reflects microwaves, it slows down cooking if the metal is covering any part of the food. Metal utensils incorrectly used can also cause some damage to the oven walls. We generally do not recommend using metal utensils other than the exceptions noted specifically in "Cooking Utensils" (page 8). Please read this page before placing any metal object in the oven.

COOKING UTENSILS

Cooking with microwaves opens up a whole new range of possibilities in convenience and flexibility of cooking utensils. Out with the pots and pans and in with cooking a sandwich on a napkin, re-warming a meal on your dinner plate, preparing soup in a thermal mug or a bowl, heating hors d'oeuvres on a hard plastic serving tray. Do not use metal utensils in the oven except when noted in the section on "Metal".

Glass and china: Category includes glass, glass-ceramic and china products. Be certain that there is no metal trim such as gold or silver anywhere on the item (including a signature on the underside of it). Some paints or glazes used by some manufacturers of various glass items do contain metallic substances and should not be used in the oven. If you have any doubts about a utensil, just place it in the oven and turn the oven on for about 15-20 seconds. If the container feels quite warm after removing it from the oven, it should not be used in the oven.

Corning products can be used in the oven except for the following items: Centura® dinnerware and Cook-n-Serve covers and the Corelle® Livingware closed handle cups.

Paper: Category includes *napkins, towels, plates, cups, cartons* containing frozen foods or take out foods, *freezer wrap* for thawing frozen foods and *heavy cardboard* used in meat packaging. Paper can be a very handy moisture absorber, which is why it is used to keep bread products from becoming soggy when they are being heated. If you do not want to use paper products, you can substitute a light towel or cloth napkin that can be easily washed.

We do not suggest making popcorn in a paper bag because it can get too hot for a paper container. If oil is used and popcorn is old, extended cooking could lead to smoking and eventually a fire.

Plastic: Category includes *dishwasher safe plastics* which are usually quite rigid material. You can use hard plastic trays, bowls, picnic ware and thermal cups and mugs. A number of dairy toppings and other products are packaged in plastic bowls that can be used in the oven. Melamine ware has a tendency to absorb energy so you should give it a 15-20 second test in the oven (see Glass) to be certain of the safety of your particular brand.

Plastic foam cups and *china foam* dishes can also be used in the oven. If you cover the dish too tightly with plastic wrap, you could cause a distortion of the plastic shape because of the steam trapped.

Plastic baby bottles can be heated with no fuss or bother.

Spatulas and *spoons* designed for non-stick pans can be left in the oven for a short time.

A rule of thumb when putting plastic in the oven: use it only when you are *heating* food to a serving temperature. Prolonged *cooking* causes food to reach a higher temperature and can distort the plastic.

Cooking Pouches: *Boil in the bag pouches* work very well in the oven. If you are simply defrosting or warming a food, you can use the pouch as it is. If the food will become so hot that steam will build up inside the pouch, cut a small slit in the pouch before cooking to let steam escape.

You can use *cooking bags* according to manufacturers' directions. These bags are designed to withstand boiling, freezing and oven heat (*not* bags designed only for storage).

There are also some *heat sealer units* that turn special plastic bags into cooking pouches.

Straw: *Baskets* can be used in the oven for the very short time it takes to heat a few rolls.

Wood: We do not recommend using wooden utensils because the moisture in them might cause a larger item, such as a steak platter, to crack. A wooden handled rubber spatula or wooden spoon becomes warm when left in the oven but it does not seem to have damaged the ones we've left in the oven during the *short* cooking time to stir puddings or sauces.

Metal: *We do not suggest using metal utensils other than the following exceptions that are noted.* A metal container slows the cooking process because microwaves are *reflected* from the metal and therefore do not reach the food inside the container (see also page 5).

In addition to slowing the cooking process, metal can cause "arcing" in the oven if there are gaps in the metal particles of an object. The walls of the oven are made of a smooth, continuous metal with no gaps. If you had a utensil that contained metal particles that were separated, the particles could set up an electrical field that would result in sparks and arcing which is a static discharge of energy.

Although metal is not generally used in the oven, it can be used under the following conditions:

1. *Aluminum foil* if the amount of food is much greater than the amount of foil. The fact that metal reflects microwaves can be used to an

advantage in some recipes. For example, foil is purposely used to slow down the cooking rate for a small part of a food item such as the wings of a roast chicken; otherwise, the wings would be overcooked before the larger parts of the chicken were cooked. Be certain the foil is not touching the walls of the oven because this could cause arcing.

2. *Metal skewers, clamps or lids* if there is a much larger amount of food in proportion to the metal. For example, shish kebab can be cooked on a metal skewer because there is a large amount of fairly dense food that will attract microwaves. You could not put a small amount of food on a metal skewer because it would cause arcing between the skewer and the walls. The clamps usually found on a frozen turkey can remain during the cooking process because there is a large amount of food in relation to the clamp. Metal lids or tops on glass jars do slow the cooking process. However, they can be left on if the amount of food is much greater than the lid or if the lid has to be on the jar as when canning.

3. *TV breakfast and dinner trays* if the containers are less than ¾ inch deep. Although cooking in TV trays occurs from the top surface only, the food and container are shallow enough that the food is adequately heated. However, foods packaged in foil containers deeper than ¾ inch should be transferred to another container before cooking. Be certain that no part of the metal tray is touching the metal walls because arcing will occur.

COVERING OF COOKING UTENSILS

The recipes indicate if food is to be cooked covered or uncovered. You will trap more heat and moisture when you use a covering.

Casserole tops: When your cooking dish has a top, it is usually the easiest covering to use. It traps in steam quite thoroughly so be careful when removing cover. You can often use a plate as a substitute for a casserole top.

Wax Paper: Can be both a cooking utensil for items such as cookies or corn on the cob or can be used as a covering. Use it when food comes in prolonged contact with covering or when you simply want to protect the oven from spatters.

Plastic Wrap: Creates a tighter seal than wax paper. Because it does hold in steam so well, be careful when removing the wrap after the cooking time. Cut a small slit in the plastic wrap to allow some steam to escape.

CLEANING OF YOUR MICROWAVE OVEN

Your microwave oven can be wiped out with dish detergent and water. Also, use any gentle all-purpose spray cleaner. Odors can be removed by boiling a cup of lemon juice and water.

ABOUT THE COOKBOOK

This is a unique cookbook to help you with microwave cooking. It is a guide and a resource full of ideas that you can pick and choose to fit into your own life style. You will probably use it most often when doing primary cooking but don't forget that it can help you in many other ways too, whether you're warming a baby bottle, reheating yesterday's dinner to taste newly made or doing a last minute defrosting of that roast in the freezer.

The recipes have been developed in our kitchens by home economists and then retested by owners of microwave ovens who prepared the recipes in their own homes. In addition, recipes were also sampled by people who were not oven owners to be sure the food met their taste and appeal requirements also. These groups were an invaluable aid and we greatly appreciate their comments and suggestions.

• Begin cooking with the section of recipes for Breakfast, Lunch, Dinner and Snacks (pages 10-36). Recipes have been chosen that will give you some idea of the basic techniques used with microwave cooking.

• The chapters have been organized according to meal format, from Appetizers to Desserts. There are also Suggestions for More Uses for Your Oven and A Convenience Foods Guide. Convenience food products are used throughout the recipe section but we have arranged a Convenience Foods Guide as a handy resource, highlighting the information about convenience food products, cooking methods, timings and additional comments.

• The book has menu suggestions throughout the Main Course section. Sometimes you might want to use your microwave oven for only one part of the meal, at other times for everything in the meal. As you get to know your oven better, you will become more aware of the great flexibility in your new style of cooking and meal planning.

• The recipes have been prepared just as they would be in a normal kitchen. Ingredients are straight from their storage places, such as eggs and butter from the refrigerator, sugar from the cupboard. If you think your ingredients might be at a different temperature than normal, it might change the cooking time just slightly.

• You may feel free to turn the cooking dish around halfway through the cooking time for more even cooking but we have felt that it is not necessary unless mentioned in a specific recipe.

• The INDEX should be your guide whenever you are looking for a particular recipe or a basic cooking technique.

• Ingredient alternates are included in some of the recipes. If you do substitute ingredients that you normally have on hand, it really shouldn't make much difference in the recipe unless you change the volume or add a number of high fat ingredients such as nuts. For example, you add 1 minute to the cooking time of four baked apples when you fill the centers with raisins, nuts or mincemeat.

• Not only does the oven cook in a short period of time, but the recipes also have a fairly short preparation time, eliminating unnecessary steps. There is also a minimum number of dishes used to save clean up time. For example, you can often use a 4-cup measure to measure and mix ingredients and sometimes to cook.

• We found in our testing that the usual high altitude adjustments are not necessary in microwave cooking. The only change might be a slight increase in cooking time.

• We suggest using All-Purpose flour rather than Self-Rising flour because Self-Rising flour's high leavening content has a more pronounced flavor when used in a microwave oven.

Please read on to Before You Begin to Cook section.

BEFORE YOU BEGIN TO COOK

Now that you've read the introductory section about microwaves and how they act, you're all ready to start your discovery of carefree cooking. It may take a little time to get used to this way of cooking so we have organized a section of beginning recipes for BREAKFAST, LUNCH, DINNER and SNACKS that will introduce you to microwave cooking as easily and thoroughly as possible. With each of the recipes we have given the *reasons why* a recipe calls for certain ingredients or cooking techniques so you will completely understand what you are doing. We have also tried to explain as many varying conditions under which you might prepare a recipe and what adjustments you can expect to make with those conditions. Following the recipe directions will assure you of cooking success. We have given some signs to look for that indicate overcooking, if, for some reason, your preparation is quite different than what is stated in the recipe.

Try the recipes that appeal to you or your family. The dinner menus provide timing helps to organize your meal preparation so all will go smoothly. The menus are only guides to give you an idea of what can be done with your oven and how foods are prepared one at a time, in sequence. If you feel like preparing only one or two of the recipes in a particular menu, by all means go ahead. The information in this section is here to acquaint you with your oven, how it cooks and some suggestions about what it can do for you.

Becoming familiar with the speed of microwave cooking may be easier if you make a practice of checking foods shortly before they should be done. In other words, tend to undercook rather than overcook when you first begin with your oven. You can always cook the food a little longer if necessary.

Because the recipes have been tested in a variety of ovens and with a variety of cooks, the recipes are very consistent. If you notice that food cooks a little slower or faster than a recipe states, it may be due to the voltage level in your home. Just as some conventional ovens seem a little slow or fast, so too your microwave oven may vary slightly, depending on the strength of your home's electrical current. Try a simple test with an 8 ounce cup of cool (50°-80°) tap water. Place it in the oven and cook for 2 minutes, 55 seconds. If the water is not boiling by that time, your oven may be cooking a little slow and recipes should be adjusted accordingly. REMEMBER, YOU CAN ALWAYS ADD MORE TIME TO A RECIPE TO GET PROPER DONENESS.

Breakfast

Hot cocoa can be made in the microwave oven using chocolate flavored milk, instant cocoa mix or combining cocoa, sugar and milk. All the same techniques apply since you are basically heating milk. These techniques are very similar to heating water for instant coffee except that the milk will boil over if it gets too hot.

A marshmallow can be added during the last seconds of heating. Because of the difference in volume as compared with the milk and because of the high sugar concentration, it would overcook before the milk was hot if added for the full time. By adding it during the last 10 to 15 seconds, the marshmallow has time to puff up and soften. When the oven shuts off, the puffed marshmallow slowly collapses.

HOT COCOA

CHOCOLATE MILK: Fill cups or mugs with chocolate flavored milk. Cook as directed below.

HOT COCOA MIX: Fill cups or mugs with milk. Cook as directed below. Stir in amount of cocoa mix as directed on package.

UNSWEETENED COCOA: In each cup or mug combine 1 tablespoon unsweetened cocoa, 2 tablespoons sugar and pinch of salt. Add enough milk to form a paste; mix until smooth. Stir in milk to fill cups. Cook as directed below.

COOKING TIMES: Cook, uncovered, until steam appears;

    1 cup — 1 minute, 15 seconds
    2 cups — 2 minutes, 20 seconds
    3 cups — 3 minutes, 25 seconds
    4 cups — 4 minutes, 30 seconds
    5 cups — 5 minutes, 40 seconds
    6 cups — 7 minutes

Stir before serving to distribute heat.

TIP: For larger quantities of cocoa, prepare and heat cocoa in a glass pitcher or tea pot. The times may be slightly longer than for the same volume heated in individual cups.

HOT INSTANT BREAKFAST

Empty envelope of instant breakfast in coffee mug. Stir in milk to fill cup. Cook, using times for hot cocoa as guide.

Pictured: Hot Cocoa, topped with marshmallow, Baked Apple, page 17, right, Hot Cereal (oatmeal), page 15, topped with fresh peaches and brown sugar, Warm Doughnut (see Warm Sweet Roll, page 13), Pancakes, page 13, reheated in microwave oven, Bacon, page 15, Scrambled Eggs, page 14.

Starting temperature of water for coffee will affect the heating time.

The cooking time necessary to heat the water will increase with the size of the cup and the number of cups.

Any type of paper, foam, mug or coffee cup can be used.

Stirring after heating (when coffee is added) distributes the heat.

We have added the coffee after the water is hot. If it were added before heating and boiled, it would taste bitter, similar to conventionally boiled coffee.

INSTANT COFFEE OR TEA

Fill coffee cups or mugs with cold tap water. Cook, uncovered, until steam appears:

        1 cup — 2¼ to 2½ minutes
        2 cups — 3¼ to 3½ minutes
        3 cups — 4¼ to 4½ minutes
        4 cups — 5½ to 5¾ minutes
        5 cups — 6¾ to 7 minutes
        6 cups — 8¼ to 8½ minutes

Add desired amount of instant coffee or tea and stir or add tea bag and steep as directed on package.

> **TIP:** Perked coffee that has cooled can be reheated using the heating chart for beverages, page 42. Some oven owners perk the coffee, unplug it, let it cool and then reheat cups as needed.

A bagel is one of the most ideal shapes to heat with microwaves. The lack of a center in a bagel or doughnut makes heating very even and quick because the center of food is the most difficult area to heat.

If serving with coffee, heat coffee first since it will hold heat while bagel is heated.

BAGELS

Place 1 bagel on paper plate or napkin. **COOK**, uncovered, **10 SECONDS** or until surface is warm. For 2 bagels, **COOK**, uncovered, **15 SECONDS.**

> **TIPS:** For heating other quantities and heating frozen bagels, see Bread chapter, page 127.
>
> ● Bagels can be split and topped with cream cheese before heating. During heating, the cream cheese will soften and can be spread easily on the warm bagel.

A whole frozen coffee cake can be thawed and heated or individual pieces can be removed to be heated and the remainder left frozen.

Frozen coffee cake is removed from the metal container to allow it to thaw and heat from all sides. Microwaves bounce off metal so it would only heat from the top side if left in the foil container.

Because microwaves are attracted to sugar, a sugar filling or topping heats very quickly and can become very hot.

The coffee cake reheats best if placed on paper or cloth that absorbs moisture. When placed directly on a plate, the moisture condenses on the cool surface and makes the bottom of the coffee cake soggy. A plate can be used if first lined with a paper or cloth napkin.

A resting time is necessary to allow heat to reach the center of the cake and thaw it without overcooking the edges. When heating 1 serving, the resting time is not necessary because it is easy to reach the center of a smaller piece.

HEATING FROZEN COFFEE CAKE

Remove a frozen coffee cake (about 11 oz.) from foil container and place on paper plate or towel. **COOK**, uncovered, **45 SECONDS; REST 30 SECONDS;** and **COOK 1 MINUTE** or until surface is warm. **LET STAND A FEW SECONDS** to distribute heat.   1 Coffee Cake

> **TIP:** To reheat 1 piece of frozen coffee cake, cut 1/6 of coffee cake and remove to a paper plate or napkin (return remainder to freezer). Cook 20 seconds or until surface is warm.

Any metal such as a cap on the syrup container is removed so it can heat from all sides. Our syrup was at room temperature. If syrup is at refrigerator temperature, the times will be a little longer.

Because the sugar concentration is high in syrup, you will notice it heats more quickly than the same amount of water.

This same technique of heating syrup can be used to heat and remove the last few drops of syrup from a bottle. The time is about 10 or 15 seconds, depending on the amount of syrup.

HEATING SYRUP

Remove metal cap from bottle of syrup. **COOK**, uncovered, **30 TO 45 SECONDS** for a 12 oz. bottle or until bubbles begin to appear. If serving from a pitcher, syrup can be heated in pitcher if it contains no metal trim.

Although pancakes, waffles and French toast need to be cooked conventionally, they are ideal for cooking ahead or cooking extras to be kept in the refrigerator or freezer for reheating in the microwave oven.

Unlike most bread products, pancakes, waffles and French toast can be heated directly on a serving plate rather than a paper napkin; excess moisture is not a problem because normally they will be served with syrup.

PANCAKES

To reheat refrigerated pancakes, stack on serving plate and cook, uncovered until center of bottom pancake is hot:

Amount	Refrigerated	Frozen
1 plate with 1 pancake	20 seconds	45 seconds
1 plate with 2 pancakes	35 seconds	1 minute, 15 seconds
1 plate with 3 pancakes	50 seconds	1 minute, 30 seconds
2 plates with 2 pancakes each	1 minute, 10 seconds	2 minutes

FRENCH TOAST

To reheat refrigerated or frozen French toast, place on serving plate in single layer and COOK, uncovered, until center of slice is hot:

Amount	Refrigerated	Frozen
1 small plate with 1 slice toast	30 seconds	1 minute
1 large or 2 small plates with 2 slices toast	45 seconds	2 minutes
1 large plate with 3 slices toast	1 minute	3 minutes
1 large plate with 4 slices toast	1 minute, 15 seconds	4 minutes

WAFFLES

Prepare and cook favorite waffles. Let cool in single layer on cooling rack. Wrap tightly and refrigerate or freeze. To reheat, cook, uncovered, on serving plate until center feels warm.

Amount	Refrigerated	Frozen
1 section	15 seconds	20 seconds
2 sections	25 seconds	35 seconds
3 sections	35 seconds	45 seconds
4 sections (2 plates)	45 seconds	60 seconds

When softening butter to be served at the table, you want to retain its shape so you allow standing times after cooking periods. If you are softening butter to be used in cooking, the shape is not important so you can cook without any standing time.

SOFTENING BUTTER

Place stick of cold butter on serving plate. **COOK 5 SECONDS, LET STAND 15 SECONDS; COOK 5 SECONDS; LET STAND 15 SECONDS.** If necessary, cook 5 more seconds.

Because sweet rolls take just seconds to heat, they should be one of the last items heated for a meal.

Bread items reheat best if placed on a paper or cloth surface that absorbs moisture. When placed directly on a glass plate, the moisture condenses and makes the bottom of the roll soggy.

The inside of sweet roll is at serving temperature when the bread surface feels warm to the touch.

For reheating, we used room temperature rolls that weighed about 2 ounces, sweet rolls that were about 5 inches in diameter and cinnamon rolls that were about 2½ inches in diameter. Other sizes take a few seconds more or less to heat.

WARM SWEET ROLLS

Place sweet rolls on napkins or paper plates. **COOK** 1 roll **15 SECONDS** or until surface is warm. **COOK** 2 rolls **20 SECONDS. LET STAND A FEW SECONDS** to distribute heat.

TIPS: For complete reheating chart for rolls, see Bread chapter, page 127.

• Since microwaves cook sugar very quickly, be careful not to overcook sweet rolls because frosting or jelly can become very hot and the roll might toughen.

Custard, rich with eggs and milk, is good at any meal. We have included it with breakfast because it is easy to mix together the night before and leave in refrigerator. Then individuals can cook or simply reheat their own custards when ready to eat breakfast.

It is interesting to watch custard cook because you can see it start to firm around sides and then puff in the center. By watching, you will have an idea of the cooking pattern within your oven and which areas of the oven may tend to cook a little faster or slower than others. You may find it desirable to remove some custards from the oven before others are cooked.

BAKED CUSTARD

1¾ cups milk
¼ cup sugar
3 eggs
¼ teaspoon salt
½ teaspoon vanilla
Nutmeg

In 4-cup measure, measure milk. Add sugar, eggs, salt and vanilla. Beat with rotary beater until well combined. Pour into four to five 5 or 6-oz. custard cups, filling ¾ full. Sprinkle with nutmeg. **COOK**, uncovered, 4¼ **TO 5 MINUTES** or until they start to bubble.

4 to 5 Custards

> **TIPS:** To cook 1 custard, cook 1 minute, 10 seconds. To cook 2 custards, cook 2 to 2½ minutes.
>
> • To bring a cooked custard that has been refrigerated to room temperature, cook 30 seconds and then let stand 1 minute to distribute heat.
>
> • To cook custard in 1-quart casserole, mix together ingredients in casserole; cook, covered, 5 minutes, or until knife inserted near center comes out clean.

Scrambled eggs are the easiest way to cook eggs because the yolks and whites, (which cook at different rates electronically) are mixed together and thus cook evenly.

Butter is added mainly for flavor so it can be melted before adding the eggs or stirred in with the eggs without melting.

Stirring is not necessary until the eggs begin to set and coagulate. This will begin about ⅔ of the way through the cooking time.

Because eggs cook so quickly, they should still be moist at end of cooking time; during standing they will finish cooking and setting. During this standing time you may want to heat coffee and a roll.

A tight fitting cover is used with the eggs to hold in the heat and help with the cooking. It is easy to reheat leftover scrambled eggs. If you are cooking them primarily for reheating, undercook them just a little.

INDIVIDUAL SCRAMBLED EGGS

In soup bowl or 20-oz. casserole, melt 2 teaspoons butter or margarine (25 sec.). Add 2 eggs and 2 tablespoons milk. Mix with fork until well scrambled together. **COOK,** covered with saucer or plastic wrap, **45 SECONDS.** Stir with fork. Cover and **COOK 30 SECONDS** more (eggs should still be moist). Stir again and **LET STAND,** covered, **1 TO 2 MINUTES** to finish cooking. Season to taste.   1 Serving

> **TIPS:** If making the eggs ahead to reheat, undercook, cool and refrigerate. Reheat by placing on serving plate and covering with small bowl. Cook 45 seconds for 2 eggs. Let stand about a minute to distribute heat.
>
> • For 2 servings (4 eggs) use 1-quart casserole or mixing bowl, 4 teaspoons butter, 4 eggs, 4 tablespoons milk. Cook 1 minute, 45 seconds, stir and then cook 50 seconds.
>
> • For other amounts of egg and times, see Egg section on page 101.
>
> • As with any dish used to cook eggs, they are difficult to clean unless soaked immediately after emptying. You may find it convenient to use a vegetable spray-on coating on the dish before cooking to make clean-up easier.

Timing for bacon will depend on thickness. If you vary brands of bacon, you may notice a slight difference in cooking times as the sugar, salt, and fat content will affect the cooking time.

Bacon can be stacked in layers if paper towels are used between, remembering that the layers should be even thickness for even cooking.

The paper towels absorb the fat as bacon cooks. You can also cook bacon without the towel in a shallow baking dish with sides such as a pie plate or 12 x 7 baking dish and then drain before eating. You may wish to cover with a towel to prevent spattering. If using a paper plate under the towel, it is best if the plate is not plastic coated because the coating would not absorb any excess fat.

We do not suggest cooking more than ½ lb. of bacon at a time because of the accumulation of grease and little time advantage.

BACON

Place 1 or 2 layers of paper towel in shallow baking dish or on paper plate. Lay strips of bacon on towel. If additional space is needed, top with 1 or 2 more layers of towel and then another layer of bacon. Top with a layer of paper towel to prevent spattering. Cook until desired crispness:

1 slice — ¾ to 1 minute
2 slices — 1½ to 1¾ minutes
3 slices — 2 to 2¼ minutes
4 slices — 2½ to 2¾ minutes
5 slices — 2¾ to 3¼ minutes
6 slices — 3¼ to 3½ minutes
8 slices — 4 to 4½ minutes

TIP: If bacon is hard to separate into slices, place the slices you are planning to cook in oven and cook about 30 seconds. Loosen and separate, reducing additional cooking time by about 30 seconds.

Both Canadian bacon and cooked ham can be heated quickly in the microwave oven. Since they are precooked, they need only be brought to serving temperature.

When heating several pieces at one time, the pieces should all be of similar size and shape; otherwise it may be necessary to remove some before the others are heated to avoid overcooking.

If serving with eggs, cook eggs first and leave covered to stay hot while cooking meat. Heat rolls or bread just before serving.

CANADIAN BACON

Place ½-inch slices of Canadian bacon on

individual glass plates or on platter. Cook, covered loosely with wax paper, until the edges of meat begin to sizzle.

1 slice — 1 minute, 15 seconds
2 slices — 2 minutes
3 slices — 3 minutes
4 slices — 4 minutes

LET STAND A FEW MINUTES to distribute the heat.

TIP: For Ham, use same guide as for Canadian bacon, but cut cooked ham into slices about ¼ inch thick and 4 to 5 inches in diameter.

Cereal is especially easy to cook in the microwave oven because it can be cooked in a serving dish.

If other types of cereal are desired, you can go by the proportions on the package. We found the oven was most convenient for the quick-cooking cereals. If the cereal is not quick-cooking, it should be covered and will need to cook after boiling for about as long as is directed on the package. The instant cereals need only to be mixed with water and then heated in the microwave oven for the time suggested on the package.

HOT CEREAL

**¾ cup water
⅓ cup quick-cooking rolled oats
Dash salt**

In cereal bowl, combine all ingredients. **COOK,** uncovered, **1 MINUTE, 30 SECONDS** or until mixture boils, stirring once. **LET STAND 1 TO 2 MINUTES** before serving.   1 Serving

TIPS: For additional servings, prepare in individual cereal bowls as directed. For 2 servings, cook 2 minutes, 30 seconds; for 3 servings, cook 3 minutes, 30 seconds; for 4 servings, cook 4 minutes, 30 seconds.

• When preparing more than one serving, the cereal can be prepared in a casserole dish and then served in individual dishes.

• Combining the cereal with cold water gives a creamy textured cereal. If you prefer more texture, first heat the water to boiling and then stir in cereal. Cook, covered, 1 minute. Stir and let stand.

• When cooking cream of wheat, use 2 tablespoons quick-cooking cream of wheat for rolled oats in recipe above and proceed as directed. Milk can be used for water, if desired.

Fruits packaged in plastic pouches are easy to thaw in the oven without transferring to the serving dish during the thawing process.

In thawing frozen fruits, it is best to still have a few ice crystals in the fruit so it retains its shape and texture.

If you find the fruit is not thawed as much as you like, just cook a few more seconds, allowing it to stand a minute to distribute the heat.

When cooking frozen vegetables in pouches, steam builds up inside the pouch so it is necessary to make a small slit in the top of the pouch to allow the steam to escape. However, when thawing fruit, it should not get hot so there is no steam and this step is not necessary.

THAWING FRUIT IN POUCHES

Place a 10-oz. pouch of frozen fruit in the oven. **COOK 30 SECONDS, LET REST 1 MINUTE** and then **COOK** another **30 SECONDS. LET STAND 1 MINUTE** to distribute heat before opening pouch and serving.

Fruits packaged in paper containers have a thicker shape than those packaged in pouches so it is necessary to stir and break up the fruit during the thawing process. Since this is not possible in the container, the fruit is transferred to a serving dish after partial thawing. Otherwise, the fruit near the outside of the package may be partially cooked and the fruit in the center still frozen solid.

Packaging for fruit does vary and if the package has metal on some sides, the thawing times may be slightly longer because the microwaves cannot pass through the metal.

A resting time is necessary in thawing fruits to allow the heat to penetrate toward the center without cooking the outside. The resting time with these directions takes place during the transfer of the fruit from the freezing container to the serving dish.

Since the fruit will not become hot, a plastic container can be used.

THAWING FRUIT IN PAPER PACKAGING

If ends of a 10-oz. carton of frozen fruit are metal, remove one end; otherwise package can be placed in oven unopened. **COOK 30 SECONDS** to loosen fruit from carton. Empty into glass or plastic serving dish, breaking up fruit with fork. **COOK**, uncovered, **30 SECONDS** and stir. **LET STAND 1 MINUTE** to distribute the heat before serving.

> **TIP:** For a 16-oz. carton of fruit, use cooking periods of 45 seconds.

Grapefruit can be heated easily in the sauce dish used for serving. Some type of dish or container is necessary to collect any juice that may run over edge of fruit during heating.

The grapefruit are left uncovered during cooking because they will not dry out with microwave cooking, there is little chance of spattering and the time would not be reduced by covering.

GLAZED GRAPEFRUIT

2 grapefruit
4 teaspoons brown sugar
2 teaspoons butter or margarine

Cut grapefruit in half, removing core and seeds. Place in sauce dishes. If desired, cut around each section to loosen. Sprinkle each half with 1 teaspoon brown sugar. Place ½ teaspoon butter in center of each half. **COOK**, uncovered, **3 MINUTES, 30 SECONDS** or until heated through. **LET STAND 1 MINUTE** to distribute heat.   4 Servings

> **TIP:** For 2 halves, cook 2 minutes, 30 seconds. For 1 half, cook 1 minute, 30 seconds.

It takes only a few minutes the night before to cook these spicy prunes.

Timing is not critical when cooking prunes because you are only heating the water to about the boiling point in order to speed the rehydrating of the dried fruit. We suggest covering with the casserole lid but a plate or other tight fitting cover would hold in the heat just as well.

By starting with hot tap water, the cooking time is shorter than if you begin with cold water.

SPICY BREAKFAST PRUNES

1½ cups dried prunes
2 cups hot water
¼ cup firmly packed brown sugar
1 stick cinnamon or 1 teaspoon ground cinnamon
10 whole allspice or ¼ teaspoon ground allspice

In 1 or 1½-quart glass casserole, combine all ingredients. **COOK**, covered with casserole lid, **4 MINUTES** or until mixture starts to boil. Allow to cool at room temperature 4 hours or overnight. Remove cinnamon stick and whole allspice before serving. Store leftovers in refrigerator.   6 Servings

> **TIP:** For a special flavor, add ½ cup port wine just before serving.

Apples are easy to cook when learning how to operate your oven and they make a quick breakfast or snack fruit.

The apples we used in testing the recipe were at refrigerator temperature. Room temperature apples may take slightly less cooking time. Cooking times will vary also with the size and shape of apple.

When additional ingredients such as raisins and nuts are added to the apples the time is increased because there is more food volume to heat and cook.

The apples have been left uncovered during cooking because they are not easy to cover and the time is not shortened appreciably by covering. There may be a little spattering which can be easily wiped up after cooking. If you prefer to prevent this spattering, place a piece of wax paper over apples during cooking.

BAKED APPLES

4 medium baking apples
4 tablespoons brown sugar
2 tablespoons butter or margarine
Cinnamon

Wash and core apples; place in 2-quart (8 x 8) baking dish or four individual custard cups or shallow coffee cups. Place 1 tablespoon brown sugar and ½ tablespoon butter in center of each apple. Sprinkle with cinnamon. **COOK,** uncovered, **5 MINUTES** or until apples are just about tender. **LET STAND SEVERAL MINUTES** to finish cooking and to cool enough to eat.

4 Baked Apples

TIPS: For 1 apple, use individual custard cup and cook 2 to 2½ minutes. For 2 apples, use individual custard cups and cook 3 to 3½ minutes. For 6 apples, use 2-quart (8 x 8 or 12 x 7) baking dish and cook 6 to 6½ minutes.

• If desired, add ½ tablespoon raisins, chopped nuts or mincemeat to filling in center of each apple, adding about 1 additional minute cooking time for 4 apples.

When thawing fruit juice, you first want to loosen the concentrate from the can and then soften it enough to easily mix it with water.

Since the can is often surrounded by metal with metal ends and foil-lined paper wrapper, it is necessary to remove one end so the microwave energy can reach the food. This process is slow because the energy can penetrate from only one side of the container. To speed the thawing, remove the concentrate from the metal can as soon as it has thawed enough to loosen.

On some types of packaging there may be a tendency for a few thin pieces of foil paper

to protrude from the can after the lid is removed. If these are not trimmed, the microwave energy may cause sparks (arcing).

In thawing there is usually a rest period to allow the heat at the outside to penetrate toward the center. With fruit juice, the resting takes place while you transfer the juice from the can to the pitcher.

If you want the concentrate to be thawed more, you can add additional cooking periods of 15 seconds with about a 1 minute rest between each period.

DEFROSTING FRUIT JUICE CONCENTRATE

Remove top from a 6-oz. can frozen juice concentrate, being sure there are no stray pieces of foil paper sticking up around edge. Place in oven and **COOK 15 SECONDS** to loosen from can. Empty concentrate into glass or plastic pitcher and **COOK 15 SECONDS** or until softened. Add water as directed on package and mix together.

TIP: For 12-oz. can, use cooking periods of 30 seconds.

The frozen breakfasts are packaged in a foil (metal) tray with a foil covering. Therefore, the foil covering must be removed before cooking and be replaced with wax paper; or you may place the uncovered tray back into its paper carton which holds in heat. The breakfast can be cooked in the foil tray because it is very shallow. Cooking times can be decreased 15 seconds by transferring the contents of the tray to a china or paper plate because it can then be cooked from all sides rather than only the top surface.

Pancakes and French toast made from home recipes are always heated uncovered to prevent sogginess. However, the manufacturer has prepared these frozen breakfasts so that covering helps heat the meat portion more quickly but does not make the pancakes or French toast soggy.

T. V. BREAKFASTS

Remove foil cover from 4½-oz. frozen T.V. breakfast. Return to outer carton or cover with wax paper. **COOK** until meat is hot:

French toast and sausage patties —
2 minutes, 30 seconds

Pancakes and sausage patties — 2 minutes, 30 seconds

Scrambled eggs, sausage patty, country style fried potatoes — 3 minutes

TIP: When cooking 2 breakfasts in foil trays, double above cooking times. Be certain that foil trays do not touch oven walls. Reduce cooking times by 30 seconds when 2 breakfasts are transferred to glass or paper plates.

Lunch

Meats that cook as quickly as ground beef patties do not have much chance to brown. We found we could achieve an attractive brown color and good flavor by first coating the meat with gravy mix. By cooking the meat and gravy mix together for a short period, the gravy mix combines with the meat juices to give a brown color and flavor.

You may find it handy to keep gravy mix on hand in an extra salt shaker.

There are other types of brown and season sprinkle ons that are available in some markets that have a similar browning effect with the meat.

If you prefer a conventionally browned beef patty, it can be browned first and then placed in the oven for a minute or two to finish the cooking.

The oven also works well for reheating leftover beef patties that have been broiled, fried or grilled. One patty takes about 45 seconds to reheat. Some oven owners tell us they cook additional patties for this purpose when barbecuing.

To defrost ground beef, see page 45.

GROUND BEEF PATTIES

Season 1 lb. ground beef with salt and pepper. Shape into 4 patties (¼ lb. each). Use 1 package (⅝ oz.) brown gravy mix to coat patties on all sides. Arrange in 2-quart (8 x 8) glass baking dish. **COOK,** covered with wax paper, **4 MINUTES** or until done. **LET STAND 2 MINUTES** to finish cooking.　　　　4 Patties

> **TIPS:** For hamburgers, place cooked patties in split and, if desired, toasted hamburger buns. Return to oven to heat buns; for 4 buns, cook, uncovered, 45 seconds; for 1 bun, cook, uncovered, 15 seconds.
>
> • For other amounts, additional seasonings, and cooking frozen patties, see page 71 in Beef section.

Wieners need only heating so the wiener and bun for a hot dog sandwich can be heated together, making these especially easy.

We suggest wrapping the sandwich loosely in a paper napkin. This wrapping holds the wiener inside the bun and helps hold in some of the heat while allowing the steam to be absorbed by the paper napkin.

To avoid cooling the hot wiener when adding relishes, add the mustard, catsup, pickles or relish before heating.

These timings are based on room temperature buns and refrigerator temperature wieners; the wieners are the size that come from 1 lb. package with 10 wieners. Larger wieners will take longer and in some cases may need to be heated separately since the bread could overheat and toughen before the larger wiener is hot.

If the buns are frozen, they can be used with the refrigerated wieners, using the same times, since the filling, not the bread, is the main factor in sandwich timing.

HOT DOGS

Place a wiener in each hot dog bun and wrap in a paper napkin. Arrange in oven and cook until the wiener feels warm:

　　1 hot dog　— 25 seconds
　　2 hot dogs — 45 seconds
　　3 hot dogs — 1 minute
　　4 hot dogs — 1 minute, 10 seconds
　　6 hot dogs — 1 minute, 45 seconds

Pictured: Ground Beef Patty on a bun and Hot Dog, recipes this page.

Mushroom soup adds a mild, creamy flavor to tuna and cheese in this easy to heat open-faced sandwich.

Bread that is first toasted has more body and supports the filling better after heating; untoasted bread tends to become very limp when heated.

For sandwich making, the firmer textured breads make the best sandwiches. Very light, airy bread can be used, but it is easier to overcook, causing the bread to become tough and chewy.

During heating of bread items, the moisture in the bread becomes hot and turns to steam. If breads are covered, this steam will make the bread and crust soggy; if left uncovered, this steam escapes into the oven.

We find the differences in melting times of cheese very slight so you can use any cheese of your choice in almost any recipe. We especially like Cheddar, American or Swiss with the tuna flavor.

TUNA 'N CHEESE SANDWICHES

1 can (6½ oz.) tuna fish, drained
Half of 10½-oz. can condensed cream of mushroom soup
4 slices bread, toasted
Onion or garlic powder
4 slices cheese

In small mixing bowl, combine tuna and soup, breaking tuna into small pieces. Place toasted bread on paper napkin covered plate or tray. Spread with tuna mixture. Sprinkle with onion powder; top with cheese slices. **COOK,** uncovered, **2 MINUTES** or until cheese is bubbly. 4 Sandwiches

TIPS: Since the tuna, soup and cheese contain salt, the sandwiches will be too salty if onion salt is used for powder.

• If desired, omit onion powder and top hot sandwiches with a few French-fried onion rings. The heat from the sandwich will warm the onions while keeping their crispness.

For chunks of ground beef in a recipe, first crumble it into the cooking dish and cook for about 5 minutes. This sets the meat which can then be stirred to break the meat into the size pieces desired.

If the recipe calls for a spice or seasoning, it is usually added during this initial cooking time; it penetrates the meat better and gives it additional color. However, if you want to drain off the fat and juices, wait to add the seasonings until after the first cooking so that you do not lose the seasoning when you drain the juices. If you use lean ground beef, there is very little excess fat and no need to drain.

If making sandwiches ahead, avoid soggy buns by toasting the buns and waiting until just before serving to fill with meat mixture and reheat.

SLOPPY JOE SANDWICHES

1 lb. ground beef
½ cup (1 med.) chopped onion or 2 tablespoons instant minced onion
½ cup (½ pepper) chopped green pepper
½ teaspoon paprika
1 cup (8-oz. can) tomato sauce
1 teaspoon salt
2 teaspoons brown sugar
Pepper
6 hamburger buns

In 1½ or 2-quart glass casserole, crumble ground beef. Sprinkle with onion, pepper and paprika. **COOK,** uncovered, **5 MINUTES;** stir to break meat into small pieces. Add remaining ingredients except buns; mix well. **COOK,** covered with casserole cover, **10 MINUTES,** stirring occasionally. Spoon onto bottom half of buns; top with other half. If necessary, return to oven and **COOK,** uncovered, **1 MINUTE** to heat through. 6 Servings

You can save washing a pan by heating soup in individual soup bowls.

For ease in adding the right amount of water, use a measuring cup or other guide to add equal amounts of soup and water.

For soups with liquid and vegetables or noodles, first divide the liquid portion equally and then divide the solids.

A 10½-oz. can of condensed soup usually contains about 1¼ cups so you can divide these amounts for the number of servings you desire.

A cover is used on the soup to hold in the heat and speed the heating process. A saucer makes an easy cover or use the plate on which you will set the soup bowl for serving.

Soup stays hot for several minutes if left covered so heat it first while assembling a sandwich. Then heat the sandwich while the soup stands.

Pictured: Cheese and Tomato Sandwich and cup of canned tomato Bisque soup, recipes this page.

CANNED SOUP

Divide contents of 10½-oz. can of condensed soup between 2 or 3 glass soup bowls. Add equal amounts of water to each. Cover with small plate and **COOK 3 TO 4 MINUTES** or until steaming hot. **LET STAND 1 MINUTE** to distribute heat.

> **TIPS:** For other types of soup, see soup chapter on page 106.
>
> • For 4 to 6 servings using 2 cans of soup, cook 6 to 7 minutes.

This easy sandwich idea is ideal for summer when tomatoes are at their peak.

Toasting the bread keeps it from becoming soggy during heating. Since there is no crust such as on a roll, the bread needs this extra firmness of toasting to support the filling.

As with the bread items for breakfast, sandwiches are best heated on a paper or cloth surface that absorbs the moisture from the roll.

The cheese is placed over the tomato in an open faced sandwich because you only want to warm the tomato, rather than cook it.

Times are similar for both open-faced and regular sandwiches with 2 pieces of bread. The filling is usually the important factor in deciding cooking times because bread heats quickly and easily.

CHEESE AND TOMATO SANDWICHES

For each sandwich, toast 1 or 2 slices of bread. Spread with mayonnaise or salad dressing and place on napkin lined plate or paper plate. Top with ½ inch thick slice of tomato and slice of cheese cut the size of bread. If desired, top with another slice of bread. **COOK** 1 sandwich, uncovered, **45 SECONDS** or until cheese starts

to melt. **LET STAND 1 MINUTE** to finish melting cheese. If desired, use crumbled bacon as garnish.

> **TIP:** If you were to overcook the sandwich, the bread would become tough and rubbery and the cheese stringy.

It is easy to make extra scrambled eggs for breakfast and then reheat leftovers for lunchtime sandwiches.

Toast the bread first to give more body to the sandwich. If using a bun which has a crust, the toasting step is optional.

Our times are based on leftover cold scrambled eggs. For warmer eggs, times are reduced slightly, depending on temperature.

If eggs have cooled completely, the sandwiches can be assembled early, loosely wrapped and stored in refrigerator.

SCRAMBLED EGG SANDWICH

For each sandwich, toast 2 slices of bread. If desired, butter and spread with catsup or mustard. Top one slice of toast with cool scrambled eggs (about 2 eggs per sandwich). Cover with other slice of toast. Place on paper napkin or plate and **COOK,** uncovered, **1 MINUTE** or until egg steams when bread is lifted. **LET STAND 1 MINUTE** to distribute the heat.   1 Sandwich

> **TIPS:** For cheese 'n egg sandwich, use only 1 scrambled egg per sandwich and top with slice of Cheddar or Swiss cheese. Reduce cooking time to 45 seconds or until cheese is melted.
>
> • Chopped ham and green pepper can be added to egg before scrambling for a Denver flavored egg sandwich.

Pictured: Tacos and Wieners in the Round, recipes this page.

Wieners are curled to form a circular holder for an easy filling of beans, macaroni or leftover casserole.

Wieners normally require a longer time to cook than any of the fillings. By placing the wieners in an outside circle, they will be heated first. The quicker cooking filling is placed in the center of the dish; since this center is the more difficult to heat spot, the filling will not be overcooked before the wieners are done. However, the filling should not be mounded too high in the center.

The temperature and density of the filling will affect heating times. These times are based on room temperature fillings.

These can be prepared and left covered on plates ready for quick, fix-yourself heating. If stored in refrigerator, add about 30 sec. to the cooking time for each plate.

WIENERS IN THE ROUND

For each serving, take 2 wieners, slice almost through at ½-inch intervals on outside edge. On serving plate with slit sides of wieners to the outside, bring the 2 wieners together to form a circle. Fasten ends together with toothpicks. Fill center with pork and beans, baked beans, canned spaghetti, macaroni and cheese, sauerkraut, German potato salad or mashed potatoes. Brush wiener with catsup or barbecue sauce. **COOK** one plate at a time, uncovered, **1 MINUTE, 30 SECONDS** or until hot. Remove toothpicks and serve. If desired, garnish with crushed potato chips or French fried onion rings.

The filling for tacos is easily cooked in the oven; then the meat filled shells are heated to serve piping hot.

This mixture should thicken during cooking, so leave uncovered to allow the steam to evaporate. To eliminate spatters in the oven, place a paper towel over the casserole dish; this is porous enough to allow some moisture to pass through or be absorbed.

During the cooking time for the ground beef filling, prepare the lettuce, tomato and cheese.

TACOS

1 lb. ground beef
1 package (1¼ oz.) taco seasoning mix
½ cup water
10 fried and shaped taco shells
Shredded lettuce
Shredded cheese
Chopped fresh tomato

In 1-quart casserole, crumble ground beef; sprinkle with seasoning mix. **COOK**, uncovered, **5 MINUTES.** Stir to break meat into small pieces. Add water and **COOK**, covered with paper towel, **5 MINUTES** or until most of liquid is evaporated. Spoon mixture into taco shells (placing filled shells in straight sided glass baking dish will help keep them upright) and return shells to oven for **1½ TO 2 MINUTES** or until heated through. Serve with lettuce, cheese and tomato to spoon onto hot filling.

10 Tacos

The oven quickly melts caramels. It can also be used to reheat and soften the caramel mixture if it becomes too thick.

Use a deep bowl for ease in dipping and coating the apples.

CARAMEL APPLES

14-oz. bag (49) caramels
2 tablespoons hot water
5 medium apples, washed and dried
Wooden sticks

Unwrap caramels and place in deep glass mixing bowl; add water. **COOK**, uncovered, **2 MINUTES, 45 SECONDS** or until caramels are melted, stirring occasionally and watching carefully so mixture does not boil over. While mixture cooks, insert sticks into stem end of apples. Dip each apple into hot caramel mixture, turning to coat. Using edge of dish, remove excess mixture from bottom of apples. Place apples on greased wax paper. (If mixture becomes too stiff, just return to oven for about 20 seconds to heat.) Refrigerate until set, about 20 minutes. Store in a cool place.

5 Apples

TIP: If wax paper is not greased, it will stick to the caramel mixture.

The oven can be used to quickly heat purchased or homemade cookies to give them a freshly baked taste.

They should be heated just until they feel warm and are a temperature that can be eaten immediately.

WARM COOKIES

Place cookies on paper napkin or plate. Cook, uncovered, just until cookie feels warm:

    1 cookie — 10 seconds
    2 cookies — 15 seconds
    3 cookies — 20 seconds
    4 cookies — 25 seconds

TIP: If you were to overcook a cookie, it would become dry and might cause raisins or dates, which attract energy because of their high sugar content, to be too hot or even burned.

Pieces of cake take on a freshly baked taste when warmed a few seconds in the oven just before serving.

Cake can be warmed on either a paper or glass plate. A little moisture may condense on the bottom of the cake on a glass plate but it will not be noticeable with the moist cake texture.

WARM CAKE SQUARES

Place squares of **UNFROSTED** cake on paper napkin, plate or glass serving plate. Cook, uncovered, just until cake feels warm:

    1 piece — 15 seconds
    2 pieces — 25 seconds
    3 pieces — 35 seconds
    4 pieces — 50 seconds

TIP: Do not use frosted cake because the frosting might melt in the time it takes for a room temperature cake to become warm.

This thick fudgy sauce uses the convenience of frosting mix. Keep on hand for quick reheating.

LICKETY THICK FUDGE SAUCE

  ⅔ cup (5-oz. can) evaporated milk
  1 package (15.4 oz.) fudge frosting mix
  ½ cup butter or margarine

In 4-cup measure, measure milk; stir in frosting mix until moistened. Add butter and **COOK,** uncovered, **4 MINUTES,** stirring occasionally and watching carefully last minute to avoid boiling over. Serve warm or cool over cake, ice cream or pudding.   3 Cups Sauce

A roll or cookie on top of prepared pie filling, canned fruit or prepared pudding makes a quick and tasty dessert that can be prepared and heated in a serving dish. The dessert should be heated just until it reaches serving temperature.

Although a roll is usually larger than a cookie, they will heat in similar times because the roll is more porous than a cookie.

QUICK COBBLER DESSERT

For each serving, spoon ½ cup prepared pie filling, canned fruit and syrup or prepared pudding into glass serving dish. Top with a sweet roll or a soft cookie. Cook, uncovered, until warm:

    1 serving — 35 seconds
    2 servings — 1 minute
    3 servings — 1 minute, 15 seconds
    4 Servings — 1 minute, 30 seconds

S'mores are easy for children or adults to make in the oven.

The marshmallow heats faster than the chocolate so they need to stand a minute after cooking to allow the heat from the marshmallow to melt the chocolate.

The S'mores are wrapped in a napkin to hold in the heat and melt the chocolate. The marshmallow puffs about 3 times its size when it heats and the napkin helps control this puffing so the marshmallow will not push the top cracker off and then roll off the bottom cracker.

S'MORES

For each S'more, place 2 squares of a milk chocolate candy bar on a graham cracker square. Top with 1 large marshmallow and then another graham cracker square. Wrap in a napkin. Cook until marshmallow melts:

    1 S'more — 15 seconds
    2 S'mores — 25 seconds
    3 S'mores — 35 seconds
    4 S'mores — 45 seconds

LET STAND 1 MINUTE to melt chocolate.

TIPS: Graham crackers can be spread with peanut butter before topping with chocolate. Use same cooking times.

• When using miniature marshmallows, use 9 marshmallows for each S'more.

• If you were to overcook a marshmallow, it would scorch. It will turn dark and scorch first in the center before any dark spot shows on the outside.

Pictured: Caramel Apples, page 21, S'Mores, page 22 and Pudding, below.

This interesting fruit tapioca has the consistency of sauce when warm and is set up like pudding when cold. It makes an easy and good addition to fresh fruits in season.

As with pudding, the stirring is necessary to distribute the heat and to distribute the tapioca that will tend to settle toward the bottom. The stirring is most important during the second half of cooking when the pudding begins to thicken.

The container is covered with a tight fitting lid to hold in the heat and speed the cooking process because you are cooking fruits as well as thickening pudding. This pudding has a water base rather than milk base so it will not boil over easily.

This is a good recipe to cook just before starting the meal so it will be warm and saucy when served. Or, if you prefer a thick pudding consistency, make early so it can cool.

Puddings and sauces cook easily in the oven because the heat comes from all sides, eliminating the possibility of scorching.

Stirring occasionally is necessary to distribute the heat and to mix in the thickening ingredients that tend to settle toward the bottom. The stirring is only necessary during the last half of the cooking time and then only about once every minute.

In selecting a cooking container, it is best to use one that holds twice the milk measurement because when the mixture starts to boil it will rise in the container. A 4-cup measure is very convenient because the milk can be measured and then the pudding added. A 1-quart (4 cup) mixing bowl can also be used, if you prefer.

A wooden spoon or rubber scraper that is being used for stirring can be left in the pudding during cooking. The wood may become a little warm, but will not affect the cooking times or the stirring utensil. Metal spoons should not be left in the oven during cooking.

Pudding can easily be put in the oven to cook while you start to prepare foods for lunch or dinner. It is then slightly warm for serving after the meal. Dress it up with toasted coconut, fresh fruits, crushed cookie crumbs (a good way to clean out the cookie jar) or baked pastry leftovers.

FRUIT TAPIOCA

3 medium apples, sliced
2 tablespoons butter or margarine
½ teaspoon salt
¼ teaspoon cinnamon or nutmeg
1 tablespoon lemon juice
⅓ cup quick-cooking tapioca
1 cup light brown sugar
2¼ cups water

In 2-quart glass casserole, combine all ingredients. **COOK,** covered with casserole lid, **10 MINUTES** or until apples are tender, stirring occasionally. Serve warm or cold.   6 Servings

TIP: Try with 3 cups cut-up rhubarb, or 3 cups (1½ pts.) blueberries. For best color, use white sugar with these fruits.

PUDDING

Select favorite flavor of 4-serving size pudding and pie filling mix. In 4-cup glass measure, measure milk as directed on package. Stir in pudding mix, stirring until dissolved. **COOK,** uncovered, **5 MINUTES** or until mixture starts to boil, stirring occasionally during last half of cooking time. Pour into 3 or 4 serving dishes and cool.   3 to 4 Servings

TIPS: For 6-serving package of pudding, use 1½-quart mixing bowl or pitcher and cook 7 minutes.

• Not stirring the pudding will cause it to be lumpy. If this happens, just beat until smooth with an egg beater or wire whip.

• Leftover refrigerated pudding can be heated in the oven to a freshly cooked temperature by heating one serving, uncovered, about 30 seconds or until warm. Let stand 1 minute to distribute the heat.

Dinner

MENU
**Fillet of Sole in Almond Butter
Parslied Rice
Tomatoes with Mayonnaise Topping
Relishes
Grand Marnier Sauce with Cake or Fruit**

This menu has quick-cooking last minute foods, which means table setting and relish or salad preparation should be done before the main dishes are begun. If expecting company, you may want to do as much preparation as possible before your guests arrive so that you can spend more time with them. If preparing the menu all at once, allow 30 to 45 minutes for the preparation and cooking.

In this menu we would suggest YOU DO WELL IN ADVANCE: THE RELISHES, ASSEMBLING THE TOMATOES AND PREPARING THE SAUCE AND FRUITS OR CAKE SQUARES. Although the Grand Marnier Sauce will be served warm, it is easier to cook first and then reheat while clearing the dishes just before serving dessert. Wait to add the liqueur until after reheating for the strongest liqueur flavor.

With these quick-cooking, last minute foods, rice may be easiest to prepare conventionally and then, if necessary, reheat in the serving dish just before placing on the table. If fixing in the oven, COOK RICE BEFORE THE FISH AND TOMATOES as it needs to stand about 10 minutes after cooking. You may want to add a little parsley to the rice just before serving. THE FIRST PART OF FISH RECIPE CAN BE DONE AHEAD: the almonds can be toasted and other sauce ingredients added and then left to stand at room temperature. ADD THE FISH about 10 minutes before serving, and continue with the cooking.
COOK THE TOMATOES AFTER THE FISH IS COOKED. The tomatoes can be sliced and topped with the mayonnaise mixture up to an hour before time to heat; keep them stored in the refrigerator. If the rice needs reheating, put it in the oven as you place other foods on the table.

While clearing the table, reheat the Grand Marnier Sauce. Reheat perked coffee or heat water for instant coffee while placing sauce and fruit or cake on the table.

The fast microwave cooking of fish retains the juices and delicate flavor, making it one of the best foods cooked in the oven.

The almonds and butter are browned in the oven before the remaining ingredients are added and give a nice golden brown color to the sauce and the fish.

In arranging fish in the baking dish, place the larger ends and pieces toward the outside and the small, thin pieces toward the center.

Fish is usually cooked covered to hold in the heat and steam which speeds the cooking process. The covering can be either plastic wrap, since it will not be touching the food, or wax paper across the top of the dish.

Since fish cooks so quickly, a standing time is necessary to distribute the heat to the center. When testing doneness, test toward the outside. If this flakes, the center should flake after the fish has been standing a couple minutes.

To defrost fish, see page 45.

FILLET OF SOLE IN ALMOND BUTTER

   **⅓ cup slivered or sliced almonds
   ⅓ cup butter or margarine
   2 tablespoons lemon juice
   2 tablespoons white wine or sherry
   ½ teaspoon dill weed or seed
   ½ teaspoon salt
   1 lb. fresh or frozen sole, halibut or perch fillets, thawed**

In 2-quart (8 x 8) glass baking dish, combine almonds and butter. **COOK**, uncovered, **5 MINUTES** or until butter and almonds are golden brown. Stir in lemon juice, wine, dill and salt. Arrange fillets in butter mixture, spooning sauce over fillets. **COOK**, covered with wax paper or plastic wrap, **5 MINUTES** or until fish flakes easily. **LET STAND**, covered, **2 MINUTES** before serving. If desired, garnish with lemon slices or dill pickle slices.   4 Servings

   TIPS: If desired, omit wine.

   • Fish is less tender and moist if it overcooks.

The tomatoes can be heated right on the serving plate or dish if it can be used in the oven.

A cover is not used on this recipe because it would stick to the topping and the tomatoes heat so quickly that a cover is not necessary.

TOMATOES WITH MAYONNAISE TOPPING

4 tomatoes
Salt
Pepper
¼ cup mayonnaise or salad dressing
2 teaspoons instant minced onion
2 tablespoons prepared mustard
Paprika

Cut tomatoes in half crosswise; place on glass serving platter or baking dish and sprinkle with salt and pepper. Combine mayonnaise, mustard and onion. Spread on tomato halves. Sprinkle with paprika. **COOK, uncovered, 3 TO 4 MINUTES** or until topping begins to bubble. **LET STAND A FEW SECONDS** to distribute heat.

> **TIPS:** Tomatoes and topping can be assembled up to an hour before heating. Store in refrigerator.
>
> • For 2 tomatoes, use half of ingredient amounts and cook 1 minute, 30 seconds.

When preparing dessert sauces such as this, use the same techniques as in cooking pudding.

Sauces are easy to cook ahead and then reheat before serving. When adding a liqueur as in this recipe, it is best added just before serving. Each time the sauce is boiled or heated, a little of the flavor evaporates.

Try this as a fondue sauce, (see Tip) or serve over fresh or canned fruit, ice cream, cake, steamed pudding or a dessert soufflé.

GRAND MARNIER SAUCE

¼ cup sugar
1 tablespoon cornstarch
¾ cup orange juice
2 to 4 tablespoons Grand Marnier or
**   other orange liqueur**

In 2-cup glass measure, combine sugar and cornstarch; stir in orange juice. **COOK, uncovered, 2 MINUTES** or until mixture boils and thickens slightly, stirring occasionally during last half of cooking time. Stir in liqueur. Serve warm or cold.   1 Cup Sauce

> **TIP:** To use as a fondue dip, reduce cornstarch to ½ tablespoon. Serve with fresh fruits, cake squares or cookie wafers.

MENU
Chicken Atop Rice
Buttered Carrots
Creamy Wilted Lettuce
Ice Cream with
Warm Topping

This dinner can be prepared in less than an hour. You can assemble most of the other foods in this menu during the half hour it takes to cook the chicken.
COOK BACON for Creamy Wilted Lettuce first because it is easier to cook before starting the other parts of the meal than at the last minute. If the salad were the only food being prepared in the oven, the bacon could be cooked just before completing the salad. While the bacon is cooking, begin preparing the chicken dish.
WHILE THE CHICKEN COOKS, prepare the buttered carrots and the salad dressing for cooking. Wash and tear the lettuce into pieces, slice the onions and return to the refrigerator; set the table.
COOK CARROTS after chicken is cooked, covered and set aside.
THE SALAD DRESSING COOKS when the carrots are done. As it is cooking, place the chicken and carrots on the table, leaving them covered to hold in the heat. When the dressing is cooked, mix with lettuce and onions and bring to the table.

When clearing the table, pour a jar of prepared ice cream topping into a serving pitcher or bowl and HEAT TOPPING in the oven about 45 seconds or until bubbles begin to appear. Stir to distribute heat and spoon over ice cream. If you are heating about a half a jar of topping, it can be left in its original container. However, a completely full jar of topping boils over very easily and can be difficult to pick up without a handle.

Chicken cooks atop a creamy, quick-cooking rice mixture for an easy family or company dish. When regular cooking rice is used, it needs more water to rehydrate.

By cutting chicken into uniform pieces, it is not necessary to turn or rearrange during the cooking process. In arranging the chicken on the rice, place the larger, thicker ends toward the outside of the dish.

If you want to cook the giblets with the chicken, tuck them under other pieces of chicken toward the center of the dish so they will not overcook.

Paprika is sprinkled on the chicken to accent the browning that will take place in the microwave oven. If you prefer more browning or a crisper skin, place the chicken under the broiler while cooking other food in the microwave oven. The chicken will brown and stay hot at the same time.

Chicken cooks with a piece of wax paper placed loosely over the top. The wax paper holds in enough heat to speed the cooking and yet the chicken pieces have a chance to brown.

CHICKEN ATOP RICE

**1½ cups quick-cooking rice, uncooked
½ cup (4-oz. can) drained mushroom
   stems and pieces
1 stalk (½ cup) celery, chopped
1 can (10½ oz.) condensed cream of
   chicken soup
1 soup can milk (1⅓ cups)
2½ to 3-lb. frying chicken, cut up
1 teaspoon salt
Paprika
Poultry seasoning**

In 2-quart (12 x 7) glass baking dish, combine rice, mushrooms, celery, soup and milk; mix well. Cut larger pieces of chicken in half for uniform size. Arrange on top of rice, skin-side up. Sprinkle with salt, paprika and poultry seasoning. **COOK**, covered with wax paper, **28 MINUTES** or until chicken is done.

5 to 6 Servings

TIPS: Other flavors of cream soup can be used; try celery and omit chopped celery, try mushroom and omit mushrooms or try asparagus soup.

• Overcooking is not critical but eventually the thin parts of chicken would develop hard, dry spots.

Most fresh vegetables are best cooked with a small amount of water and then seasoned before serving. Salt added during the cooking would draw moisture out of the carrots.

When adding seasonings toward the end of cooking the vegetable, you can use part of the cooking time to double as a heating time to blend the seasonings.

Vegetables are cooked covered and with a small amount of liquid. This provides steam in the cooking dish so that they will not become dry. The stirring helps them cook evenly and keeps them moist from the liquid in the bottom of the dish. When not stirred or if overcooked, the top carrots may become slightly withered.

BUTTERED CARROTS

**4 to 5 medium carrots, sliced
2 tablespoons water
2 tablespoons butter or margarine
¼ teaspoon salt
¼ teaspoon dill weed, if desired**

In 1-quart glass casserole, combine carrots and water. **COOK**, covered with casserole cover, **6 TO 7 MINUTES** or until carrots are just about tender, stirring occasionally. Add butter, salt and dill weed. **COOK**, uncovered, **1 MINUTE**, stirring once after butter melts to glaze carrots. **LET STAND**, covered, **SEVERAL MINUTES** to finish cooking.   5 to 6 Servings

The bacon and warm dressing can be cooked in the same salad dish used for serving. If you are planning to use a wooden salad bowl, cook bacon and dressing in a glass bowl and then assemble the salad in the wooden bowl because the wooden bowl would dry out and might crack with repeated use in the oven.

CREAMY WILTED LETTUCE

**6 slices bacon
½ cup sour cream
1 egg, slightly beaten
¼ cup vinegar
2 tablespoons sugar
Dash salt
1 head (6 cups) lettuce, torn
3 to 4 medium green onions, sliced**

In large mixing bowl or serving bowl, **COOK** bacon between pieces of paper towel **3 MINUTES, 15 SECONDS** or until crisp. Remove paper and bacon, leaving about 3 tablespoons drippings in dish. Stir in sour cream, egg, vinegar, sugar and salt. **COOK**, uncovered, **3 MINUTES** or until thickened, stirring occasionally during last half of cooking. Add lettuce, onions and crumbled bacon, tossing until well coated. Serve immediately.

6 Servings

TIPS: When fresh spinach is available, use half spinach and half lettuce.

• Extra dressing can be refrigerated for reheating. It is delicious served over sliced fresh tomatoes. Use crumbled bacon as a garnish.

MENU
Ham Slice in Orange Sauce
Simple Scalloped Potatoes
Fresh or Frozen Broccoli
Salad
Apple Pie

MAKE THE APPLE PIE AHEAD because it is easy to reheat after cutting and placing on serving plates. When pie is prepared early, allow ¾ to 1 hour to fix dinner. However, it can be prepared just before starting the main part of dinner; allow 1¼ hours to fix dinner. While it is in the microwave oven, you can begin preparing other foods to go into the oven.
COOK POTATOES BEFORE HAM AND BROCCOLI because potatoes cook the longest of the main meal foods and hold the heat while they are standing covered. They can be peeled and mixed with other ingredients while the pie is in the microwave oven. Then they will be ready to cook when the pie comes out. While the potatoes cook, prepare the ham slice and set the table.
COOK THE HAM SLICE when the potatoes are finished cooking. The ham is cooked now because it holds the heat better than the vegetable. While the ham slice cooks, prepare the broccoli and fix a salad of your choice.
COOK THE BROCCOLI after the ham is cooked and covered with a tight fitting cover or foil to hold in heat. If foods are still piping hot, place them on table, removing covers just before sitting down to eat. If they have cooled, return to oven for about 1 minute to heat before placing on table along with broccoli.

When it is time for dessert, HEAT COFFEE BEFORE THE PIE because the coffee will take longer to heat and will hold the heat better than the pie.

A simple orange glaze makes an attractive and tasty dress-up for ham.

A specially purchased ham slice can be used for this or buy a ready-to-eat boned ham and cut a slice of about the same thickness. If you can use the remaining ham, this is probably a better buy than the ham slice.

The cooking time allows the sauce to boil and thicken and the ham to heat through. If the slices are thinner than in this recipe, the time needed to heat will be less.

Since ham shapes and sizes vary, you can use any shallow dish that will hold the ham slice easily. If you are using smaller individual slices of ham, use a 1½-quart (10 x 6 or 8-inch round) baking dish.

HAM SLICE IN ORANGE SAUCE
  ½ cup firmly packed brown sugar
  1 tablespoon cornstarch
  ⅛ teaspoon ground ginger
  1 cup orange juice
  8 to 10 whole cloves
  1 ham slice, cut 1-inch thick

In shallow glass baking dish (a size that ham slice will fit), combine brown sugar, cornstarch and ginger. Stir in orange juice. Add ham slice, turning to coat both sides. Sprinkle with cloves. **COOK**, uncovered, **9 MINUTES** or until hot and bubbly, ocasionally spooning sauce over ham. **LET STAND**, covered, **2 MINUTES** to finish cooking.   4 to 5 Servings

> **TIPS:** For 1½-inch thick ham slice, cook 12 minutes — serves 6 to 8.
>
> • For ½-inch thick ham slice, use half the orange sauce and cook 6 minutes — serves 3 to 4.

In this easy recipe for scalloped potatoes, the ingredients for a white sauce cook and thicken as the potatoes cook.

The casserole called for may seem a little large, but the extra space is necessary to allow the milk to boil. With a smaller casserole, part of the milk may boil over, making it necessary to add more milk toward the end of the cooking time.

The potatoes are occasionally stirred to mix those at the outside that cook first with those in the center that cook more slowly. The stirring also helps mix the white sauce as it cooks. In a recipe such as this, you may want to stir 3 or 4 times during the cooking process.

SIMPLE SCALLOPED POTATOES
  5 cups (4 medium) peeled and sliced
    potatoes
  1 tablespoon flour
  1 teaspoon salt
  ¼ cup chopped onion or 1 tablespoon
    instant minced onion
  1½ cups milk
  1 tablespoon butter or margarine

In 2½ or 3-quart glass casserole, arrange sliced potatoes. Add flour, salt, and onion; toss lightly. Stir in milk and dot with butter. **COOK**, covered with casserole cover, **15 MINUTES** or until potatoes are desired doneness, stirring occasionally. If desired, sprinkle with paprika or parsley. **LET STAND**, covered, **5 MINUTES** to finish cooking.   4 to 5 Servings

> **TIP:** For 2 to 3 servings, use half the ingredients in 1½ or 2-quart casserole and cook about 10 minutes.

Frozen and fresh vegetables cook quickly in the oven and retain a fresh flavor and bright color.

The vegetables are covered to hold in the heat and steam and to prevent dehydration. By placing frozen vegetables in the container, icy side up, the moisture runs over the vegetables as they cook.

With frozen broccoli, additional water is not necessary during the cooking process. With fresh, a little extra moisture is needed to keep the vegetables from dehydrating. This water addition varies with each vegetable.

Salt tends to draw moisture out of foods, so we suggest adding it after cooking. If it is more convenient to put on before cooking, place it in the bottom of the dish before adding the vegetable.

Where it is possible to arrange the spears in the cooking dish, as with a fresh vegetable, the part that takes the longest to cook (stalk) is placed toward the outside of the dish.

BROCCOLI

Place frozen broccoli spears from a 10-oz. package in 1-quart glass casserole, icy side up. **COOK,** covered, **6 TO 7 MINUTES** or until just about tender, rearranging once. **LET STAND,** covered, **1 TO 2 MINUTES** to finish cooking. Drain and season as desired.

4 Servings

TIPS: For 2 packages of broccoli spears, use 1½-quart casserole and cook, covered, 9 to 10 minutes.

• For fresh broccoli, split stalks to make uniform in size. Place in 1½-quart casserole with stalks toward outside of dish. Add ¼ cup water. Cook, covered, 7 to 9 minutes or until just about tender. Let stand 1 to 2 minutes to finish cooking. Drain and season as desired.

• If you overcook broccoli, it loses some of its green color.

We recommend a combination of microwave and conventional cooking with some foods where browning is important and we are not able to achieve this browning using the microwave oven alone. Two crust pies are an example of this. Cooked only in the microwave oven, the crust would not brown and would not be crisp. A pastry shell of a one crust pie can become crisp because the filling is cooked separately (see page 155). However, when there is moisture from a filling as in a two crust pie, some conventional cooking is needed to dry and crisp the crust.

Since the filling cooks very quickly in the microwave oven, the crust will be more crispy and flaky than when cooked just conventionally. Also, since the crust is evenly hot when it goes into the conventional oven, the browning is especially even.

For a golden brown color, use the pie crust stick or mix that has a yellow color to the dough, or add 7 to 8 drops yellow food color to the water for your home recipe pastry.

FRESH APPLE PIE

Prepare favorite recipe for two crust fresh apple pie in 9-inch glass pie plate. Preheat conventional oven to 450°. While preheating, **COOK** pie, uncovered in microwave oven, **7 TO 8 MINUTES** or until apples are just about tender or juice begins to bubble through slits in the crust. Transfer to preheated oven and **COOK 10 TO 15 MINUTES** or until light golden brown.

9-inch Pie

TIPS: To cook other fruit pies or unbaked frozen fruit pies, see page 156.

• To reheat slices of pie, cook 1 slice 15 seconds; cook 2 slices 25 seconds.

MENU
One Dish Macaroni and Beef
Tossed Salad
Hot Dinner Rolls
Pineapple Upside Down Cake

This meal can be prepared, including dessert, in less than 45 minutes.

FIRST COOK UPSIDE DOWN CAKE so it can cool while the rest of the meal is being cooked. When time for dessert, the cake should still be slightly warm. If you care to reheat it, see the times in the Lunch section for warm cake.

While the cake is cooking, mix together the macaroni and beef casserole. When the cake comes from the oven, begin cooking the casserole.

WHILE CASSEROLE COOKS, prepare the salad, set the table and arrange rolls in basket for heating.

PLACE ROLLS IN OVEN 30 seconds to heat when casserole is cooked and other foods are on the table.

While clearing dishes from the table, reheat perked coffee or heat water for instant coffee.

This tasty macaroni and beef casserole is mixed together in one step and cooked in just 15 minutes.

You may prefer to use lean ground beef because the ground beef in this casserole is not precooked to drain the fat. Otherwise, you may want to skim off excess fat before serving. Paper towels work nicely for blotting up any excess fat on the top of foods.

A tight fitting lid is used to hold in heat and moisture.

The casserole is stirred once about halfway through cooking to distribute the heat evenly in the casserole. The stirring before serving is for the same purpose.

ONE DISH MACARONI AND BEEF

½ lb. ground beef
1 cup uncooked macaroni
1 small (¼ cup) onion, chopped, or
1 tablespoon instant minced onion
1 cup (8-oz. can) tomato sauce
1½ cans water (1½ cups)
⅓ cup catsup
1 can (7 oz.) whole kernel corn, undrained
1 tablespoon brown sugar
½ teaspoon salt
¼ teaspoon pepper
¼ teaspoon chili powder

In 2-quart glass casserole, combine all ingredients, mixing well. **COOK,** covered with casserole cover, **15 MINUTES** or until macaroni is tender, stirring once. Stir before serving. **LET STAND SEVERAL MINUTES** to finish cooking.

4 Servings

TIPS: If desired, other cooked vegetables can be used for corn.

• The meat in this casserole will be in fine pieces. If you prefer larger pieces of meat, cook ground beef, uncovered, 3 minutes; stir to break into pieces; add remaining ingredients and continue as directed.

HOT DINNER ROLLS

Place baked dinner rolls in cloth or paper napkin lined basket. **COOK,** uncovered, about **30 SECONDS** or until surface of rolls feels warm.

TIP: If you were to overcook rolls, they would become tough and rubbery.

Many cake mixes can be cooked in the oven, but we would suggest starting with upside down cake since the timing is less critical. Upside down cake has an exceptionally moist, delicate texture. When a sweet pineapple or other fruit layer is added to the bottom of the cake, part of the energy is attracted to the sweet fruit layer, allowing the cake to cook more slowly and evenly.

Most cakes and baked type products are cooked uncovered. The top has more of a crust-like appearance when moisture can escape.

PINEAPPLE UPSIDE DOWN CAKE

2 tablespoons butter or margarine
⅓ cup firmly packed brown sugar
¾ cup (8-oz. can) drained crushed pineapple (use syrup for part of liquid in cake)
½ package (about 2⅓ cups) yellow cake mix

In 2-quart (8 x 8) glass baking dish, melt butter (20 sec.). Blend in brown sugar and pineapple; spread evenly over bottom of dish. Prepare cake mix as directed on package using half the ingredient amounts. Pour over pineapple mixture in pan, spreading to cover pineapple. **COOK,** uncovered, **8 MINUTES, 30 SECONDS** or until toothpick comes out clean. **LET STAND 1 MINUTE** before loosening edge and inverting onto serving plate. Serve warm or cold with whipped cream.   8-inch Square Cake

TIPS: About 1 cup (half of 21-oz. can) of prepared pie filling can be used for the brown sugar and pineapple. Cake will take about 8 minutes to cook. It's especially good with cherry, pineapple and apple. You might like to add a little cinnamon or apple pie spice with the apple.

• The Pineapple Upside Down Cake Mix can be prepared as directed on package and cooked, using above times.

MENU
Meat Loaf
German Potato Salad
French-cut Green Beans
Easy Rice Pudding

You should allow at least an hour to prepare this dinner when you are first learning to use your new oven. It is better to have too much time because any of the foods can be returned to the oven for quick reheating.

PREPARE RICE PUDDING FIRST because it needs to cool and other foods need to be prepared near serving time.

THE GERMAN POTATO SALAD IS NEXT because it has more preparation steps and takes longer than the meat loaf. The potatoes take about 10 minutes to cook and during this time you can combine the meat loaf mixture and leave it in the refrigerator. By keeping it refrigerated, the recipe cooking times still apply. If it stood at room temperature long enough to start to warm, the times may be less than the directions state. You may also want to set the table during this time.

COOK THE MEAT LOAF after the potato salad is cooked and has been set aside, covered, to hold the heat. While it cooks, finish setting the table and put the canned green beans into a serving dish that can also be used in the oven, draining off most of the liquid. Cover the beans with a plate to hold in the heat and speed the heating process. The vegetable can be cooked conventionally, but a simple canned vegetable that only needs reheating is convenient to put in the oven during the standing time for the meat loaf.

When the meat loaf comes out and is standing for 5 minutes, HEAT THE BEANS by cooking about 3 minutes or until steaming hot. Return the potato salad to the oven for about 1 minute to heat through.

This tasty meat loaf has an attractive tangy topping of brown sugar, catsup and mustard. To keep this attractive appearance when served, keep this top side up when meat loaf is transferred to serving platter.

When mixing in the baking dish, the mixture should always be spread evenly before cooking. If not, the food may overcook in some places before other areas are cooked. Small food pieces that cling to the sides of the dish may overcook or burn.

For covering use a piece of wax paper over the top of the dish during cooking. This helps hold in the heat and prevents spattering in the oven.

To check doneness, make a cut near the center of meat loaf. A pink center will finish cooking and lose its pinkness during standing but a red center indicates more cooking time is needed.

MEAT LOAF

  1½ **lbs. ground beef**
  ⅔ **cup milk**
   1 **egg**
   3 **tablespoons onion soup mix**
  ¼ **teaspoon salt**
   3 **tablespoons brown sugar**
  ½ **teaspoon dry or prepared mustard**
   3 **tablespoons catsup**

In 1½-quart (8 x 4) glass loaf dish, combine ground beef, milk, egg, soup mix and salt; mix well. (Mixture will be very moist.) Press evenly in pan. Combine brown sugar, mustard and catsup; spoon and spread over top of meat. **COOK,** covered with wax paper, **8 MINUTES** or until center is done. **LET STAND,** covered with same wax paper, **5 MINUTES** to finish cooking. With spatulas, remove to serving platter and slice.   4 to 5 Servings

> **TIPS:** Meat loaf can be prepared several hours ahead and stored in the refrigerator. Cook as directed.
>
> ● For other meat loaf recipes, see page 73 in Beef section.

German Potato Salad takes a while to make, but we have found it convenient in the oven because the potatoes, bacon and dressing can be quickly cooked. Also, it need not be a last minute preparation since it can easily be reheated.

Potatoes should still feel a little firm when they are removed from the oven. They continue to cook before they are peeled and sliced and cook a little more when added to the hot dressing.

When the bacon drippings add flavor to a recipe, cook the bacon in the same dish used to prepare the remainder of the recipe. You can regulate the amount of drippings that are left in the pan by the amount of paper towels in the bottom of the dish. Here you want part, but not all, of the drippings so use only one layer of towels.

GERMAN POTATO SALAD

>   **4 medium potatoes**
>   **4 slices bacon**
>   **½ cup (1 med.) chopped onion or 6 green onions, sliced**
>   **2 tablespoons sugar**
>   **1 tablespoon flour**
>   **1 teaspoon or cube beef bouillon**
>   **1 teaspoon salt**
>   **¼ teaspoon ground allspice, if desired**
>   **Dash pepper**
>   **¼ cup vinegar**
>   **½ cup water**

Cook potatoes as directed on page 35; set aside. In glass mixing bowl (can be bowl in which you will serve the salad) place 1 layer of paper towel. Cut bacon into pieces so that it will lie in a single layer in bowl. Cover with another paper towel. **COOK** about **2 MINUTES, 30 SECONDS** or until crisp. Remove towel and bacon leaving drippings in bowl. Add onion to drippings and **COOK,** uncovered, **1 MINUTE.** Stir in sugar, flour, bouillon, salt, allspice and pepper. Blend in vinegar and water. **COOK,** uncovered, **3 MINUTES** or until mixture boils and thickens, stirring twice. While mixture cooks, peel potatoes. Slice potatoes into hot mixture and toss lightly to coat potatoes. Crumble bacon over top and serve warm.

4 to 5 Servings

>   **TIPS:** Salad can be prepared several hours ahead and then heated, covered, in oven about 1 minute.
>
>   • For 2 to 3 servings, use half of ingredients, cook bacon 1½ to 2 minutes, and dressing mixture 2 minutes.

By using a pudding mix, you can make rice pudding that has the flavor of the old-fashioned baked type and the preparation ease of a pudding mix. If you have not prepared pudding in the oven, you may want to refer to page 23 in the lunch section for more background on the preparation.

The cooking times and directions for preparing plain custard mix are similar to the pudding directions.

EASY RICE PUDDING

>   **1 package (4-serving size) vanilla pudding and pie filling mix**
>   **2½ cups milk**
>   **½ cup raisins**
>   **½ cup quick-cooking rice**

In 4-cup glass measure or casserole combine all ingredients. **COOK,** uncovered, **6 MINUTES** or until mixture boils, stirring occasionally during last half of cooking time. Serve warm or cool.

4 to 6 Servings

>   **TIP:** A 3-oz. package custard mix can be used for pudding mix, preparing and cooking as directed. The custard mix needs to cool before it will set.

MENU
Bacon-Wrapped Water Chestnuts
Hot Cheese Snacks
Broiled or Grilled Steak
Baked Potatoes
Tossed Salad
Frozen Lemon Dessert

This menu is an example of combining microwave cooking with other types of cooking to make meal preparation easier. It is a good meal to serve to guests because there is very little last minute preparation.
PREPARE THE FROZEN DESSERT EARLY IN THE DAY or the night before to allow time to freeze.
HORS D'OEUVRES CAN BE ASSEMBLED EARLY, using the make ahead suggestions on the recipes so that only last minute heating is necessary.
SALAD GREENS CAN BE PREPARED AHEAD and placed in the refrigerator with a damp paper towel over the top to keep them crisp. Then, just before serving, toss with dressing.

Plan your schedule around the time it takes to BROIL THE STEAK. We do not suggest cooking steak in the microwave oven because it cooks too fast to brown and it takes only minutes to broil or grill conventionally.* The microwave oven can be used after broiling or grilling steak to finish cooking to the right degree of doneness.
It will take only a few seconds; remember that it will continue to cook after being removed from the oven. If you grill extra steaks, they can quickly be reheated in the microwave oven the next day. A cold cooked steak will take about 1½ to 2 minutes to reheat.

To defrost steak, see page 45.
COOK THE POTATOES in the microwave oven while the steak is being broiled. When cooked, wrap potatoes in foil or place them in the conventional oven away from the broiler to keep warm.

After clearing the table, cut and place the dessert on serving plates. If desired, use the suggestion in the recipe Tips to remove icy chill from the dessert before serving. If heating coffee, heat it first, since the dessert should be served while it is still cold.

*With Micro-Browner™ Steak Grill you may broil steak in microwave oven.

Partially cooked bacon, wrapped around water chestnuts or pineapple chunks, makes an easy hot hors d'oeuvre that can be made ahead.
If you are not familiar with cooking bacon in the oven, see the Breakfast section for additional information.

BACON-WRAPPED WATER CHESTNUTS
1 can (5 oz.) water chestnuts, drained
¼ cup soy sauce
6 slices bacon, cut in half

Cut each water chestnut in half and marinate in soy sauce about 30 minutes. Meanwhile, arrange bacon on paper towel-lined glass or paper plate or baking dish. **COOK**, covered with paper towel, about **2 MINUTES, 30 SECONDS** or until partially cooked. Wrap each water chestnut piece with a bacon slice and secure with a toothpick. Place on paper towel-lined plate. **COOK**, uncovered, **2 TO 3 MINUTES** or until bacon is desired crispness.

12 Hors d'oeuvres

TIPS: To make ahead, marinate water chestnuts, partially cook bacon and wrap around water chestnuts. Cover and refrigerate. To serve, arrange on paper towel-lined plate. Cook for final cooking time as directed.

● If hors d'oeuvres become cold during serving, just return to oven a few seconds or until the bacon begins to sizzle.

● If desired, use pineapple chunks for water chestnuts.

Cheese is easy to melt on crackers in the oven. They can be assembled early and be popped into the oven when ready to serve.
Crackers contain very little moisture and so can be heated directly on the serving plate.

HOT CHEESE SNACKS

Place about 12 crackers on a glass or paper serving plate. Top each with a small cheese slice. **COOK**, uncovered, about **30 SECONDS** or until outside of cheese melts. **LET STAND 1 MINUTE** to distribute the heat and finish melting cheese.

12 Snacks

Potatoes cook quickly in the oven, but remember that with each added potato, the cooking time increases because of the additional food load.

The potatoes are placed on paper towels during cooking to absorb some of the moisture that will collect in the oven. Potatoes are composed of a high percentage of water and, during cooking, part of this water turns to steam in the oven. If the paper towel is not used, there will be more steam collecting in the oven.

Potatoes are best cooked until still a little firm. After being removed from the oven, they should be wrapped tightly in something that will hold in the heat while standing 5 minutes or until served to finish cooking. If cooked until completely done in the oven, they will overcook before being eaten and start to shrivel. If they are wrapped in foil during the standing time, the foil can easily be reused.

Because there is moisture in the oven as the potatoes cook, they will not have a crisp skin. If you prefer a drier potato, you can place in the conventional oven for 10 to 15 minutes rather than wrapping in foil. This is especially convenient if the oven is on for other foods and you would like to use the microwave oven for cooking a vegetable.

Potatoes need to be of the same size to cook in the same time. If some potatoes are smaller, check a few minutes early and remove when the potatoes just begin to feel soft. If there are several potatoes in the oven, the smaller ones can be placed closer together and in the center. This will help all the potatoes to cook at a more uniform speed.

BAKED POTATOES

Wash and dry medium sized potatoes. Place on 1 or 2 layers of paper towel, leaving at least 1 inch between potatoes. Cook until potatoes just begin to feel soft when pressed:

1 potato	— 3½ to 4 minutes
2 potatoes	— 6½ to 7 minutes
3 potatoes	— 8½ to 9 minutes
4 potatoes	— 10½ to 11 minutes
6 potatoes	— 15 to 16 minutes

Wrap potatoes in foil and **LET STAND 5 MINUTES** or until served to finish cooking.

Your microwave oven can be handy to cook the egg yolk custard for this frozen dessert. Prepare early to allow time to freeze.

The mixture cooks quickly and needs to be stirred 2 or 3 times during the cooking to keep the mixture creamy. If not stirred, the outside part overcooks and becomes curdled.

FROZEN LEMON DESSERT

> **¾ cup (10 squares) graham cracker crumbs**
> **3 eggs, separated**
> **¼ cup sugar**
> **1 tablespoon grated lemon peel**
> **¼ cup lemon juice**
> **⅛ teaspoon salt**
> **¼ cup sugar**
> **1 cup whipping cream, whipped, or**
> **2 cups (4½-oz. pkg.) frozen whipped topping, thawed**

Line ice cube tray, 9 x 5 inch loaf pan or 8-inch square pan with ½ cup of cracker crumbs. Separate eggs, placing whites in small mixer bowl; yolks in 1 or 2-cup glass measure. Add sugar, lemon peel, lemon juice and salt to egg yolks, mixing until well blended. **COOK,** uncovered, **1 MINUTE, 30 SECONDS** or until mixture thickens, stirring occasionally. Cool slightly. Beat egg whites until frothy. Gradually beat in ¼ cup sugar until mixture forms stiff peaks. Fold in lemon mixture and whipped cream. Pour into pan; sprinkle remaining crumbs over top. Freeze at least 4 hours or until served.

6 Servings

TIP: A dessert such as this is best if it has been at room temperature about 20 minutes to remove the icy chill. You can also do this quickly in the microwave oven by heating 1 piece on serving plate, 10 seconds or 2 pieces on 2 plates, 15 seconds.

Snacks

These snacks on a toothpick are fun for children to make. The oven eliminates any chance of burned fingers.

CHOCOLATE COCONUT MARSHMALLOWS

> **1 cup (6-oz. pkg.) semi-sweet chocolate pieces**
> **¼ cup milk**
> **½ lb. large marshmallows (25 to 30)**
> **1 cup coconut**

In small, shallow, glass casserole or mixing bowl, combine chocolate pieces and milk. **COOK, uncovered, 1 MINUTE, 30 SECONDS** or until chocolate melts, stirring twice. Place a toothpick in each marshmallow. Dip marshmallows in chocolate and roll in coconut. Serve warm or cold.   25 to 30 Marshmallows

> **TIPS:** Chocolate coated marshmallows can also be rolled in chopped nuts, graham cracker crumbs or crushed peanut brittle.
>
> • If chocolate mixture begins to cool while dipping marshmallow, return to oven for a few seconds.

The best percentage of popped corn can be achieved by conventional methods.

POPCORN (not recommended)

The successful cooking of popcorn in a microwave oven has always been dependent on many variables, including type, temperature and age of corn. Attempting to pop corn in a casserole dish for longer than 5 minutes will not increase percentage of corn popped but just cause it to burn. Extended cooking may also cause the dish to get too hot to handle and eventually cause breakage.

Do not attempt to cook popcorn in a paper bag. If oil is used and popcorn is old, extended cooking could lead to smoking and eventually a fire.

These easy candy-like treats set firmly after being refrigerated 30 minutes. Use the oven to quickly melt the butterscotch pieces.

CRUNCHY PEANUT-SCOTCH TREATS

> **½ cup peanut butter**
> **1 cup (6-oz. pkg.) butterscotch pieces**
> **3 cups (5-oz. can) chow mein noodles**
> **½ cup peanuts**

In large glass bowl, combine peanut butter and butterscotch pieces. **COOK, uncovered, 1 MINUTE.** Remove and stir until smooth. Stir in chow mein noodles and peanuts, mixing well to coat. Drop by teaspoons onto wax paper. Refrigerate until set, about 30 minutes. Store in refrigerator.   24 to 30 Treats

Since crackers contain little moisture, they do not need to be placed on a paper or cloth surface as do breads.
The amount of filling will determine the time it takes for heating. The filling should be just hot enough to be eaten easily.

SNACK CRACKERS

Top a cracker with peanut butter, slice of bologna or piece of cheese. Heat on plate, napkin, or directly on bottom of oven, cooking until topping is hot:

> 1 cracker — 5 to 10 seconds
> 4 crackers — 20 to 25 seconds
> 6 crackers — 30 to 35 seconds

A single serving of porous products such as these can be thawed without a resting time during the thawing cycle. If you were thawing an entire cake, a resting time would be necessary to thaw the center without starting to cook the edges.

HEATING FROZEN COOKIES, BROWNIES OR CAKE

Keep baked cookies, brownies or unfrosted cake in the freezer. For a quick snack, remove the amount you want and leave the remainder frozen. To thaw and warm, cook on paper napkin or plate, uncovered:

> 1 cookie or brownie — 30 seconds
> 1 piece cake — 45 seconds

LET STAND A FEW SECONDS to distribute the heat.

> **TIP:** If cake is frosted, resting times are necessary to prevent frosting from melting and running off cake. See page 162 for thawing pieces of frosted cake.

Appetizers

This chapter includes suggestions for canapes, hors d'oeuvres, dips served hot, snacks and also appetizers that can be served as the first course for dinner. Many appetizers are very convenient because they can be made ahead and then heated right on a plastic tray, paper plate or in a serving bowl or dish. You can heat or reheat just the amount that you need at a time. The fillings for canapes can be made ahead and the base toasted but they should be assembled just before heating and serving to prevent any sogginess. Refresh any limp potato chips or crackers by heating a plateful about 45 seconds to 1 minute; let stand another minute to crisp.

Wiener slices in a peppy sauce make tasty hot snacks served on toothpicks.

TANGY WIENER PICK UPS

   1 package (⅝ oz.) homestyle or brown
      gravy mix
½ cup cold water
½ cup apple or currant jelly
   2 tablespoons catsup
   1 lb. wieners or smokie links, cut into
      ½ inch slices

In 1½-quart casserole, combine gravy mix and water; mix well. Stir in remaining ingredients. COOK, uncovered, 7 MINUTES or until sauce thickens and wieners are heated through, stirring occasionally. Serve with toothpicks.

8 to 10 Servings

This appetizer can be cooked in the casserole and then transferred to a chafing dish for serving. If chafing dish is appropriate for the oven, cook and serve in same dish.

WIENERS IN MUSTARD SAUCE

   1 lb. wieners, cut into ½-inch slices
   1 can (10½ oz.) condensed cream
      of celery soup
   1 cup (½ pt. or 8 oz.) sour cream
¼ cup prepared mustard
   1 teaspoon prepared horseradish

In 1½-quart casserole, combine wieners, soup, sour cream, mustard and horseradish; mix well. COOK, covered, 5 MINUTES or until sauce begins to bubble around edge of dish, stirring occasionally. Serve with toothpicks.

6 to 8 Servings

TIP: For half a recipe, use 1-quart casserole and cook, covered, 3 minutes.

If convenient, prepare ahead to allow flavors to blend.

SWEET-SOUR TIDBITS

   1 can (13¼ oz.) pineapple chunks,
      undrained
½ cup firmly packed brown sugar
½ teaspoon salt
   4 teaspoons cornstarch
¼ cup vinegar
½ cup water
   2 cans (5 oz. each) Vienna sausages,
      drain and cut into 1-inch chunks
½ green pepper, cut into ¾-inch squares

Drain pineapple, reserving ½ cup syrup. In 1½-quart casserole, combine brown sugar, salt and cornstarch. Stir in pineapple syrup, vinegar and water. COOK, uncovered, 2 TO 3 MINUTES or until mixture boils, stirring occasionally. Add pineapple, sausages and green pepper. COOK, covered, 3 MINUTES, 30 SECONDS or until hot, stirring occasionally. Serve with toothpicks.

6 to 8 Servings

TIP: This recipe can be made ahead through adding pineapple and sausages; refrigerate. At serving time, cook 3 minutes, 30 seconds.

PARTY SNAX

   2 cups bite-size shredded corn cereal
   2 cups oat puffs cereal
   2 cups bite-size shredded wheat cereal
   4 oz. thin pretzel sticks
1½ cups (½ lb.) Spanish peanuts
½ cup butter or margarine
   2 tablespoons Worcestershire sauce
   1 teaspoon each, celery, onion and
      garlic salt

In 3-quart casserole or mixing bowl, combine cereals, pretzel sticks and peanuts. In 1-cup measure or bowl, combine butter, Worcestershire sauce and salts. COOK, uncovered, 45 SECONDS or until melted. Drizzle in fine stream over cereal mixture, stirring to coat evenly. COOK, uncovered, 8 MINUTES or until warm, stirring occasionally. Serve warm or cold.

About 8 Cups

This popular Mexican snack can be heated, a plate at a time, in just seconds.

NACHOS

Place a single layer of taco or corn chips on a paper plate or plastic tray. Cut ¼ inch thick slices of cheese into 1-inch squares. Place a square of cheese on each corn chip. COOK, uncovered, 45 SECONDS TO 1 MINUTE or until cheese is melted. Serve. Prepare additional nachos as needed.

MIXED SPICED NUTS

    ¾ cup firmly packed brown sugar
    ¾ teaspoon salt
    1 teaspoon cinnamon
    ½ teaspoon ground cloves
    ¼ teaspoon ground allspice
    ¼ teaspoon nutmeg
    2½ tablespoons water
    1 cup walnut halves
    1 cup pecan halves
    1 cup Brazil nut halves

In 1-quart casserole, combine brown sugar, salt, spices and water. **COOK,** uncovered, **1 MINUTE, 30 SECONDS,** stirring once. Add about ½ cup nuts at a time to syrup mixture. Stir with fork until coated. Lift out cup of nuts, draining off excess syrup and place in single layer in oblong glass utility dish. **COOK** 1 cup of nuts at a time, uncovered, **4 MINUTES** or until syrup begins to harden slightly (nuts will be somewhat soft yet). Transfer nuts to wax paper to cool until crisp. Continue until all nuts have been cooked. 3 Cups Nuts

PEPPERONI CHIPS

Arrange thin slices of pepperoni or hard salami on paper plate or several layers of paper towel. **COOK,** covered with paper towel, about **1 MINUTE** for each 10 to 15 slices or until meat is crisp. Serve warm or cold with dips.

> **TIP:** Regular salami will not become crisp so be sure to use the hard salami.

HOT CLAM DIP

    1 package (8 oz.) cream cheese
    1 can (8 oz.) minced clams, drained
    2 tablespoons chopped almonds
    1 tablespoon instant minced onion
    1 tablespoon prepared horseradish
    ¼ teaspoon garlic salt
    ¼ teaspoon salt
    Dash pepper
    3 tablespoons milk

In 1½-quart mixing bowl or serving dish, soften cream cheese (30 sec.). Stir in remaining ingredients. **COOK,** uncovered, **2 MINUTES** or until hot, stirring occasionally. If desired, garnish with paprika or parsley.

About 2½ Cups Dip

> **TIP:** To make ahead, mix ingredients together and refrigerate. Heat when ready to serve.

This hot dip is good with crackers, chips or raw vegetables.

CHICKEN 'N CHEESE DIP

    1 can (5 oz.) chicken spread
    2 packages (3 oz. each) cream cheese
    ¼ teaspoon poultry seasoning
    ¼ teaspoon chives, if desired

In small bowl, combine chicken spread, cream cheese and poultry seasoning. **COOK,** uncovered, **3 MINUTES** or until hot, stirring occasionally. Garnish with chives.

About 1 Cup Dip

(A) Tangy Wiener Pick Ups, page 37, (B) Escargot, page 41, (C) Teriyaki Wrap Ups, page 41, (D) Crab on the Half Shell, Clam Dip, above, with crackers.

This hot dip can easily be put in the oven to reheat when it has cooled.

CHEESY CLAM DIP

    2 tablespoons minced onion
    2 tablespoons butter or margarine
    1 can (8 oz.) minced clams, undrained
    1 cup (4 oz.) cubed American cheese
    2 tablespoons chopped, pitted ripe olives
    1 tablespoon catsup
    1 teaspoon Worcestershire sauce

In 2-cup casserole or small bowl, combine onion and butter. **COOK,** uncovered, **1 MINUTE** or until onion is tender. Drain clams, reserving 1 tablespoon liquid. To onion, add clams and liquid, cheese, olives, catsup and Worcestershire sauce, mixing well. **COOK,** uncovered, **2 MINUTES** or until bubbly around edges of dish, stirring occasionally. Serve hot with crackers or chips.   1¼ Cups Dip

MEAT 'N CHEESE DIP

    1 can (4½ oz.) corned beef spread
    ½ cup sour cream
    1 tablespoon cornstarch
    1 tablespoon milk
    ⅓ cup shredded cheese

In small bowl or serving dish, combine corned beef spread, sour cream and cornstarch. Stir in milk and cheese. **COOK,** uncovered, **4 TO 5 MINUTES** or until thickened, stirring once.   About 1 Cup Dip

HOT CHEDDAR DIP

    1 can (10¾ oz.) condensed Cheddar cheese soup
    2 tablespoons catsup
    ⅛ teaspoon leaf oregano
    ½ small clove garlic, minced, or 1/16 teaspoon garlic powder

In small bowl, blend all ingredients. **COOK,** uncovered, **2 MINUTES** or until hot, stirring occasionally.   1½ Cups Dip

HOT TACO DIP

    1 cup (8 oz. or ½ pt.) sour cream
    1 can (10½ oz.) condensed bean and bacon soup
    ½ cup (2 oz.) shredded Cheddar or American cheese
    2 tablespoons dry taco seasoning mix
    ½ teaspoon instant minced onion

In 1½-quart mixing bowl or serving dish, combine all ingredients; mix well. **COOK,** uncovered, **2 MINUTES, 30 SECONDS** or until heated through, stirring occasionally. Serve warm with corn or taco chips.   About 3 Cups Dip

TIPS: For a hotter flavored dip, use 3 tablespoons (1 pkg.) dry taco seasoning mix.

• Dry taco dip mix can be used for taco seasoning mix.

• To make ahead, mix ingredients together and refrigerate. Heat when ready to serve.

page 41, (E) Cheese and Shrimp Puffs, page 40, (F) Hot Liver Canapes, page 40, (G) Nachos, page 37 and (H) Hot

Almonds make a toasty, tasty stuffing for mushroom caps. They are good as snacks or as garnishes for a main course.

STUFFED MUSHROOMS

    2 cups (16 oz. or 1 pt.) whole fresh mushrooms
    2 tablespoons butter or margarine
    ¼ cup chopped almonds
    2 tablespoons chopped onion or
       1½ teaspoons instant minced onion
    ½ teaspoon salt
    1 teaspoon lemon juice
    ½ cup (1 slice) crumbled bread crumbs
    1 tablespoon sherry or water

Wash mushrooms and remove stems (save and use in sauces, soups or with vegetables). Arrange mushroom caps, hollow side up in pie plate or shallow baking dish. In small mixing bowl, combine butter and almonds. **COOK,** uncovered, **3 MINUTES** or until golden brown. Add remaining ingredients except mushroom caps; mix well. Spoon into mushrooms. **COOK,** covered with wax paper, **2 MINUTES** or until hot.

                      6 to 8 Servings

    TIP: To make ahead, stuff mushrooms and refrigerate. When ready to serve, cook as directed, increasing time 30 seconds when mushrooms are completely cold.

Shrimp are tucked between toast squares and a buttery cheese topping. Very tasty hot or cold.

CHEESE SHRIMP PUFFS

    8 slices bread or 32 crackers
    ¼ cup butter or margarine
    2 cups (8 oz.) shredded Cheddar cheese
    1 egg, separated
    1 can (4½ oz.) small cooked shrimp

Toast bread and cut each slice into 4 squares. Arrange on 2 napkin-lined plates or trays. In mixing bowl, soften butter (10 sec.). Cream together butter and cheese. Mix in egg yolk, placing white in small mixing bowl. Beat egg whites until soft mounds form. Fold into cheese mixture. Drain shrimp well and divide among toast squares. Top each, with spoonful of cheese mixture so there is space for spreading during heating. **COOK** 1 plate at a time, uncovered, about **1 MINUTE** or until hot.

                      32 Snacks

    TIPS: Large shrimp can be used, but they are usually more expensive. If using the large shrimp, cut into pieces to divide among the pieces of bread.

    • These can be assembled up to two hours ahead and left at room temperature until ready to heat.

HOT CRABMEAT CANAPES

    1 cup (7¾-oz. can) crabmeat
    ½ cup mayonnaise or salad dressing
    ½ teaspoon prepared mustard
    ½ teaspoon Worcestershire sauce
    1 teaspoon prepared horseradish
    ½ cup grated Parmesan cheese
    6 slices bread, toasted, or 24 crackers

In small mixing bowl, flake crabmeat. Add mayonnaise, mustard, Worcestershire sauce and horseradish; mix well. Cut each slice bread into 4 squares. Arrange on 2 napkin-lined plates or trays. Top each with about 1 teaspoon crab mixture; sprinkle with Parmesan cheese. **COOK** 1 plate at a time, uncovered, **1 MINUTE** or until edges of filling begin to bubble.   24 Canapes

    TIP: To make ahead, toast bread and combine crab mixture. Assemble and heat just before serving.

Chicken livers with broth are cooked in the oven before chopping to make the topping for these hot canapes.

HOT LIVER CANAPES

    8 oz. chicken livers
    ½ cup water
    1 cube or teaspoon chicken bouillon
    1 tablespoon chopped onion
    2 tablespoons cream or chicken broth
    2 tablespoons butter or margarine, softened
    ¼ teaspoon salt
    4 slices bread or 16 crackers

In 1-quart casserole, combine chicken livers, water and bouillon. **COOK,** covered, **4 MINUTES,** stirring once. **LET STAND 5 MINUTES** to finish cooking. Remove livers from broth. Chop fine or process in blender until fine. Add remaining ingredients except bread, mixing well. Toast bread and cut each slice into 4 squares. Place squares on napkin-lined plate or tray. Top each square with teaspoon of liver mixture. Garnish if desired (see Tip). **COOK,** uncovered, **1 MINUTE, 15 SECONDS** or until hot.

                      16 Canapes

    TIP: For garnish, use sliced stuffed green olives, pickled onions, pickle slices, chopped almonds, pimiento strips, sliced water chestnuts or add parsley sprigs after heating.

This bacon-cheese mixture can be put on toast rounds ahead of time because there is no liquid to make the toast soggy.

HOT BACON APPETIZERS

½ lb. bacon (about 12 slices)
¾ cup (3 oz.) shredded American or
Cheddar cheese
2 teaspoons caraway seed
30 melba toast rounds

In 2-quart (12 x 7) baking dish, layer bacon between layers of paper towels. **COOK 8 MINUTES** or until crisp. Crumble bacon into small bowl. Mix in cheese and caraway seed. Arrange toast rounds on tray or plates. Top each with a heaping teaspoonful of cheese mixture, spreading to edges. **COOK,** uncovered, **1 MINUTE** or until cheese is melted.

30 Appetizers

TIP: If cooking a plate at a time (about 10 appetizers), cook, uncovered, 15 to 20 seconds, or until cheese is melted.

Thin strips of sirloin steak marinate in a teriyaki mixture and are then wrapped around water chestnuts.

TERIYAKI WRAP UPS

1 tablespoon sugar
1 tablespoon chopped onion or
1 teaspoon instant minced onion
1 clove garlic, minced, or ⅛ teaspoon
instant minced garlic
¼ teaspoon ginger
¼ cup soy sauce
½ lb. sirloin steak, cut into thin strips
1 can (5 oz.) water chestnuts, drained

In small bowl, combine sugar, onion, garlic, ginger and soy sauce; mix well. Add steak strips, tossing to coat with soy mixture. **LET STAND 15 TO 30 MINUTES,** stirring occasionally. Drain steak strips and wrap each around water chestnut (cut larger water chestnuts in half), fastening with toothpicks. Place on plate or shallow baking dish. **COOK,** uncovered, **3 MINUTES** or until steak is desired doneness.

About 16 Snacks

TIPS: To make ahead, marinate the steak strips and wrap around water chestnuts. Refrigerate until ready to cook. Increase cooking time to 3 minutes, 30 seconds.

• If desired, use ⅓ cup bottled prepared teriyaki sauce for the sugar, onion, garlic, ginger and soy sauce.

This French delicacy is usually served as a first course. The pottery escargot dishes can be used in the oven. This recipe allows 6 snails per serving.

ESCARGOT

½ cup butter or margarine
½ to 1 teaspoon garlic powder or
instant minced garlic
1 teaspoon parsley flakes
Dash nutmeg
1 can (4½ oz.) snails (about 24)

In 1-cup measure or small bowl, combine butter, garlic, parsley and nutmeg. **COOK,** uncovered, **1 MINUTE** or until butter bubbles. Place snails in the compartments of four special 6-hole dishes or in four sauce dishes. Half fill compartments with seasoned butter, or in sauce dishes pour ¼ of sauce into each dish. **COOK,** covered loosely with wax paper, **45 SECONDS TO 1 MINUTE** or until butter begins to bubble.

4 Servings

TIP: When using snails in shells, follow above times.

This colorful appetizer can be served along with cocktails or as a first course. Make ahead for quick reheating.

CRAB ON THE HALF-SHELL

¼ cup butter or margarine
3 tablespoons flour
1 cup (7¾-oz. can) crabmeat
Milk
1 tablespoon minced pimiento
2 tablespoons minced green pepper
½ teaspoon salt
Parmesan cheese
Paprika

In 2-cup measure or bowl, melt butter (30 sec.). Blend in flour. Reserve crab liquid and add milk to make 1 cup. Add liquid to butter and flour and **COOK,** uncovered, **2 MINUTES, 30 SECONDS** or until thickened, stirring occasionally. Add flaked crabmeat, pimiento, green pepper and salt; mixing well. Spoon mixture into about 12 small or 6 medium shells, top with grated Parmesan cheese and sprinkle with paprika. Place filled shells on hard plastic tray or platter. **COOK,** loosely covered with wax paper, **2 MINUTES** or until bubbly.

6 Medium or 12 Small Shells

TIPS: To reheat from refrigerator, cook, loosely covered with wax paper, 3 minutes or until bubbly.

• If frozen after assembling, thaw and heat by cooking loosely covered with wax paper 4 minutes or until bubbly.

OYSTERS ROCKEFELLER

1 package (10 oz.) frozen creamed spinach
12 large oysters
Tabasco sauce
Salt
2 tablespoons butter or margarine
¼ cup grated Parmesan cheese
¼ cup dry bread crumbs

Make small slit in pouch of frozen spinach and place in oven. **COOK 5 MINUTES.** Place each oyster in individual shell or dish for appetizers; 3 oysters in each shell or small serving dish for main course. Sprinkle with Tabasco sauce and salt. In small bowl, melt butter (15 sec.). Stir in cheese and bread crumbs. Top oysters with cooked spinach. Sprinkle with crumb mixture. **COOK,** covered with wax paper, **5 MINUTES** or until oysters are done.

12 Appetizer or 4 Main Course Servings

TIPS: If desired, 2 tablespoons slivered almonds can be toasted with butter for topping; cook, uncovered, about 3 minutes, stirring occasionally.

• If you prefer Oysters Rockefeller without a cream sauce, use frozen chopped spinach for creamed spinach. Cook as directed, squeeze spinach in paper towels to drain and use it to top oysters.

This seafood dish can be served as a first course or as an appetizer. The clams are cooked right in the shell with a crumb topping.

CLAMS CASINO

24 hard-shell clams
3 slices bacon, cooked and crumbled
¼ cup grated Parmesan cheese
¼ cup dry bread crumbs
2 tablespoons minced parsley
2 tablespoons minced green pepper
1 tablespoon minced onion
½ teaspoon leaf oregano
Paprika

Wash clams. Open clams, discarding top shell and loosening meat from bottom shell. Drain well on paper towels. In small bowl, combine remaining ingredients except paprika. Place clams on tray or two plates. Top each clam with a heaping teaspoon of crumb mixture. **COOK,** loosely covered with wax paper, **3 MINUTES** or until clams are set. Sprinkle with paprika.

4 Servings (6 Clams each)

TIPS: If two plates are used, cook, 12 clams at a time, 1 minute, 45 seconds.

• If clams are quite large, you may need additional crumbs and cooking time.

Beverages

You can heat beverages in a pitcher, mugs, juice jar, paper cups, brandy snifters or everyday coffee cups. Heat a total recipe amount or individual servings as needed. The timings in the general heating chart are helpful when you are adapting a home recipe for a beverage with a similar amount. The recipes in this chapter include those for both alcoholic and non-alcoholic beverages and those with a fruit or a milk base. Don't forget that you can simply reheat any beverage that has cooled. See the Breakfast section for coffee and hot cocoa (pages 11, 12).

HEATING TIMES FOR BEVERAGES

MUGS OR CUPS	TIMES
1	1 to 1½ minutes
2	2 to 2½ minutes
3	3¼ to 4 minutes
4	4¼ to 5 minutes
5	5½ to 6½ minutes
6	6½ to 7½ minutes
7	8 to 9 minutes
8	9 to 10 minutes
9	10 to 12 minutes

Use minimum time for ingredients at room temperature, maximum for refrigerated ingredients. Stir before serving to distribute heat.

HOT BUTTERED MILK

2 teaspoons sugar or honey
2 teaspoons butter or margarine
1 cinnamon stick
About 1 cup milk
½ teaspoon vanilla
1 tablespoon rum or brandy, if desired
Nutmeg

In mug, combine sugar, butter and cinnamon stick. Fill with milk. **COOK,** uncovered, **1 MINUTE, 15 SECONDS** or until hot. Stir in vanilla and rum; sprinkle with nutmeg. 1 Serving

TIPS: For other amounts, use heating chart above.

• If desired, use ¼ teaspoon rum or brandy flavoring for rum or brandy.

• Prepared eggnog can be used for milk; omit flavorings and use half the sugar amount.

TOM AND JERRYS

2 eggs, separated
1 cup powdered sugar
½ teaspoon vanilla
Dash nutmeg
Rum
Brandy

For Tom and Jerry batter, beat egg whites with ½ cup powdered sugar until soft peaks form. Beat egg yolks with remaining ½ cup powdered sugar until thickened, about 5 minutes. Blend in vanilla and nutmeg. Pour over egg whites and by hand, fold together until well blended. (Can be covered and stored in refrigerator for up to two weeks.)

To make Tom and Jerrys, fill mugs ¾ full with water and heat, uncovered, using chart on page 42. Add 1 heaping tablespoon of batter and 1½ tablespoons each rum and brandy to each cup; stir to combine. Sprinkle with nutmeg.

About 15 (1 cup) Servings

TIP: The prepared batter that you buy can be used for this home recipe batter.

Red cinnamon candies give the peppy flavor to this cranberry punch. It is also good chilled and served over ice.

CRANBERRY SIPPER

½ cup sugar
½ cup red cinnamon candies
1 quart (4 cups) cranberry juice
1 can (6 oz.) frozen pineapple or orange juice concentrate, undiluted
1 can (¾ cup) water
1 tablespoon lemon juice

In 1½-quart pitcher or bowl, combine all ingredients. **COOK**, uncovered, **7 MINUTES** or until hot, stirring occasionally. If desired, garnish with orange slices.   6 (1 cup) Servings

TIP: For individual servings, place 4 teaspoons sugar, 4 teaspoons cinnamon candies, 2 tablespoons juice concentrate, 2 tablespoons water and ½ teaspoon lemon juice in each mug. Fill with cranberry juice. Heat, using chart on page 42.

HOT BUTTERED RUM

In each mug, place 1 tablespoon brown sugar; fill mugs ¾ full with water or apple cider. Heat, using chart on page 42. Add 1 jigger (1½ tablespoons) rum and top with 1 teaspoon butter or margarine.

This after-dinner coffee uses brandy which is flamed before serving. Serve this along with ice cream.

CAFÉ BRÛLOT

¾ cup brandy
1 cinnamon stick
6 whole cloves
6 to 8 sugar cubes or 3 to 4 teaspoons sugar
2 strips lemon peel
2 strips orange peel
3 cups hot strong coffee

In 1½-quart bowl, combine brandy, cinnamon stick, cloves, sugar cubes, lemon and orange peel. **COOK**, uncovered, **1 MINUTE** or until warm. Ignite brandy and stir to dissolve sugar. Slowly pour in coffee. Serve in small demitasse cups. If desired, top with whipped cream or ice cream.   7 (½ cup) Servings

BOUILLON SIPPER

2 cans (10½ oz. each) condensed beef bouillon
1⅓ cups (1 soup can) hot water
2 to 3 tablespoons sherry

In 1½ or 2-quart pitcher or bowl, combine all ingredients. **COOK**, uncovered, **4 MINUTES** or until hot, stirring occasionally. If desired, garnish with lemon slices and parsley.

4 (1 cup) Servings

TIP: For individual servings, fill mugs ⅔ full with bouillon. Finish filling with water, adding about 1 tablespoon sherry to each. Heat, using chart on page 42.

Spices and almond flavoring turn hot chocolate into a special beverage. Marshmallows make it light and foamy.

MEXICAN CHOCOLATE

1½ squares (1½ oz.) semi-sweet chocolate
¼ cup water
2 tablespoons sugar
¼ teaspoon ground cinnamon
⅛ teaspoon ground nutmeg
Pinch of salt
1 quart milk
4 large marshmallows
¼ teaspoon almond extract

In 2-quart pitcher or bowl, combine chocolate, water, sugar, cinnamon, nutmeg and salt. **COOK**, uncovered, **4 MINUTES** or until mixture has boiled 2 minutes, stirring occasionally. Stir in milk and **COOK**, uncovered, **6 MINUTES** or until hot. Add marshmallows and almond extract. Beat with rotary beater until foamy. **COOK**, uncovered, **2 TO 3 MINUTES** or until hot.   4 (1 cup) Servings

A spicy apple cider that is easy to keep on hand for quick reheating. The clove studded orange makes a pretty garnish for the punch bowl or pitcher.

WASSAIL BOWL

1 orange
½ teaspoon whole cloves
1½ quarts apple cider or juice
2 tablespoons lemon juice
3 cinnamon sticks

Insert cloves into peel of orange. Place in 2-quart pitcher or bowl. COOK, uncovered, 2 MINUTES. Add remaining ingredients and COOK, uncovered, 8 MINUTES or until hot.

6 (1 cup) Servings

TIPS: If desired, add 1 to 1½ cups vodka and ¼ cup brandy before serving. Or, pour a little Vodka and Brandy into each mug before filling with the hot punch.

• For individual servings, place 1 orange slice, 4 whole cloves, 1 teaspoon lemon juice and ½ cinnamon stick in each mug. Fill with apple cider and heat, using chart on page 42.

This hot punch is good served plain or with the addition of rum.

MULLED APRICOT NECTAR

5¾ cups (46-oz. can) apricot nectar
1 cup orange juice
4 cinnamon sticks
⅛ to ¼ teaspoon whole cloves
¼ teaspoon whole allspice
1 lemon, sliced, if desired

In 2-quart pitcher or bowl, combine all ingredients except sliced lemon. COOK, uncovered, 15 MINUTES or until hot. Stir and remove spices. Garnish with lemon slices.

7 (1 cup) Servings

TIPS: Rum can be added to hot nectar. Fill cups ¾ full with mulled nectar; add rum, according to taste, mixing well.

• For individual servings, place ½ cinnamon stick, 2 whole cloves, 2 whole allspice and 1 tablespoon orange juice in each mug. Fill with apricot nectar. Heat, using chart on page 42. Garnish with lemon slice.

This beefy tomato juice cocktail makes a good pre-dinner drink or appetizer.

TOMATO NOGGINS

1 can (46 oz.) tomato juice
2 cans (10½ oz. each) beef broth
1 lemon, sliced
Vodka

Fill mugs ⅔ full with tomato juice; finish filling with beef broth. Heat, using chart on page 42. Add lemon slice and 2 tablespoons vodka to each mug.

9 (1 cup) Servings

TIP: 3 cubes or teaspoons beef bouillon and 2½ cups water can be used for beef broth.

This hot punch is terrific for cold weather entertaining. Try it after skiing when warming up around the fireplace.

MULLED ROSÉ PUNCH

1 tablespoon whole cloves
1 tablespoon whole allspice
2 cinnamon sticks
1 cup water
1 teaspoon instant tea
1 can (6 oz.) frozen tangarine juice concentrate, undiluted
1 can (6 oz.) frozen Hawaiian punch, undiluted
3⅓ cups (4/5 quart) Rosé wine
Lemon slices

In 2-quart pitcher or bowl, combine spices, water and tea. COOK, uncovered, 5 MINUTES. Remove spices. Stir in tangarine juice, punch and wine. COOK, uncovered, 8 MINUTES or until hot. Serve with lemon slices.

6 (1 cup) Servings

HOT SPICED CIDER

2 quarts (½ gallon) apple cider or juice
4 cinnamon sticks
16 whole allspice
16 whole cloves
2 tablespoons brown sugar
2 lemons, sliced
2 oranges, sliced

In 3-quart pitcher or bowl, combine all ingredients. COOK, uncovered, 15 MINUTES or until hot. Stir and remove spices.

8 (1 cup) Servings

TIP: For making individual servings, place ½ cinnamon stick, 2 whole allspice, 2 whole cloves, scant teaspoon brown sugar, 1 lemon slice and 1 orange slice in each mug. Fill with cider. Heat, using chart on page 42.

GUIDE FOR DEFROSTING MEAT, POULTRY AND FISH

Use the following times as a guide when defrosting these or similar cuts of frozen meat, poultry or fish. Since shape of cut and package, starting temperature and total weight will vary, it may be necessary to make slight adjustments in the times.

With items as dense as meats, a rest period (standing time) after each cooking period is necessary to allow the heat to penetrate the center of the meat without cooking the outside edges. **REST PERIODS SHOULD BE AT LEAST 2 MINUTES FOR LARGER, MORE DENSE CUTS AND 1 MINUTE FOR SMALLER, LESS DENSE CUTS.** With smaller cuts, you can separate or rearrange the pieces to speed the defrosting of the center.

Large items such as roasts can begin with cooking periods of 2 to 3 minutes. As the roast thaws on the outside, the cooking times must be decreased to avoid cooking these thawed areas. Once the outside of the meat feels warm and is thawed, the cooking periods should be reduced to 30 seconds to 1 minute, depending on the size of the cut. It is more difficult to know when the center of a large cut is thawed but a meat thermometer will quickly tell you if the temperature has climbed above 32°.

With these times, there may be some cooking that begins on the outside edge. This is acceptable if the meat will be cooked immediately. If not planning to cook the meat immediately, it is better to use shorter cooking periods while defrosting to eliminate the chance of spoilage during additional storage.

MEAT	WEIGHT	COOKING TIMES*
Chops	2 lbs.	2 min; 1 min; 1 minute
Ground	2 lbs.	2 min; 1 min; 1 min; 1 min; 30 seconds
	1 lb.	2 min; 1 min; 30 sec; 30 seconds
Ribs	2 lbs.	2 min; 1 min; 1 min; 1 minute
	1 lb.	2 min; 1 min; 30 seconds
Roast	4 lb.	3 min; 3 min; 2 min; 2 min; 1 min; 1 min; 1 minute
	3 lb.	3 min; 3 min; 2 min; 1 min; 1 min; 30 seconds
Steak (¾ inch thick)	1½ - 2 lbs.	2 min; 1 min; 1 minute
Steak (1½ inch thick)	1½ - 2 lbs.	2 min; 2 min; 2 min; 1 minute

POULTRY		
Chicken, Breasts (4)	1 lb.	2 min; 1 min; 1 minute
Chicken, Fryer	2½ to 3 lbs.	3 min; 2 min; 2 min; 1 min; 1 minute
Cornish Hens (2)	1 lb. each	2 min; 2 min; 2 min; 1 min; 1 minute
(4)	1 lb. each	3 min; 2 min; 2 min; 2 min; 1 min; 1 minute
Goose	10 lb.	3 min; 3 min; 3 min; 3 min; 3 min; 2 min; 2 min; 2 min; 2 min; 2 min; 2 minutes
Turkey, Boneless Rolled Roast	4 lb.	3 min; 2 min; 2 min; 2 min; 2 min; 2 minutes
Turkey, Breast (1)	2 lb. 2 oz.	3 min; 2 min; 2 min; 1 min; 1 min; 1 minute
Turkey, Thighs (1)	1 lb. 7 oz.	3 min; 2 min; 1 min; 1 minute
Turkey, whole	See Page 67	
Turkey, Wings (2)	2 lb. 7 oz.	3 min; 2 min; 2 min; 1 min; 1 minute

FISH AND SEAFOOD		
Fillets	1 lb.	2 min; 1 min; 1 min; 30 seconds
Whole Fish	12 oz.	30 seconds; 30 seconds; 30 seconds
Lobster Tail	8 - 10 oz.	30 seconds; 30 seconds; 30 seconds
Shrimp	8 - 10 oz.	1 minute; 30 seconds

*Allow a rest period of at least 2 minutes for larger cuts and 1 minute for smaller cuts after each cooking period.

This chart *does not* pertain to automatic defrost features.

Fish and Seafood

You have to taste fish and seafood prepared in a microwave oven to realize what a superior product it is. Delicate, flaky fish and tender seafood will highlight many of your menus.

Your meal planning will have to take into account the speed with which fish cooks. Because it is a fairly last minute food, the table should be set and other foods completely prepared or ready to go into the oven immediately after removing the fish or seafood. If you think that you will find it necessary to reheat fish, try to undercook it the first time.

Most fish and seafood need covering during cooking and standing time. Fish is cooked most often in shallow baking dishes that usually don't have covers so the recipes indicate using wax paper or plastic wrap as a cover. Seafood is most often cooked in a casserole that has an accompanying cover. The covering is especially important during standing time to hold in the heat to cook the center without drying the outside of fish.

Fish: The recipes use whole fish, fillets, steaks and canned fish. Steaks can be substituted for fillets with a slight increase in time, remembering with both to keep the larger end of the fish toward the outside of the cooking dish. The following are some fish that can be used interchangeably in the recipes: sole, perch, halibut, snapper, flounder and whitefish.

Seafood: The recipes include a variety of seafood such a lobster, crab, shrimp, scallops, oysters and clams. Many recipes mention frozen seafood because of its wide availability, but of course, fresh seafood can always be substituted. Seafood cooked in the shell has no different timing than seafood cooked without a shell. Also, serving dishes of natural shell can be used in the oven.

MENU

Fish Fillets in Cucumber Sauce
Rice* (132)
Peas with Onions and
Mushrooms (123)
Hot Rolls (127)
Lemon Cloud Pie (156)

1. Early in day, cook pie and refrigerate.
2. About 45 minutes before serving, cook rice* and let stand.
3. Cook fish for first cooking.
4. Cook peas.
5. Finish cooking fish and sauce.
6. Reheat rice if necessary.
7. Heat rolls.
*It may be more convenient to cook Rice conventionally.

Bits of cucumber and fresh tomato in mushroom soup make an attractive and tasty sauce with fish. In our test kitchen, this was one of our most popular fish recipes.

FISH FILLETS IN CUCUMBER SAUCE

   1 medium cucumber, unpeeled and diced
  ½ teaspoon dill weed
   2 tablespoons butter or margarine
   1 can (10½ oz.) condensed cream of
     mushroom soup
  ⅓ cup sour cream
   1 medium tomato, chopped
   2 tablespoons butter or margarine
  ½ teaspoon salt
   2 teaspoons anchovy paste, if desired
   2 lbs. fresh or frozen fish fillets
     (sole, haddock or pike), thawed

In 4-cup measure, combine cucumber, dill and 2 tablespoons butter. **COOK**, uncovered, **4 MINUTES**, stirring once. Stir in soup, sour cream and tomato; set aside. In 2-quart (12 x 7) baking dish, melt butter with salt and anchovy paste (20 sec.). Mix together. Arrange fish in dish turning over in butter to coat. **COOK**, covered with wax paper or plastic wrap, **8 MINUTES** or until fish is almost done. Spoon sauce over top; **COOK**, covered with wax paper or plastic wrap, **3 MINUTES** or until sauce is hot.   **6 to 8 Servings**

  TIP: Recipe can be cut in half, using half the ingredient amounts and 2-quart (8 x 8) baking dish. Decrease cooking time to 3 minutes for cucumber, 4 minutes for fish and 2 minutes after sauce is added.

The hint of lemon in this creamy mushroom sauce goes well with the mild fish flavor.

FISH FILLETS WITH MUSHROOM LEMON SAUCE

    ¼ **cup butter or margarine**
    2 **cups (1 pt. or 16 oz.) fresh mushrooms, sliced**
    ¼ **cup sliced green onion**
    2 **tablespoons flour**
    1 **teaspoon salt**
    1 **teaspoon parsley flakes or 1 tablespoon minced parsley**
    1 **teaspoon grated lemon peel**
    ⅛ **teaspoon pepper**
    1 **cup milk**
    2 **lbs. fresh or frozen fish fillets (sole, haddock or pike), thawed**

In 2-quart (12 x 7) baking dish, combine butter, mushrooms and onion. **COOK**, uncovered, **3 MINUTES**, stirring once after butter melts. Stir in flour, salt, parsley, lemon and pepper. Blend in milk, stirring until well mixed. **COOK**, covered with wax paper or plastic wrap, **3 MINUTES** or until mixture boils. Stir well. Arrange fish fillets in pan, spooning sauce over each fillet. **COOK**, covered with wax paper or plastic wrap, **10 MINUTES** or until fish flakes easily. **LET STAND**, covered, **2 MINUTES** to finish cooking.   **6 to 8 Servings**

> **TIPS:** If desired, 1 cup canned sliced mushrooms can be used for fresh.
>
> • For 3 to 4 servings, use 2-quart (8 x 8) baking dish and half the ingredients; reduce cooking times to 2 minutes for mushrooms, 2 minutes for sauce, and 5 minutes for fish.

Garlic in butter sauce gives this dish an added zest.

HALIBUT WITH PIQUANT SAUCE

    ¼ **cup butter or margarine**
    ½ **teaspoon dry mustard**
    1½ **teaspoons parsley flakes or 1 tablespoon minced parsley**
    ⅛ **teaspoon garlic powder or instant minced garlic**
    1½ **teaspoons lemon juice**
    1 **lb. fresh or frozen halibut fillets, thawed**

In 1½-quart (10 x 6) or 2-quart (8 x 8) baking dish, melt butter (30 sec.). Add mustard, parsley, garlic and lemon juice. Break apart or cut fillets into 4 or 5 pieces. Dip each piece in butter mixture, turning butter side up. **COOK**, covered with wax paper or plastic wrap, **5 MINUTES** or until fish flakes easily. **LET STAND**, covered, **2 MINUTES** to finish cooking.   **4 to 5 Servings**

Fillet of sole cooks in a creamy sauce sparked by green onions, parsley and a hint of bay leaf.

FILLET OF SOLE IN WINE SAUCE

    1 **lb. fresh or frozen sole fillets, thawed**
    ½ **teaspoon salt**
    2 **green onions, sliced**
    1 **teaspoon parsley flakes or 1 tablespoon minced parsley**
    ⅓ **cup white wine**
    2 **teaspoons flour**
    ½ **bay leaf**
    2 **tablespoons cream**

In 1½-quart (10 x 6) baking dish, arrange fillets. Sprinkle with salt, onions and parsley. Mix together wine and flour until dissolved. Crumble in bay leaf. Pour around fish. **COOK**, covered with wax paper or plastic wrap, **5 MINUTES** or until fish flakes easily, spooning sauce over fish once or twice. Remove fish from baking dish; stir cream into sauce in pan. Pour over fish on serving plate or if serving from baking dish, return fish to dish.   4 Servings

Lemon flavored rice and fish fillets combine in this quick dish that cooks in only 10 minutes. When you add additional ingredients, such as rice, the cooking time increases over the same amount of fish cooked in a small amount of sauce.

FISH FILLETS WITH LEMON RICE

    1½ **cups quick-cooking rice, uncooked**
    ¼ **cup chopped onion or 1 tablespoon instant minced onion**
    1 **teaspoon salt**
    1 **teaspoon parsley flakes or 1 tablespoon minced parsley**
    ½ **teaspoon powdered thyme or poultry seasoning**
    2 **tablespoons lemon juice**
    1¼ **cups water**
    1 **lb. fresh or frozen fish fillets, thawed**
    2 **tablespoons butter or margarine**
Paprika

In 2-quart (8 x 8) baking dish, combine uncooked rice, onion, salt, parsley, thyme, lemon juice and water; mix well. Arrange fillets on mixture. Dot with butter; sprinkle with paprika. **COOK**, covered with wax paper or plastic wrap, **10 MINUTES** or until fish flakes easily. **LET STAND**, covered, **2 MINUTES** to finish cooking.   4 Servings

Frozen shrimp newburg adds flavor to the stuffing for sole fillets. The newburg also doubles as sauce to serve over the fish.

FILLET OF SOLE MARGUERY

> **2 pouches (6½ oz. each) frozen shrimp newburg**
> **1 tablespoon finely chopped celery**
> **1 tablespoon water**
> **1 slice bread, crumbled**
> **1 tablespoon parsley flakes or**
>   **2 tablespoons minced parsley**
> **1 tablespoon milk**
> **½ lb. fresh or frozen sole fillets, thawed**
> **Salt**
> **2 tablespoons butter or margarine**
> **Paprika**

Place frozen newburg in oven and COOK 4 TO 5 MINUTES or until thawed. In medium mixing bowl, combine celery and water. COOK, covered, 1 MINUTE. Add bread, parsley and milk. Measure ½ cup of newburg (taking as many shrimp as you can) and add to bread mixture, mixing well. Cut each fillet in half lengthwise and salt lightly. Divide stuffing among fillets and spread evenly; roll up beginning at widest end. Place seam side down in buttered casserole dish. Brush with butter and sprinkle with paprika. COOK, covered with wax paper or plastic wrap, 4 TO 5 MINUTES or until fish flakes easily. Let stand, covered, while COOKING remaining newburg, covered, 1 MINUTE, 30 SECONDS or until hot. Serve over fillets.

2 Servings

An oriental flavored sauce that tastes a little like teriyaki adds color and flavor to this easy family fish dish.

ORANGE 'N SOY FILLETS

> **2 tablespoons soy sauce**
> **2 tablespoons frozen orange juice concentrate**
> **1 tablespoon lemon juice**
> **1 tablespoon catsup**
> **⅛ teaspoon instant minced garlic or 1 clove garlic, minced**
> **1 lb. fresh or frozen fish fillets, thawed**

In 2-quart (8 x 8) baking dish, combine soy sauce, orange and lemon juice, catsup and garlic. Arrange fish in dish, turning over to coat with sauce. COOK, covered with wax paper or plastic wrap, 5 MINUTES or until fish flakes easily. LET STAND, covered, 2 MINUTES to finish cooking. Serve extra sauce over rice.

3 to 4 Servings

TIP: Recipe can be doubled and cooked in 2-quart (12 x 7) baking dish for 10 minutes.

This dish is actually 4 individual servings of fish and stuffing cooked in custard cups. They are cooked right side up but inverted for serving. Great for entertaining.

TURBAN OF SOLE

> **2 tablespoons butter or margarine**
> **½ cup (1 stalk) finely chopped celery**
> **¼ cup finely chopped onion or 1 tablespoon instant minced onion**
> **1½ teaspoons parsley flakes or**
>   **3 tablespoons minced parsley**
> **¼ teaspoon chervil, if desired**
> **1 teaspoon lemon juice**
> **Dash white or black pepper**
> **Dash thyme**
> **1½ cups (1½ slices) soft bread cubes**
> **1 package (1 lb.) fresh or frozen sole fillets, thawed**
> **Sauce**
>   **Half of 10½-oz. can condensed cream of mushroom soup**
>   **1 tablespoon chopped pimiento or ripe olives**
>   **1 tablespoon milk or cream**

In 1-quart bowl or casserole, combine butter, celery, onion, seasonings and lemon juice. COOK, covered, 3 MINUTES, stirring once. Mix bread cubes with mixture. Butter four 6-oz. custard cups. Line sides and bottoms with thin pieces of fish, reserving small scraps for top. (You may have to cut thick pieces in half.) Evenly divide stuffing between the 4 custard cups (about ½ cup each). Top with any leftover pieces of fish. Place custard cups on a dinner plate. COOK, covered with a dinner plate, 4 MINUTES or until fish flakes easily. When done, with both hands, invert dinner plates with custard cups between them. Let stand covered while making sauce.

   Combine all ingredients for sauce. COOK, uncovered, 1 MINUTE, 30 SECONDS or until mixture bubbles. Remove top plate and custard cups. Spoon sauce over turbans and serve.

4 Servings

TIPS: The stuffing can also be used to stuff four 8 to 10 oz. whole fish.

● You can use preseasoned bread cubes and eliminate seasonings in recipe.

Pictured, top to bottom: Stuffed Walleyed Pike, page 50, Turban of Sole, above, Salmon Ring, page 52, topped with Creamy Dill Sauce, page 133, and Halibut Divan, page 50.

Frozen broccoli and fish are thawed in packages, then cooked together and topped with an easy and colorful sauce made from shrimp soup. Ready to serve in about 20 minutes.

HALIBUT DIVAN

   **1 can (10 oz.) frozen condensed cream of
     shrimp soup**
   1 package (1 lb.) frozen halibut fillets
   1 package (10 oz.) frozen broccoli spears
   ½ teaspoon leaf tarragon, if desired

To loosen soup from edges of can, let stand in container of hot water while thawing and cooking fish. Place packages of frozen fillets and broccoli in oven and **COOK 3 MINUTES.** Remove from packages and separate, placing fillets in bottom of 2-quart (8 x 8) baking dish. Top with broccoli, placing stems toward outside of dish, but not extending beyond edge of fish (if they extend beyond, they may overcook). Sprinkle with tarragon. **COOK,** covered with wax paper or plastic wrap, **11 MINUTES** or until fish flakes easily. Let stand covered. Remove frozen soup from container and place in 2-cup measure or dish and **COOK,** uncovered, **4 TO 5 MINUTES** or until thawed and heated, stirring occasionally. Pour sauce over fillets and broccoli.   4 Servings

> **TIPS:** If fish is fresh, omit first cooking time that is primarily for thawing. Cook frozen broccoli 2 minutes to thaw and separate.
>
> • If broccoli is fresh, place in covered casserole with 1 tablespoon water and cook for the 3 minute time to start cooking.

FILLET OF SOLE IN LEMON PARSLEY BUTTER

   2 lbs. fresh or frozen sole fillets, thawed
   ½ cup butter or margarine
   2 tablespoons cornstarch
   3 tablespoons lemon juice
   **1 teaspoon parsley flakes or 1 tablespoon
     chopped parsley**
   Celery salt
   White or black pepper

In 2-quart (12 x 7) baking dish, melt butter (45 sec.). Add cornstarch, lemon juice and parsley; blend well. Dip each fillet in sauce, turning sauce side up. Sprinkle fillets with celery salt and pepper. **COOK,** covered with wax paper or plastic wrap, **7 MINUTES, 30 SECONDS** or until fish flakes easily. **LET STAND,** covered, **2 MINUTES** to finish cooking. Spoon butter sauce over each serving.

6 to 8 Servings

> **TIP:** For even cooking, place thickest ends of fish toward edges of dish.

A snappy tomato sauce made with tomato soup is a perfect accompaniment to the mildly flavored white fish. If you don't have a use for the extra soup, add all of it to the fish and then serve the additional sauce over rice.

CREOLE FISH

   2 tablespoons butter or margarine
   **¼ cup chopped onion or 1 tablespoon
     instant minced onion**
   ½ cup (1 stalk) chopped celery
   ¼ cup chopped green pepper
   ¼ teaspoon salt
   ½ teaspoon leaf basil or Italian seasoning
   1 lb. fresh or frozen fish fillets, thawed
   Half of 10¼ -oz. can condensed tomato soup

In 1½ -quart (8-inch round) baking dish, combine butter, onion and celery. **COOK,** uncovered, **2 MINUTES,** stirring after butter melts. Stir in green pepper, salt and basil. Arrange fish in dish. Top with tomato soup. **COOK,** covered with wax paper or plastic wrap, **6 MINUTES** or until fish flakes easily, occasionally spooning sauce over fish. **LET STAND,** covered, **2 MINUTES** to finish cooking.

4 Servings

This recipe can be used for many types of pike, such as Northern, Channel, Pickerel, as well as perch or trout. The stuffing enhances the mild flavor of the fish.

STUFFED WALLEYED PIKE

1½ -lb. whole walleyed pike
Salt
   2 tablespoons butter or margarine
   **2 tablespoons (1 med.) chopped green
     onion**
   ⅛ teaspoon fennel, if desired
   ⅓ cup white wine
   1 cup crumbled herb seasoned stuffing

Cut off large fin on back (dorsal) since it's very sharp. Salt inside of fish. In medium bowl, melt butter (20 sec.). Add onion and fennel; **COOK,** covered with a plate, **1 MINUTE, 30 SECONDS.** Add white wine and crumbled stuffing, tossing to combine. Stuff fish and secure with string, toothpicks or small metal skewers. Place fish diagonally on wax or parchment paper. Wrap fish in paper and secure ends if necessary with rubber bands. **COOK 8 MINUTES** or until fish flakes easily, turning once. **LET STAND,** wrapped, **2 MINUTES** to finish cooking.

4 Servings

> **TIP:** Place several towels in bottom of oven for absorption of moisture and easy removal of fish after cooking.

This recipe also can be used with turbot or cod. The tang of Hollandaise gives excellent flavor to the fish.

POACHED HALIBUT WITH HOLLANDAISE

**1 lb. fresh or frozen halibut fillets, thawed
Hollandaise sauce (see page 133)**

Cut fillets into 4 pieces and arrange in 1½-quart (10 x 6) or 2-quart (8 x 8) baking dish. **COOK,** covered with wax paper or plastic wrap, **5 MINUTES** or until fish flakes easily. **LET STAND,** covered, **2 MINUTES** to finish cooking. Prepare Hollandaise sauce and spoon over fillets.   4 Servings

> **TIP:** You can use the dry packaged Hollandaise sauce mix, cooking in oven 2 minutes, 30 seconds or until mixture boils, stirring 3 times.

Shrimp adds special flavor to fish stuffing. This recipe can be used for flounder, white fish or catfish as well.

SHRIMP STUFFED TROUT

**2 tablespoons (1 med.) chopped green
onion or 1 teaspoon instant minced onion
¼ cup (½ stalk) finely chopped celery
1 tablespoon finely chopped pimiento
2 tablespoons butter or margarine
1 tablespoon lemon juice
⅛ teaspoon celery salt
¼ teaspoon chervil, if desired
Dash white or black pepper
¾ cup (4½-oz. can) chopped shrimp
1½ cups dry bread cubes, coarsely crushed
1 egg, slightly beaten
4 (8 to 10 oz. each) trout**

In 1-quart bowl or casserole, combine onion, celery, pimiento, butter, lemon juice and seasonings. **COOK,** covered, **3 MINUTES,** stirring once. Add shrimp and bread cubes, mixing well. Mix in beaten egg. Stuff each fish with approximately ⅓ cup stuffing. Secure openings with string, toothpicks or small metal skewers. Wrap fish individually in wax paper or place in 2-quart (12 x 7) baking dish covered with wax paper or plastic wrap. **COOK 11 MINUTES** or until fish flakes easily. **LET STAND,** covered, **2 MINUTES** to finish cooking.   4 Servings

> **TIP:** When cooking less fish, use these cooking times:
> 1 fish — 3 minutes
> 2 fish — 5 minutes, 30 seconds
> 3 fish — 8 minutes

When freshly caught trout is used for this recipe, the poached trout turns a brilliant blue color. The broth is good for poaching other fish such as salmon, whiting or sole.

POACHED TROUT

**3 cups water
¼ cup vinegar
¼ cup minced carrot
¼ cup minced onion or 1 tablespoon
instant minced onion
2 teaspoons salt
4 to 5 peppercorns
1 tablespoon parsley flakes
1 bay leaf
Dash thyme
4 (8 to 10 oz. each) trout**

In 2-quart baking dish (12 x 7), combine all ingredients except trout. **COOK,** uncovered, **15 MINUTES;** strain. Bring back to a boil, about 2 minutes. Add trout; **COOK,** covered with wax paper or plastic wrap, **6 MINUTES, 30 SECONDS** or until fish flakes easily. **LET STAND,** covered, **2 MINUTES.** Remove from broth with wide slotted spatula and serve plain or with a sauce.   4 Servings

> **TIP:** To eliminate need to strain broth, tie peppercorns, carrot, onion, parsley and bay leaf in small square of cheese cloth and remove after cooking.

Here we've used red snapper topped with a traditional Amandine sauce but the sauce is also good with trout or sole. You can cook (and brown) the butter almond sauce in only 4 minutes.

RED SNAPPER AMANDINE

**1 lb. fresh or frozen red snapper fillets,
thawed
1 teaspoon lemon juice
Salt
⅓ cup slivered or sliced almonds
⅓ cup butter or margarine**

Place fillets in 1½-quart (10 x 6) or 2-quart (8 x 8) baking dish. Rub lemon juice into fillets and salt lightly. **COOK,** covered with wax paper or plastic wrap, **5 MINUTES** or until fish flakes easily. Let stand, covered, while making sauce. In 1-cup measure or bowl, **COOK** almonds and butter, uncovered, **4 MINUTES** or until light brown, stirring twice. Serve Amandine sauce over fillets.   4 Servings

Salmon, either fresh or frozen, cooks very nicely in the oven. This recipe has a flavorful mushroom and bread stuffing that forms a topping on each steak. The mixture would make a good stuffing for part of a whole salmon, too.

SALMON STEAKS WITH MUSHROOM STUFFING

4 salmon steaks, cut ¾ inch thick
¼ teaspoon salt
¼ cup butter or margarine
¼ cup chopped onion
1 stalk (½ cup) celery, chopped
3 cups (3 slices) soft bread cubes
2 cups (1 pt.) sliced fresh mushrooms
2 teaspoons parsley flakes or ¼ cup minced parsley
¼ teaspoon salt
⅛ teaspoon pepper
1 tablespoon lemon juice
½ cup light cream

In 2-quart (12 x 7) baking dish, arrange salmon steaks with thin ends toward center; sprinkle with ¼ teaspoon salt. In mixing bowl, combine butter, onion and celery. **COOK**, uncovered, **3 MINUTES**, stirring once after butter melts. Stir in bread cubes, mushrooms, parsley, ¼ teaspoon salt, pepper and lemon juice. Toss to mix well. Spoon on top of salmon steaks. Pour cream over top. **COOK**, covered with wax paper or plastic wrap, **10 MINUTES** or until salmon flakes easily. Garnish with lemon slices.

4 Servings

> **TIPS:** If desired, add 2 tablespoons sherry to stuffing.
>
> ● For 2 servings, use 2-quart (8 x 8) baking dish, half of the ingredients and cooking times of 2 minutes and 6 minutes.

Cream style corn makes a very easy and tasty sauce for salmon.

SALMON WITH CREAM SAUCE

4 salmon steaks, cut ¾ inch thick
2 tablespoons chopped green pepper
1 cup (8-oz. can) cream style corn

In 2-quart (12 x 7) baking dish, arrange salmon steaks with thin ends toward center. Place green pepper in small custard cup and **COOK**, covered, **1 MINUTE**. Sprinkle green pepper over salmon. Spoon corn over salmon. **COOK**, covered with wax paper or plastic wrap, **6 MINUTES** or until fish flakes easily. **LET STAND**, covered, **2 MINUTES** to finish cooking.

4 Servings

This recipe has a mild, pleasant salmon flavor with colorful bits of carrot, celery and onion. You need only add rice or noodles and a fruit salad to complete the meal. Allow about 20 minutes for cooking.

SAUCY SALMON AND VEGETABLES

4 medium carrots, thinly sliced
3 stalks celery, sliced ¼ inch thick
5 to 6 small white onions, cut in half
1 cup water
1 teaspoon salt
3 tablespoons flour
1 can (1 lb.) salmon
1 cup milk
1 tablespoon Worcestershire sauce
Dash pepper
½ cup shredded Cheddar cheese

In 2 or 2½-quart casserole, combine carrots, celery, onions, water and salt. **COOK**, covered, **10 MINUTES** or until partially cooked. Combine flour with liquid from salmon. Add milk, flour mixture, salmon, Worcestershire sauce and pepper to vegetables. **COOK**, covered, **10 MINUTES** or until vegetables are desired doneness and sauce boils and thickens. Stir in cheese. **LET STAND**, covered, **2 MINUTES** to melt cheese.

5 to 6 Servings

This salmon loaf gets its ring shape from a casserole dish with a glass in the center. Canned tuna may be used, also.

SALMON RING

3 eggs, beaten
2 cups (1-lb. can) red salmon, drained and flaked
1 cup fine dry bread crumbs
½ cup (1 stalk) chopped celery
¼ cup chopped green pepper
2 tablespoons minced onion or 2 teaspoons instant minced onion
1 tablespoon lemon juice
¾ cup milk

In 1½-quart casserole, combine all ingredients; mix well. Move mixture away from center and place glass in center to make the ring shape. **COOK**, uncovered, **8 MINUTES** or until mixture around glass is set. Remove glass and invert onto serving plate.

6 Servings

> **TIPS:** You can use 2 cans (7 oz. each) tuna fish for salmon.
>
> ● The center of the ring can be filled with creamed peas or other vegetables before serving.

MENU
Salmon Steaks with Lemon-Dill Sauce
Stuffed Baked Potatoes (123)
Sliced Tomatoes
Relishes
Cherries Jubilee over cake or
ice cream (137)

1. About 30 minutes before serving, cook potatoes first cooking, then stuff.
2. Cook salmon and sauce.
3. Finish cooking stuffed potatoes.
4. While clearing table, cook cherries (assemble earlier).

SALMON STEAKS WITH LEMON-DILL SAUCE

4 salmon steaks, cut ¾ inch thick
1 medium onion, sliced
1 cube or teaspoon chicken bouillon
1 tablespoon lemon juice
1 teaspoon dill weed
½ teaspoon salt
1 cup water
2 tablespoons butter or margarine
2 tablespoons flour
½ teaspoon salt
½ cup whipping cream
2 tablespoons lemon juice

In 2-quart (12 x 7) baking dish, arrange salmon steaks with thin ends toward center. Top with onion. Crumble bouillon and sprinkle over top along with 1 tablespoon lemon juice, dill weed, ½ teaspoon salt and water. **COOK**, covered with wax paper or plastic wrap, **10 MINUTES** or until fish flakes easily. In 2-cup measure, melt butter (20 sec.). Blend in flour and salt. Stir in cream, mixing until smooth. Add juices from fish; stir in lemon juice. **COOK**, uncovered, **3 MINUTES** or until mixture boils, stirring occasionally. Arrange salmon steaks on serving plate; pour sauce over top and garnish with sprigs of parsley. 4 Servings

TIP: For 2 servings, use 1½-quart (8-inch round) baking dish, half the ingredients (can use 1 cube bouillon) and cooking times of 6 minutes and 2 minutes.

Biscuits start out on the bottom of this casserole, but during cooking, they rise to the top with an attractive glaze from the cheese soup. Prepare and cook in about 15 minutes.

TUNA AND CHEESE CASSEROLE

1 can (8 oz.) refrigerated biscuits
1 can (10¾ oz.) condensed Cheddar cheese soup
2 cans (6½ oz. each) tuna fish, drained
1 cup milk
1 teaspoon parsley flakes or 1 tablespoon minced parsley

In 1½-quart (10 x 6) baking dish, arrange biscuits in 2 rows along length of dish. Combine soup, fish, milk and parsley. Spoon over biscuits. **COOK**, uncovered, **12 MINUTES** or until biscuits are no longer doughy, spooning sauce over biscuits once during last half of cooking. 6 Servings

TIP: To reheat, cook, uncovered, about 5 minutes or until hot.

TUNA NOODLE CASSEROLE

1½ cups uncooked noodles
1 cup water
1 cup (6½-oz. can) drained tuna fish
1 can (10½ oz.) condensed cream of mushroom soup
½ cup (4-oz. can) drained mushroom stems and pieces
2 cups (1 lb. 1-oz. can) drained green beans or peas
½ cup coarsely crushed potato chips, if desired

In 2-quart casserole, combine noodles and water. **COOK**, covered, **10 MINUTES**, stirring once. Stir in tuna fish, soup, mushrooms and green beans. **COOK**, covered, **6 MINUTES** or until heated through, stirring once. Sprinkle with potato chips just before serving. 6 to 8 Servings

LOBSTER TAILS

Split each 9 oz. thawed tail through top shell. Pull lobster meat out of shell, placing on top and leaving connected to shell at end. Brush with melted butter and sprinkle with paprika. Arrange in shallow casserole dish. Cook, covered:

1 tail — 3½ minutes
2 tails — 6 minutes
4 tails — 10 minutes

TIP: To thaw, see page 45.

Bouillabaisse

MENU

Bouillabaisse
Garlic French Bread (129)
Artichoke Hearts on Lettuce Salad
Butterscotch Fondue Sauce (135)
with Fruits

1. About 30 minutes before serving, cook butterscotch fondue sauce and let stand.
2. Cook Bouillabaisse.
3. Heat French Bread.
4. Reheat Fondue Sauce if necessary.

SCALLOPED OYSTERS

  ½ cup butter or margarine
1½ cups coarsely crushed dry bread or cracker crumbs
  ½ cup grated Parmesan cheese
  ⅛ teaspoon pepper
Dash mace
  2 cups (two 8-oz. cans) oysters and liquor
  ¼ cup cooking sherry

In 4-cup measure or 1-quart casserole, melt butter (30 sec.). Blend in bread crumbs, cheese, pepper and mace. In 1½-quart (10 x 6) baking dish, arrange half of bread crumb mixture in layer. Spoon oysters evenly over crumbs. Pour oyster liquor and sherry over oysters; top with remaining crumbs. COOK, uncovered, 5 MINUTES or until oysters are hot.

4 to 6 Servings

TIP: Canned whole clams can be used for oysters.

LIVE LOBSTER

  ½ cup water
  ½ teaspoon salt
1½-lb. live lobster, pegged

In 2-quart (12 x 7) baking dish or 3-quart casserole, bring water and salt to a boil (1½ min.). Place live lobster in dish and cover with another 2-quart (12 x 7) baking dish or casserole cover. COOK, covered, 9 MINUTES. LET STAND, covered, 2 MINUTES to finish cooking. Split tail and if meat is still translucent in center, cook 30 to 45 seconds. Serve whole lobster or remove meat from tail and claws. Serve with melted or drawn butter.

1 to 2 Servings

TIP: A 1½-lb. live crab, such as Dungeoness, can be cooked as above using 3-quart casserole. Pry off shell after cooking.

This is a fish stew to serve for company. Use some seafood still in the shell if it is available.

BOUILLABAISSE

  ½ cup (1 med.) chopped onion
  1 clove garlic or ⅛ teaspoon instant minced garlic
  2 tablespoons olive or cooking oil
  1 cup (8-oz. can) tomato sauce
  4 cups water
  2 tablespoons parsley flakes or ¼ cup minced parsley
  ¼ teaspoon saffron or curry
2½ teaspoons salt
  ¼ teaspoon pepper
  1 teaspoon lemon juice
  1 lb. fish fillets, cut into 2-inch pieces
12 oz. shrimp
  6 oz. crab or lobster meat
  1 pint oysters or clams

In 4 or 5-quart casserole, combine onion, garlic and oil. COOK, uncovered, 2 MINUTES. Add remaining ingredients and mix to distribute evenly. COOK, covered, 15 TO 20 MINUTES or until seafood is done, stirring occasionally. Serve in large soup bowls.   10 to 12 Servings

TIPS: The fish and seafood can be added either fresh or frozen. In using the frozen, you can add while still frozen and use the maximum cooking time. If they are thawed or fresh the minimal time will be about right.

• Any combination of fish or seafood can be used for this dish. Select the available kinds that are favorites. Cooking times may vary slightly but should fall within the range given. If some pieces are much larger than others, such as lobster tails, cut into smaller pieces.

Fresh clams cooked in a small amount of water will actually be "steamed clams". Overcooking will toughen clams.

CLAMS OR OYSTERS IN THE SHELL

  ¼ cup water
  6 fresh clams or oysters, thoroughly washed

In 2-quart casserole, bring water to a boil (45 sec.). Arrange clams evenly in casserole and COOK, covered, 3 MINUTES. LET STAND, covered, 1 TO 2 MINUTES to finish cooking. Check for doneness (clam meat should be firm) and if necessary cook longer, about 30 seconds.

2 Servings

Allow 12 minutes to cook this spicy curry. If cooking rice in the oven, cook rice first while mixing together the curry and then cook curry while the rice rests. Since the curry is highly seasoned, serve with buttered asparagus or other mildly seasoned vegetable.

SHRIMP CURRY

¼ cup butter or margarine
¼ cup chopped onion or 1 tablespoon instant minced onion
½ cup (1 stalk) chopped celery
2 tablespoons chopped green pepper or pimiento
3 tablespoons flour
2 teaspoons curry powder
1 cube or teaspoon chicken bouillon
½ cup water
½ cup milk
3 cups (12 oz.) frozen uncooked shrimp

In 1½ or 2-quart casserole, combine butter, onion and celery. **COOK, uncovered, 2 MINUTES.** Stir in green pepper, flour, curry, bouillon, water, milk and frozen shrimp. **COOK, covered, 12 MINUTES** or until shrimp turn pink. Serve over rice along with condiments.

4 to 5 Servings

> **TIPS:** If desired, 10-oz. pkg. frozen cooked shrimp can be used. Cook 8 minutes or until mixture boils and thickens. If shrimp are thawed, time will be about 2 minutes less.
> • For condiments, pass small dishes of toasted coconut, chopped peanuts, pickle relish, chutney, sliced green onions, raisins or crumbled crisp bacon.

This makes an easy luncheon dish. You can cook it ahead and then just reheat for serving over toast points or patty shells. Lobster, crab, shrimp or a combination of these go well with the sauce.

NEWBURG

¼ cup butter or margarine
1½ tablespoons flour
½ teaspoon salt
1½ cups half and half or light cream
2 egg yolks
¼ cup sherry or white wine
2 cups (12 oz.) cooked lobster, crab or shrimp
1 teaspoon lemon juice

In 1½-quart casserole, melt butter (30 sec.). Stir in flour and salt. Beat cream with egg yolks until well mixed. Stir into flour mixture. Add sherry and lobster. **COOK, covered, 7 MINUTES** or until mixture starts to boil and thicken, stirring occasionally. Stir in lemon juice. Serve over toast points, patty shells or rice.

5 to 6 Servings

This can be served as a main dish for a light lunch or as an appetizer for dinner. Cream of shrimp soup eliminates making a sauce.

SEAFOOD THERMIDOR

1 can (10 oz.) frozen condensed cream of shrimp soup
½ cup (4-oz. can) drained sliced mushrooms
1 cup (6 to 6½-oz. can) drained, diced cooked lobster meat
¼ cup milk
¼ teaspoon dry mustard
Dash cayenne pepper
Grated Parmesan cheese
Paprika

Remove one end from can of frozen shrimp soup. Place can in 1-quart casserole or bowl; add water to ¾ cover can. **COOK 3 MINUTES** or until soup loosens in can. Discard water and slide soup into the casserole or bowl. Cook in 30 second intervals with rest periods of at least 1 minute until thawed (4 or 5 times). Add mushrooms, lobster, milk, mustard and pepper. Spoon into 4 individual casseroles, sauce dishes or shells. Sprinkle with Parmesan cheese and paprika. **COOK, uncovered, 3 MINUTES** or until edges bubble.

4 Servings

> **TIP:** To reheat 2 dishes from refrigerator, cook, uncovered, 2 minutes, 30 seconds.

SHRIMP FLAMENCO

1 package (6 oz.) herb or Spanish rice mix
2 cups (1-lb. can) undrained tomatoes
2 tablespoons butter or margarine
1 cup water
4 cups (16 to 20 oz.) frozen uncooked shrimp
1 package (⅝ oz.) golden gravy mix
¼ cup water
½ cup milk
½ cup cream or evaporated milk
1 tablespoon dry white wine
Dash cayenne pepper
1 tablespoon parsley flakes or 2 tablespoons minced parsley

In 2-quart casserole, combine herb rice mix, tomatoes, butter and water. **COOK, covered, 8 MINUTES,** stirring once. Let stand, covered. Meanwhile, defrost shrimp in 45 second cook and 1 minute rest intervals until thawed (4 to 5 times). In 1½-quart casserole, combine gravy mix, water and milk. **COOK, uncovered, 1 MINUTE, 30 SECONDS** or until thickened, stirring twice. Add cream, white wine, pepper, parsley and defrosted shrimp. **COOK, covered, 6 MINUTES** or until shrimp turn pink, stirring once. Serve with the rice.

4 to 5 Servings

Shrimp cooked in a tomato creole sauce goes especially well with rice. With frozen shrimp there is about ½ cup liquid added from the juices that cook out during thawing and cooking. If your shrimp are thawed and drained, you may have to add this amount of liquid.

SHRIMP CREOLE

   3 tablespoons cornstarch
   ¼ cup chopped onion 1 tablespoon instant minced onion
   ½ cup chopped green pepper
   ½ teaspoon salt
   ½ teaspoon paprika
   ½ teaspoon chili powder
   ⅛ teaspoon instant minced garlic or 1 clove garlic
   ⅛ teaspoon pepper
   ½ teaspoon leaf basil or marjoram
   3½ cups (1 lb. 12-oz. can) undrained tomatoes
   3 cups (12 oz.) frozen uncooked shrimp

In 1½ or 2-quart casserole, combine all ingredients; mix well. **COOK**, covered, 12 **MINUTES** or until shrimp are done and mixture boils, stirring occasionally during last half of cooking time. Serve over rice.   4 to 5 Servings

Shrimp is accented by the flavors of a sweet-sour sauce. Allow about 12 minutes for cooking.

SWEET 'N SOUR SHRIMP

   ¼ cup sugar
   3 tablespoons cornstarch
   ½ teaspoon ground ginger
   1 teaspoon paprika
   2 tablespoons soy sauce
   ¼ cup vinegar
   1½ cups (13¼-oz. can) undrained pineapple tidbits
   3 cups (12 oz.) frozen uncooked shrimp
   3 medium green or 1 small onion, sliced
   2 stalks celery, sliced
   1 green pepper, cut into strips
   1 large tomato, cut into small pieces

In 2-quart casserole, combine sugar, cornstarch, ginger, paprika, soy sauce and vinegar; mix well. Stir in pineapple, frozen shrimp, onions, celery and green pepper. **COOK**, covered, 12 **MINUTES** or until shrimp is done. Stir in tomato and leave covered a few minutes to heat tomato.   4 to 5 Servings

   TIPS: If desired, 10-oz. pkg. frozen cooked shrimp can be used. Cook 8 minutes or until vegetables are desired doneness.

   • For crisp green pepper, add during last 5 minutes of cooking.

The red color of crabmeat gives this luncheon dish or appetizer a very colorful appearance.

CRAB REGAL

   ¾ to 1 cup (6 to 8 oz.) drained and flaked cooked crabmeat
   ¼ to ½ cup shredded Cheddar or Swiss cheese
   2 tablespoons dry bread crumbs
   2 tablespoons chopped celery
   2 tablespoons salad dressing or mayonnaise
   2 tablespoons milk or cream
   1 tablespoon chopped pimiento, if desired
   ½ teaspoon instant minced onion
   ½ teaspoon lemon juice
   ⅛ teaspoon salt
   Dash pepper

In 1-quart casserole or mixing bowl, combine all ingredients. Spoon into 2 individual casseroles, sauce dishes or shells. **COOK**, uncovered, 1 **MINUTE, 30 SECONDS** or until edges bubble.
                                        2 Servings

   TIPS: It is easy to double or triple recipe, cooking 2 at a time.

   • This dish can be made ahead and refrigerated. To reheat, cook:
      1 dish   — 1 minute, 15 seconds
      2 dishes — 2 minutes
      3 dishes — 3 minutes
      4 dishes — 4 minutes

Scampi is in the same family as shrimp but usually a little larger. The easier-to-find shrimp can be used in this recipe.

WINE SCAMPI

   2 cups (8 or 10-oz. pkg.) frozen uncooked scampi
   2 tablespoons butter or margarine
   1 clove garlic, minced
   3 tablespoons white wine
   Dash parsley

To defrost scampi, place in a single layer on layer of paper towel; cook 1 minute, 30 seconds or until almost thawed. Set aside. In 1½-quart (8 or 9-inch round) baking dish, combine butter, garlic, wine and parsley. **COOK**, uncovered, 2 **MINUTES**. Add scampi and **COOK**, uncovered, 2 **MINUTES** or until hot, stirring once.   2 to 3 Servings

   TIP: If you wish to reduce liquid after scampi is cooked, remove scampi to prevent toughening and cook liquid, uncovered, 2 minutes, 30 seconds or until reduced. Return scampi to liquid.

SCALLOPS POULETTE

¼ **cup butter or margarine**
1 **tablespoon minced onion or ½ teaspoon instant minced onion**
½ **cup (4-oz. can) drained mushroom stems and pieces**
¼ **cup flour**
½ **cup white wine**
½ **teaspoon salt**
⅛ **teaspoon pepper**
1 **lb. fresh or frozen sea scallops, thawed and cut into quarters**
1 **bay leaf**
2 **teaspoons lemon juice**
½ **cup light or whipping cream**
1 **egg yolk**
1 **tablespoon chopped parsley or parsley flakes**

In 1½ or 2-quart casserole, combine butter and onion. COOK, uncovered, 2 MINUTES. Stir in mushrooms, flour, wine, salt, pepper, scallops, bay leaf and lemon juice; mix well. COOK, covered, 5 MINUTES or until scallops are just about done, stirring occasionally. Remove bay leaf. Blend cream with egg yolk. Stir into hot mixture. COOK, covered, 3 MINUTES or until hot, stirring twice. Stir in parsley.   4 Servings

TIPS: Fresh mushrooms can be used for canned; use 1 cup sliced fresh mushrooms and add with onion, increasing cooking time to 3 minutes.

• For Clams Poulette, use 2 cans (7 oz. each) minced clams, undrained, for scallops. Prepare and cook as directed.

This will give you a good guide for reheating prebreaded scallops in the oven as well as an idea for a snappy and easy sauce to serve with scallops or other fish. Watch the time carefully because scallops heat very quickly.

SCALLOPS WITH DEVILED SAUCE

¾ **cup milk**
2 **teaspoons sugar**
2 **teaspoons chopped chives**
2 **teaspoons Dijon mustard or 1 teaspoon dry mustard**
1 **package (1½ oz.) sour cream sauce mix**
2 **packages (7 oz. each) frozen prebreaded scallops**

In 2-cup measure, combine milk, sugar, chives, mustard and sauce mix; stir until blended. COOK, uncovered, 1 MINUTE, 45 SECONDS or until mixture thickens slightly. Set aside. Place frozen scallops on paper towel on serving platter. COOK, uncovered, 2 MINUTES or until hot. Remove paper towel and pour sauce over scallops or serve sauce in dish along with scallops.   4 to 5 Servings

TIP: The sauce will make the scallops a little soggy on standing. If they are not going to be eaten immediately, we would recommend keeping sauce and scallops separate.

Scallops in a creamy wine sauce make a delicious main course or appetizer served in shells or small sauce dishes. You may find it convenient to make ahead and refrigerate or freeze for easy reheating.

COQUELLES ST. JACQUES

¼ **cup butter or margarine**
¼ **cup (½ stalk) chopped celery**
1 **cup sliced fresh mushrooms**
2 **medium green onions, sliced or 2 tablespoons chopped onion**
2 **tablespoons green pepper**
2 **tablespoons flour**
½ **teaspoon salt**
⅛ **teaspoon pepper**
½ **bay leaf**
½ **cup white wine**
1 **lb. fresh or frozen sea scallops, thawed**
¼ **cup whipping cream**
1 **egg yolk**
1 **tablespoon chopped pimiento**
2 **tablespoons butter or margarine**
2 **tablespoons bread crumbs**
2 **tablespoons grated Parmesan cheese**

In 2-quart casserole, combine butter, celery, mushrooms and onion. COOK, uncovered, 3 MINUTES, stirring occasionally. Stir in green pepper, flour, salt, pepper, bay leaf and wine; mix well. Add thawed scallops. COOK, covered, 5 MINUTES or until mixture boils and thickens. Beat together cream and egg yolk until well mixed. Stir into scallops along with pimiento. COOK, covered, 2 MINUTES or until hot. Remove bay leaf. Spoon into 4 shells or individual serving dishes that each hold 1 cup. In small dish or measure, melt butter (20 sec.). Stir in bread crumbs and cheese. Sprinkle about 1 tablespoon of mixture on each serving. COOK, uncovered, 1 MINUTE to heat through, or place under broiler a few minutes to brown crumbs.   4 Servings

TIP: ½ cup (4-oz. can) drained sliced mushrooms can be used, but wait and add along with green pepper. They will tend to pop if added during the first cooking.

Poultry

The natural tenderness and moistness of poultry are preserved with microwave cooking. This section includes recipes for chicken, turkey, duck, Cornish hen, pheasant and goose.

Frying Chicken: Most of the recipes have a one step method that simplifies the preparation and enhances flavors. All the recipes provide for some browning. If additional browning is desired, you can pre-brown chicken in a flame proof dish or brown under a broiler just before serving. The larger pieces of a chicken are cut to make all the parts more even in size. When arranging chicken pieces, put the larger part of each piece toward the outside of the cooking dish and the smaller part toward the center to aid even cooking.

We suggest using a frying chicken to make a delicious stew because a stewing chicken will remain too tough during the relatively short cooking time.

See Dinner section for another poultry recipe, Chicken Atop Rice, page 27.

Roasting Chicken and Turkey: All whole birds are turned over once during the cooking period to assure even cooking. During the first half of the cooking time, foil is used to cover the thinner parts of the bird (wing tips and end of legs) to prevent overcooking. However, do not use foil if it will touch the walls of the oven because it might cause pitting of the walls. If you have overcooked a bird and notice hard spots, you can let it stand overnight in the refrigerator (after removing any stuffing). The moisture of the bird tends to equalize and the dry parts will gather more moisture after standing. The giblets from a roast should be cooked conventionally because they need long, slow cooking to become tender and also because they tend to pop in the microwave oven.

Most stuffing recipes are interchangeable. This is only a sample because stuffings adapt quite easily to microwave cooking.

To keep the oven clean from spatters, you can loosely cover a bird with wax paper. All roasted birds rest on something to keep them out of drippings. You can improvise your own device such as crisscrossed wooden spoons or overturned sauce dishes.

If you use a thermometer to check doneness, place it in the meaty inside part of the thigh, *after* removing the bird from the oven. The temperature should be about 20° less than it will be after the standing time for the larger birds because they will continue to cook. The smaller birds will read closer to 10° less than their final temperature.

Duck and Goose: The fat in duck and goose is cooked out during the cooking time in the recipes. It is their high fat content that enables duck and goose to have a shorter cooking time than a comparable amount of leaner poultry such as chicken or turkey.

See page 45 for directions for defrosting all poultry except a whole turkey (page 67).

A mild, tomato-flavored chicken dish. Canned soups make this traditional dish very easy.

CHICKEN MARENGO

  2½ to 3-lb. frying chicken, cut up
  1 can (10½ oz.) condensed golden
    mushroom soup
  1 can (10¾ oz.) condensed tomato soup
  1 clove garlic, minced, or ⅛ teaspoon
    garlic powder or instant minced garlic
  1 lb. (about 16) small whole onions or
    1⅔ cups (1-lb. can) drained pearl onions

In 2 or 3-quart casserole, combine all ingredients. **COOK**, covered, **28 MINUTES**, stirring once. If desired, thicken sauce with 1 to 2 teaspoons cornstarch dissolved in 2 tablespoons water.   4 to 6 Servings

CHILIED CHICKEN

  2½ to 3-lb. frying chicken, cut up
  1 can (10¾ oz.) condensed tomato soup
  ½ cup chopped green pepper
  ½ cup chopped onion or 2 tablespoons
    instant minced onion
  1 tablespoon flour
  ½ teaspoon salt
  1 teaspoon chili powder
  1 tablespoon vinegar

Cut larger pieces of chicken in half for uniform size. Arrange in 2-quart (12 x 7) baking dish. Combine remaining ingredients and spoon over chicken. **COOK**, covered with wax paper, **28 MINUTES** or until done.   4 to 6 Servings

  TIP: Two turkey wings (about 2¼ to 2½ lbs.) can be used with half this sauce. Cook in 2-quart covered casserole 20 minutes or until done, occasionally spooning sauce over turkey.

The microwave oven can be used to partially cook chicken before placing on the grill to reduce the total cooking time and to prevent the barbecued chicken being too brown on the outside before the center of the pieces are done.

CHICKEN FOR BARBECUING

Arrange a 2½ to 3-lb. cut up frying chicken in 2-quart (12 x 7) baking dish with larger pieces toward outside of dish. **COOK,** uncovered, 15 MINUTES. Dip pieces in favorite barbecue sauce and grill over hot coals **15 TO 20 MINUTES,** turning occasionally until chicken is done and browned.   4 to 6 Servings

TIP: This same idea can be used when broiling chicken.

> **MENU**
> **Chicken Magnifico**
> **Baked Potatoes (117)**
> **Spinach Delish (125)**
> **Bananas Royale (136)**
> **over ice cream**
>
> 1. Cook chicken for half of time.
> 2. Cook potatoes and let stand.
> 3. Cook first cooking of spinach.
> 4. Finish cooking chicken.
> 5. Finish cooking spinach.
> 6. While clearing table, add bananas to Bananas Royale and cook (assemble earlier).

Cheese and tomato make an attractive and tasty sauce for chicken.

CHICKEN MAGNIFICO

   2½ to 3-lb. frying chicken, cut up
   1 can (10½ oz.) condensed Cheddar cheese soup
   1 cup (8-oz. can) undrained stewed tomatoes
   ¼ cup instant minced onion or 1 cup chopped onion
   1 teaspoon leaf basil
   ½ teaspoon salt
   ⅛ teaspoon pepper
   2 oz. (½ cup) chopped ham
   Paprika

Cut larger pieces of chicken in half for uniform size. Arrange skin side up in 2-quart (12 x 7) baking dish. Combine remaining ingredients except paprika. Spoon over chicken. Sprinkle generously with paprika. **COOK,** covered with wax paper, **28 MINUTES** or until chicken is done.   4 to 5 Servings

TIP: If you do not have ham on hand, it can be omitted. Other luncheon meats or 1 tablespoon bacon-flavored bits can be used, if desired.

Bananas, orange juice and cashew nuts team with chicken for an unusual and tasty treat. Serve over rice and add a vegetable such as pea pods or broccoli. Cook the vegetable in the oven just before you add the bananas and nuts to the chicken.

ISLANDER CHICKEN

   2½ to 3-lb. frying chicken, cut up
   1 can (6 oz.) frozen orange juice concentrate, thawed
   1 tablespoon cornstarch
   1 teaspoon salt
   ¼ teaspoon cinnamon
   1 tablespoon lime or lemon juice
   2 bananas, sliced
   ½ cup chopped cashew or macadamia nuts

Cut larger pieces of chicken in half for uniform size. Arrange skin side up in 2-quart (12 x 7) baking dish. Combine juice concentrate, cornstarch, salt, cinnamon and lime juice. Pour over chicken. **COOK,** covered with wax paper, **28 MINUTES** or until chicken is done, spooning sauce over chicken during last half of cooking time. Add bananas and nuts. **COOK,** uncovered, **1 MINUTE, 30 SECONDS.**   4 to 5 Servings

TIPS: If browner chicken is desired, place under broiler a few minutes before adding bananas and nuts.

• If fixing ahead, add bananas and nuts just before serving because bananas are easy to overcook and the nuts lose their crunchy texture.

An easy chicken dish with a rich, golden flavor and color from mushroom soup. It cooks in just 28 minutes.

GOLDEN CHICKEN

   2½ to 3-lb. frying chicken, cut up
   1 stalk (½ cup) celery, chopped
   1 teaspoon salt
   1 can (10½ oz.) condensed golden mushroom soup

Cut larger pieces of chicken in half for uniform size. Arrange skin side up in 2-quart (12 x 7) baking dish. Sprinkle with celery and salt. Spoon soup over top of chicken. **COOK,** covered with wax paper, **28 MINUTES** or until chicken is done.   5 to 6 Servings

TIP: A 2 to 2½-lb. turkey breast can be used with half this sauce. Cook in 2-quart covered casserole 20 minutes or until done, occasionally spooning sauce over turkey.

This sauce is mild flavored; increase the oregano and garlic if you prefer a zestier sauce.

CHICKEN CACCIATORI

    2½ to 3-lb. frying chicken, cut up
     2 cups (16-oz. can) tomato sauce
     ¾ cup (6-oz. can) tomato paste
     2 tablespoons instant minced onion or
       ½ cup chopped onion
     1 teaspoon salt
    1¼ teaspoons leaf oregano
     ½ teaspoon garlic powder or instant
       minced garlic or 2 cloves garlic
     ¼ teaspoon pepper
     ¼ teaspoon powdered thyme
     2 cups water

Cut larger pieces of chicken in half for uniform size and set aside. Combine remaining ingredients in 4-quart casserole or Dutch oven. Stir in chicken pieces, coating with sauce. COOK, covered, 40 MINUTES or until chicken is done, stirring once. Serve plain or over spaghetti.   4 to 6 Servings

> **TIP:** If desired, use ¼ cup red wine for part of water.

ORANGE GLAZED CHICKEN

    2½ to 3-lb. frying chicken, cut up
     1 can (6 oz.) frozen orange juice
       concentrate, thawed
     ½ cup (4-oz. can) drained mushroom
       stems and pieces
     ½ tablespoon cornstarch
     1 teaspoon dry or prepared mustard
    1½ teaspoons paprika

Cut larger pieces of chicken in half for uniform size. Arrange chicken in 2-quart (12 x 7) baking dish. Combine juice concentrate, mushrooms, cornstarch, mustard and paprika; spoon over pieces of chicken. COOK, covered with wax paper, 28 MINUTES or until chicken is done, spooning glaze over chicken during last 10 minutes of cooking.   4 to 6 Servings

APRICOT GLAZED CHICKEN

    2½ to 3-lb. frying chicken, cut up
     ½ cup apricot preserves
     ½ tablespoon cornstarch
     1 teaspoon leaf marjoram or ½ teaspoon
       powdered marjoram
     ½ teaspoon salt
     1 tablespoon soy sauce

Cut larger pieces of chicken in half for uniform size. Arrange skin side up in 2-quart (12 x 7) baking dish. Combine remaining ingredients and spoon over chicken. COOK, covered with wax paper, 28 MINUTES or until done.   4 to 6 Servings

Chicken goes well with this soy flavored sauce. Bamboo shoots and water chestnuts add a crunchy texture.

ORIENTAL CHICKEN

    2½ to 3-lb. frying chicken, cut up
     ¼ teaspoon salt
     ⅛ teaspoon pepper
     ½ cup chicken broth or bouillon*
     ¼ cup soy sauce
     1 medium onion, cut into wedges
     1 tablespoon cornstarch
     1 tablespoon sugar
     2 tablespoons water
     ¾ cup (5-oz. can) drained bamboo shoots
     ⅔ cup (5-oz. can) drained and sliced
       water chestnuts

Cut larger pieces of chicken in half for uniform size. In 2-quart (12 x 7) baking dish, combine salt, pepper, chicken broth, soy sauce and onion. Place chicken in dish, skin side down. COOK, covered with wax paper, 30 MINUTES, turning chicken over once. Remove chicken to serving platter. Combine cornstarch, sugar and water. Add to juices. COOK, covered, 1 MINUTE, 30 SECONDS, stirring once. Add bamboo shoots and water chestnuts. COOK 2 MINUTES or until hot, stirring once. Serve over rice along with chicken.   4 to 6 Servings

> **TIP:** *For bouillon you can add 1 chicken bouillon cube or ½ teaspoon instant chicken bouillon to ½ cup water.

This is a good company casserole; vermouth gives it a special flavor.

CHICKEN BASQUE

    2½ to 3-lb. frying chicken, cut up
     ¾ cup chopped onion
     1 clove garlic, crushed, or ⅛ teaspoon
       garlic powder or instant minced garlic
    1⅓ cups (two 4-oz. cans) undrained
       mushroom stems and pieces
       (or 1 lb. fresh mushrooms)
     3 cups (1 lb. 12-oz. can) undrained
       tomatoes, broken up
     1 cup vermouth or dry white wine
     1 teaspoon salt
     ¼ teaspoon pepper
     ½ teaspoon each powdered basil
       and thyme
     1 bay leaf, crumbled

Cut larger pieces of chicken in half for uniform size. Combine all ingredients in 4-quart casserole. COOK, covered, 30 MINUTES or until done, stirring once. If desired, thicken sauce with 1 tablespoon cornstarch.
                4 to 6 Servings

This dish is especially nice for company. The orange sauce goes well with rice and a mild flavored green vegetable. If you like crisper chicken skin, just place the chicken dish under the broiler while you cook a vegetable in the oven. The chicken browns and stays warm at the same time.

ORANGE BURGUNDY CHICKEN

2½ to 3-lb. frying chicken, cut up
½ cup orange marmalade
½ cup orange juice
½ cup burgundy or red wine
2 tablespoons brown sugar
2 tablespoons cornstarch
1 tablespoon lemon juice
1 teaspoon salt

Cut larger pieces of chicken in half for uniform size. Arrange skin side up in 2-quart (12 x 7) baking dish. Combine remaining ingredients. Pour over chicken. **COOK**, covered with wax paper, **28 MINUTES** or until chicken is done, spooning sauce over chicken during last half of cooking time. If desired, place under broiler for additional browning. Serve over rice.

4 to 5 Servings

> **TIPS:** For half recipe, use 2-quart (8 x 8) baking dish and cook 20 minutes.
>
> • A 1¼ to 1½ -lb. turkey thigh can be used with half this sauce. Cook in 1½ -quart covered casserole 15 minutes or until done, occasionally spooning sauce over turkey.

Rabbit is similar to chicken, but has a little more pronounced flavor. For our testing, we used the domestic rabbit that is available frozen. If you have wild rabbit, we would suggest marinating it in the sauce overnight before cooking. This will help tenderize the meat.

RABBIT IN SAVORY SAUCE

2 to 2½ -lb. rabbit, cut up
1 onion, sliced
1 stalk celery, sliced
⅓ cup red wine
1 can (10½ oz.) condensed golden
   mushroom soup
½ teaspoon salt
1 clove garlic, minced, or ⅛ teaspoon
   instant minced garlic
1 teaspoon Worcestershire sauce
½ bay leaf, crumbled

In 2-quart (12 x 7) baking dish, arrange rabbit. Top with onion and celery. Pour wine over pieces. Combine soup with salt, garlic, Worcestershire sauce and bay leaf; spoon over rabbit. **COOK**, covered with wax paper, **35 MINUTES** or until done.   4 to 5 Servings

A fryer makes a quick and often economical chicken stew. We found the flavor as good as with stewing chicken cooked conventionally.

SPEEDY CHICKEN STEW

2½ to 3-lb. frying chicken, cut up
2 stalks celery, cut into 1-inch pieces
1 medium onion, sliced
1 bay leaf
4 peppercorns
1 tablespoon salt
3 cubes or teaspoons chicken bouillon
3 cups water
4 carrots, cut into thin slices
¼ cup flour
Dumplings
1½ cups unsifted all purpose flour
2 teaspoons baking powder
½ teaspoon salt
1 teaspoon parsley flakes
⅔ cup milk
1 egg, slightly beaten
2 tablespoons oil

In 4-quart casserole or Dutch oven, combine fryer, celery, onion, bay leaf, peppercorns, salt, bouillon and water. **COOK**, covered, **24 MINUTES**, stirring once. Add carrots. Combine ¼ cup flour with ½ cup water. Stir into chicken mixture. **COOK**, covered, **8 MINUTES**. (Meanwhile, prepare Dumplings.) Remove bay leaf and peppercorns; if desired, remove meat from bone at this point. Spoon Dumplings by rounded tablespoons onto hot chicken mixture. **COOK**, covered, **6 MINUTES** or until dumplings are no longer doughy on underside.

Dumplings: In mixing bowl, combine flour, baking powder, salt and parsley flakes. Combine milk, egg and oil; add to dry ingredients and mix just until moistened. (Mixture will be soft.)

4 to 6 Servings

> **TIPS:** For stewed chicken without vegetables and dumplings, cook chicken 28 minutes or until tender.
>
> • For variety, add ½ cup raisins and ⅛ teaspoon nutmeg to flour mixture for Dumplings.

Pictured, top to bottom: Stuffed Cornish Hens, page 64, Orange Burgundy Chicken, left, Speedy Chicken Stew, above.

An especially easy chicken dish with a gourmet flavor. Add broccoli and a fruit salad for an easy guest dinner. We found the chicken breast bone did not affect cooking time.

CHICKEN BREASTS IN WINE SAUCE

> **4 chicken breasts, skinned and boned, if desired**
> **½ teaspoon salt**
> **Pepper**
> **½ cup (4-oz. can) drained mushroom stems and pieces**
> **3 medium carrots, thinly sliced**
> **¼ cup white wine or milk**
> **1 can (10½ oz.) condensed cream of chicken soup**
> **Parsley**

Arrange chicken breasts in 1½-quart (10 x 6 or 8-inch round) baking dish. Sprinkle with salt and pepper. Top with mushrooms, carrots and wine. Spoon soup over top, spreading to cover. **COOK**, covered with wax paper, **15 MINUTES** or until carrots and chicken are done. Garnish with parsley. Serve with rice or noodles.

4 Servings

This recipe was given to us by a microwave oven owner. She likes to serve it to guests with asparagus spears garnished with pimiento. Ready to serve in 20 minutes.

CHICKEN DOUBLE

> **½ cup slivered or sliced almonds**
> **4 slices bacon**
> **4 chicken breasts, skinned and boned, if desired**
> **1 can (10½ oz.) condensed cream of chicken soup**
> **2 tablespoons sherry or white wine, if desired**

Toast almonds by spreading in thin layer in 2-quart (12 x 7) baking dish. **COOK**, uncovered, **4 MINUTES** or until toasted, stirring 4 times. Remove from dish. **COOK** bacon in dish between layers of paper towel, **1 MINUTE, 30 SECONDS** or until still limp. Discard paper towels and wrap 1 piece of bacon around each chicken breast. Arrange in baking dish. **COOK**, covered with wax paper, **10 MINUTES** or until chicken is done. Mix soup with sherry and juices from chicken. Spoon over top of chicken. Return to oven and **COOK**, covered, **3 MINUTES** or until soup is hot. Top with toasted almonds. Serve on bed of rice.

4 Servings

> **TIP:** To make ahead, toast almonds, cook bacon and wrap chicken breasts. Refrigerate until ready to cook.

We've used a crunchy almond stuffing here for contrast with the hens; you may also like to try half the Rice Pilaf recipe, page 132 as stuffing, or the wild and white rice mix, prepared as directed on package. 4 hens will take about 25 minutes to cook plus 5 to 10 minutes standing time.

STUFFED CORNISH HENS

> **4 cornish hens (1 lb. each)**
> **1 teaspoon salt**
> **Almond Stuffing**
> **¼ cup butter or margarine, melted**
> **1 teaspoon paprika**

Wash hens and set aside giblets (use however you prefer, but they are best cooked conventionally). Sprinkle the inside of cavities with salt; fill body and neck cavity with stuffing. Secure openings with toothpicks or metal skewers. On each, tie legs together and wings to body with string. Cover the end of legs with small pieces of foil. Place inverted saucers or small casserole lids in 2-quart (12 x 7) baking dish to hold hens out of juices. Place hens, breast side down, on saucers. Brush with mixture of butter and paprika. **COOK**, covered with wax paper, **12 MINUTES**. Turn breast side up and reverse outside edges to inside. Brush with remainder of butter mixture. **COOK**, covered with wax paper, **12 MINUTES** or until meat thermometer registers 185° (will increase to 190° during standing). **LET STAND**, covered, **5 TO 10 MINUTES** to finish cooking. 4 Servings

> **TIPS:** For variety, use water chestnuts for almonds in stuffing and brush with a glaze of 2 tablespoons butter, 2 tablespoons soy sauce and 2 tablespoons dark corn syrup.
>
> • Do not use meat thermometer in oven when cooking.

ALMOND STUFFING

> **⅓ cup butter or margarine**
> **½ cup (1 stalk) chopped celery**
> **¼ cup chopped onion or 1 tablespoon instant minced onion**
> **½ cup chopped almonds**
> **4 cups (4 slices) soft bread cubes**
> **1 tablespoon parsley flakes**
> **¼ teaspoon salt**
> **1 cube or teaspoon chicken bouillon (crumble cube)**
> **⅓ cup water**

In mixing bowl, combine butter, celery, onion and almonds. **COOK**, uncovered, **2 MINUTES**, stirring once. Stir in remaining ingredients. Stuffing for 4 Cornish Hens or 1 Roasting Chicken

A pineapple sweet-sour sauce adds flavor and color to the split cornish hens.

TANGY CORNISH HENS

2 cornish hens, split in half
1 cup (8-oz. can) undrained crushed
  pineapple
¼ cup firmly packed brown sugar
1 tablespoon cornstarch
2 tablespoons lemon juice
1 tablespoon prepared mustard
1 tablespoon soy sauce

Arrange hens in 2-quart (12 x 7) baking dish, tucking giblets under hens, if desired. Combine remaining ingredients and spoon over hens. **COOK,** covered with wax paper, **18 MINUTES** or until done, spooning sauce over hens during last half of cooking time. If additional browning is desired, place under broiler. Serve with rice.

4 Servings

> **TIP:** Pineapple tidbits can be used for crushed pineapple.

An easy cornish hen and wild rice dish that cooks in just 25 minutes. Since the rice takes longer to cook than the hens, it is cooked partially before adding the hens.

CORNISH HEN AND RICE BAKE

1 package (6 oz.) white and wild rice mix
½ cup (1 stalk) chopped celery
½ cup (4-oz. can) drained mushroom
  stems and pieces
1¾ cups water
¼ cup butter or margarine
2 cornish hens (1 lb. each)
2 tablespoons butter or margarine

In 2-quart (12 x 7) baking dish, combine uncooked rice mix (with seasonings), celery, mushrooms and water; dot top with ¼ cup butter. **COOK,** covered with wax paper, **10 MINUTES.** Meanwhile, cut cornish hens in half lengthwise down side of breast-bone (kitchen shears work well). Arrange on top of rice, tucking giblets and neck under each half. Brush with 2 tablespoons butter. **COOK,** covered with wax paper, **15 MINUTES** or until done.

4 Servings

> **TIP:** If desired, reserve 2 teaspoons of seasonings from rice mix and add to butter for brushing hens.

MENU

Glazed Turkey Roast
Peachy Yams (124)
Broccoli (115)
with Hollandaise Sauce (133)
Gelatin Salad
Cranberry Sauce (134)
Pumpkin Pie (157)

1. Early in day, cook pie, gelatin salad, cranberry sauce and cook yams if fresh.
2. About 45 minutes before serving, cook turkey and let stand.
3. Cook broccoli and sauce.
4. Cook Peachy yams.
5. Reheat broccoli if necessary.

A 3-lb. turkey roast can be ready to serve in 25 minutes. Use leftovers for cooked turkey recipes on page 69. We found it hard to judge by feel if the turkey roast was thawed so have suggested the use of a thermometer. If it is not thoroughly thawed, these cooking times will not be correct.

GLAZED TURKEY ROAST

3 to 4-lb. boneless rolled turkey roast
Glaze, see below

Be sure roast is thoroughly thawed by checking with meat thermometer which should register around 40-50°. Place skin side up on inverted saucers in 2-quart (12 x 7) baking dish. **COOK,** uncovered, **15 TO 20 MINUTES** (5 minutes per pound) or until meat thermometer registers 180° (will increase to 195° during standing), brushing with desired glaze during last 5 minutes of cooking. **LET STAND 10 TO 15 MINUTES** before slicing.
Curry Peach Glaze: Combine ¼ cup pineapple preserves with 2 tablespoons butter or margarine and ½ teaspoon curry powder. **COOK 2 MINUTES** to melt butter.
Ginger Peach Glaze: Combine ¼ cup peach preserves with 2 tablespoons butter or margarine and ½ teaspoon ground ginger or 2 tablespoons chopped candied ginger. **COOK 2 MINUTES** to melt butter.
Cinnamon Apricot Glaze: Combine ¼ cup apricot preserves with 2 tablespoons butter or margarine and ½ teaspoon cinnamon. **COOK 2 MINUTES** to melt butter. 10 to 12 Servings

> **TIP:** Do not use meat thermometer in oven when cooking.

A 5-lb. roasting chicken will take about 40 minutes to cook plus 10 to 15 minutes to rest. In this time, there will be some browning and the meat will be tender and especially juicy. Stuffing does not affect the cooking time.

ROAST CHICKEN

5 to 5½-lb. roasting chicken*
Stuffing For Chicken
1 teaspoon salt
Butter or margarine

Wash chicken and set aside giblets (use however you prefer, but best cooked conventionally). Prepare stuffing, or leave unstuffed. Sprinkle inside of cavity with salt. Fill cavity and neck opening with stuffing. Secure openings with toothpicks or metal skewers. Tie legs together and wings to body with string. Cover the end of legs, tail and the wings with small pieces of foil. Place inverted saucers or small casserole lids in 2-quart (12 x 7) baking dish to hold chicken out of juices. Place chicken breast side down on saucers. Brush with butter. **COOK,** uncovered, **20 MINUTES.** Remove chicken, using paper towels as hot pads, to platter or cutting board. Drain juices. Remove foil pieces from chicken. Turn chicken breast side up, brush with butter and **CONTINUE COOKING 20 MINUTES** or until meat thermometer registers 180° (will increase to 195° during standing). If necessary, cover with wax paper to prevent spattering. **LET STAND,** covered with foil, **10 TO 15 MINUTES** before carving to allow chicken to finish cooking and make carving easier.   6 to 8 Servings

> **TIPS:** *For other weights of chicken, figure about 8 minutes cooking time per pound.
>
> • Do not use meat thermometer in oven when cooking.

STUFFING FOR CHICKEN

¼ cup butter or margarine
¼ cup chopped onion or 1 tablespoon instant minced onion
½ cup (1 stalk) chopped celery
4 cups (4 slices) soft bread cubes
½ teaspoon salt
½ teaspoon poultry seasoning
¼ cup broth or water

In mixing bowl, combine butter, onion and celery. **COOK,** uncovered, **3 MINUTES,** stirring once. Stir in bread cubes, salt, seasoning and broth.

Stuffing for 1 Roasting Chicken
or 4 Cornish Game Hens

We used apples and prunes for stuffing, but you may have other favorite stuffings for goose. Note that stuffing will not affect the total cooking time. Allow 6 minutes per pound for goose; this is less than for turkey because of the attraction of the microwaves to the additional fat in goose. Cooking and resting take about 1¼ hours.

ROAST GOOSE

10 to 11-lb. domestic goose
1 teaspoon salt
3 to 4 medium apples
8 to 10 dried prunes
1 teaspoon leaf marjoram

Wash goose and set aside giblets (use however you prefer, but they are best cooked conventionally). Sprinkle inside of cavity with salt. Fill cavity with whole or quartered apples and prunes. Sprinkle with marjoram. Secure openings with toothpicks or metal skewers. Tie legs together and wings to body with string. Cover legs and wings with small pieces of foil. Place inverted saucers or small casserole lids in 2-quart (12 x 7) baking dish to hold goose out of juices. Place goose, breast side down, on saucers. **COOK,** uncovered, **30 MINUTES.** Remove goose, using paper towels as hot pads, to platter or cutting board. Drain juices and fat. Remove foil pieces from goose. Turn goose, breast side up and **CONTINUE COOKING 30 MINUTES** or until meat thermometer registers 180° (will increase to 195° during standing). If necessary, cover with wax paper to prevent spattering. **LET STAND,** covered with foil, **10 TO 15 MINUTES** before carving to allow the goose to finish cooking and to make carving easier.   10 to 12 Servings

Here is one recipe for turkey stuffing . . . you may have another that you prefer. Cooking times will not be affected by dressing.

SAVORY MUSHROOM STUFFING

½ cup butter or margarine
½ cup chopped onion or 2 tablespoons instant minced onion
1 cup chopped celery
1 cup (8-oz. can) drained mushroom stems and pieces
8 cups dry bread cubes
2 tablespoons parsley flakes
1 teaspoon salt
2 teaspoons poultry seasoning or ground sage
¼ teaspoon pepper
½ cup broth or water

In large bowl, combine butter, onion and celery. **COOK,** uncovered, **5 MINUTES** or until onion is tender. Stir in remaining ingredients, mixing well.   Stuffing for 12 to 15-lb. Turkey

Turkey is in the oven for an adequate time to get a golden brown skin. Because beginning temperatures and type of turkey may vary, we suggest using a thermometer to test doneness. If you are not familiar with using one, see page 59. Turkey will be easiest to cook after you have a few weeks experience with the oven so you can best judge doneness. If you notice any dark brown spots developing on the breast bone, we would suggest covering the spots with foil as this indicates overcooking in these areas.

ROAST TURKEY

Select a turkey between 8 and 20 pounds. Larger birds can be cooked in the oven if your baking dish and lids or saucers used to hold turkey out of juices will allow the turkey, **when** breast side down and breast side up, to fit in the oven.

Wash turkey and set aside giblets (use however you prefer, but they are best cooked conventionally). Sprinkle inside with salt. If stuffing is desired, prepare and stuff main cavity and neck cavity with stuffing. Secure openings with toothpicks or metal skewers. Tie legs together and wings to body with string. Cover legs and wings with small pieces of foil. Place inverted saucers or small casserole lids in 2-quart (12 x 7) baking dish to hold turkey out of juices. Place turkey, breast side down, on saucers. **COOK,** uncovered, for **HALF OF COOKING TIME.** Using paper towels as hot pads, turn turkey breast side up. Remove foil pieces. Continue **COOKING** for **REMAINING HALF OF COOKING TIME** or until meat thermometer registers 175° (will increase to 195° during standing). If necessary, cover with wax paper to prevent spattering. **LET STAND,** covered with foil, **20 TO 30 MINUTES** to allow the turkey to finish cooking and to make carving easier.

Cooking times (Stuffed or Unstuffed):
  8 to 10-lb. turkey — 7 minutes, 30 seconds per pound
  10 to 12-lb. turkey — 7 minutes per pound
  12 to 20-lb. turkey — 6 minutes, 30 seconds per pound
Times are same for stuffed and unstuffed birds.

TIPS: Turkey can be cooked a day ahead for reheating at serving time. Cook as directed, remove stuffing and cool. Refrigerate until ready to use. Place turkey in baking dish or on platter. Cook, uncovered, 15 minutes or until heated through. Heat stuffing, covered, 7 minutes or until heated through. Turkey is easier to carve while cold, so you may prefer to slice the cold turkey, arrange on serving platter and then reheat about 5 minutes, depending on amount.

• Do not use meat thermometer in oven when cooking.

• If you prefer crisper skin, cook turkey as directed, but reduce cooking time 30 seconds per pound. Then finish in preheated conventional oven at 450° for 15 to 20 minutes or until skin is brown and crisp.

• The pop-up doneness indicators that are in some turkeys can be left in during cooking in the microwave oven.

THAWING TURKEY

Turkey is large, so you can start with fairly long cooking periods for thawing. During the thawing process, some cooking may begin which is acceptable if you are planning to cook turkey immediately. When not planning to cook turkey immediately, use shorter thawing times to avoid beginning the cooking process. The plastic wrap and metal staple can be left on turkey for first part of thawing time.

How we thawed a 13-lb. turkey:
  Cook 5 minutes, rest 5 minutes, cook 5 minutes, rest 5 minutes and turn over.
  Cook 5 minutes, rest 5 minutes, cook 5 minutes, rest 5 minutes and turn over, removing plastic wrap and placing turkey in baking dish.
  Cook 3 minutes, rest 3 minutes, cook 3 minutes, rest 3 minutes and remove giblets from neck and loosen legs from holder.
  Cook 3 minutes, rest 3 minutes, cook 3 minutes, rest 3 minutes and remove neck from main cavity.
  Cook 3 minutes, let rest 10 minutes while preparing stuffing. Stuff and cook.
  Total thawing time: About 1 hour, 20 minutes.

TURKEY PARTS

Turkey is available in parts such as thighs, drumsticks or breasts. We felt the flavor was best when cooked with a sauce as with the frying chicken recipes. To give you a guide, we have included times for cooking turkey parts with the following chicken recipes:

Turkey Breast — Golden Chicken, page 60
Turkey Wings — Chilied Chicken, page 59
Turkey Thigh — Orange Burgundy Chicken, page 62

This can be served as a brunch or luncheon dish. Broccoli keeps its green color when cooked in the oven.

TURKEY DIVAN

2 packages (10 oz. each) frozen broccoli or asparagus spears
6 slices cooked turkey (or enough for 4 to 6 servings)
3 oz. (6 slices) sliced American cheese
1 can (10½ oz.) condensed cream of chicken soup
1 can (3½ oz.) French-fried onion rings

Place packages of frozen broccoli spears in oven and COOK 6 MINUTES or until partially cooked. Place broccoli in bottom of 2-quart (12 x 7) baking dish. Top with turkey and then cheese. Spoon soup over all. COOK, covered with wax paper, 10 MINUTES. Add onion rings and COOK, uncovered, 1 MINUTE.

4 to 6 Servings

By using quick-cooking rice, you can eliminate pre-cooking the rice. Plan about 15 minutes to prepare and cook this casserole.

EASY CHICKEN RICE

⅓ cup chopped onion or 1 tablespoon instant minced onion
1 can (10½ oz.) condensed chicken broth*
1 teaspoon soy sauce
1 cup quick-cooking rice, uncooked
1 to 1½ cups cubed cooked chicken or turkey
1 cup (7-oz. can) drained green beans, if desired
⅔ cup (5-oz. can) drained and sliced water chestnuts, if desired

In 1½ or 2-quart casserole, combine onion, broth, soy sauce, rice and chicken. COOK, covered, 8 MINUTES. Stir in beans and water chestnuts. COOK, covered, 1 MINUTE or until hot.

4 Servings

TIP: *You can use 1¼ cups water and either 2 chicken bouillon cubes or 1 teaspoon chicken stock base.

Pictured, clockwise: Uses for leftover turkey — Turkey Noodle Bake, above, Day After Turkey Sandwiches, page 109, Easy Chicken Rice, above (made with turkey), and Roast Turkey, page 67, as cooked totally in the microwave oven.

An easy casserole for leftover turkey or chicken. Heats in just 4 minutes.

TURKEY NOODLE BAKE

1 can (10½ oz.) condensed cream of chicken soup
¼ cup water
2 cups cubed cooked turkey or chicken
1 cup (2 stalks) chopped celery
½ cup coarsely chopped cashew nuts, if desired
1 tablespoon instant minced onion or ¼ cup chopped onion
1 tablespoon chopped pimiento or green pepper
2 cups (3-oz. can) chow mein noodles

In 1½ or 2-quart casserole, combine all ingredients, using only 1 cup chow mein noodles. COOK, uncovered, 4 MINUTES or until heated through, stirring once. Sprinkle with remaining noodles and serve. 4 Servings

MENU
Huntington Chicken
Honey Glazed Carrots (122)
Wilted Lettuce Salad (131)
Pineapple Cakettes (152)

1. About 40 minutes before serving, cook cakettes.
2. Cook bacon for salad.
3. Cook chicken casserole.
4. Cook carrots.
5. Cook dressing for salad.

This cheesy noodle casserole using leftover chicken and uncooked noodles takes only 15 minutes to cook.

HUNTINGTON CHICKEN

1 cup chicken stock*
½ cup milk or light cream
1½ cups uncooked noodles
2 to 3 cups cubed cooked chicken or turkey
2 tablespoons chopped pimiento
½ teaspoon salt
⅛ teaspoon pepper
1 cup (4-oz. pkg.) shredded Cheddar cheese

In 1½ or 2-quart casserole, combine all ingredients except cheese. COOK, covered, 15 MINUTES or until noodles are tender. Stir in cheese. 6 Servings

TIP: *You can use 1 cup water and either 2 chicken bouillon cubes or 1 teaspoon chicken stock base.

The fat in duckling cooks out without the excessive spattering that is sometimes present in conventional cooking. The skin browns some and has some crispness; however, if you like crisper skin, you may prefer to put it under the broiler while you are cooking a vegetable in the oven. Plan about 40 minutes for cooking duck.

DUCKLING A LA ORANGE

  4½ to 5-lb. duckling
   1 teaspoon salt
   2 unpeeled oranges, quartered
   1 clove garlic or ⅛ teaspoon instant minced garlic
   3 peppercorns
   3 to 4 tablespoons orange marmalade
Orange Sauce
   2 tablespoons brown sugar
   1 tablespoon cornstarch
   1 tablespoon grated orange peel
  ⅔ cup orange juice
   3 tablespoons duck drippings
   3 tablespoons Curacao, Cointreau or Grand Marnier

Wash duckling and set aside giblets (use however you prefer, but best cooked conventionally). Fasten neck skin with toothpicks or metal skewers. Sprinkle inside of cavity with salt. Stuff main cavity with oranges, garlic and peppercorns. Close cavity securely with toothpicks or metal skewers. Tie legs together and wings to body with string. Cover the ends of legs, tail and the wings with small pieces of foil. Place inverted saucers or small casserole lids in 2-quart (12 x 7) baking dish to hold duck out of juices. Place duck breast side down on saucers. COOK, uncovered, 20 MINUTES. Remove duck using paper towels as hot pads to platter or cutting board. Drain juice. Remove foil pieces from duck. Turn duck breast side up and CONTINUE COOKING 20 MINUTES or until done. If necessary, cover with wax paper to prevent spattering. Spread skin with marmalade and COOK 4 MINUTES, or for crisper skin, place under the broiler for a few minutes. Let stand while preparing orange sauce. Serve cut in half or quarters (kitchen shears work well) or carved like turkey with Orange Sauce spooned over meat.
Orange Sauce: In 2-cup measure, combine brown sugar and cornstarch. Stir in orange peel, juice and drippings. COOK, uncovered, 3 MINUTES or until mixture boils and thickens. Stir in liqueur.   4 Servings

The orange sauce gives this classic pheasant dish flavor and color. It's very quick and simple to reduce the sauce in the oven after cooking the pheasant.

MANDARIN PHEASANT

   1 pheasant (about 2 lb.), split in half
   1 cup (11-oz. can) undrained mandarin oranges
   1 tablespoon cornstarch
   1 teaspoon grated lemon peel
   1 tablespoon lemon juice
  ½ teaspoon salt

In 2 or 3-quart casserole, arrange pheasant skin side down. Sprinkle with salt. In 2-cup measure or bowl, combine liquid from oranges, cornstarch, lemon peel, lemon juice and salt. COOK, uncovered, 1 MINUTE, 45 SECONDS or until thickened, stirring once. Add oranges and pour mixture over pheasant. COOK, uncovered, 20 MINUTES or until pheasant is done, turning pheasant once. Remove pheasant to serving platter. COOK remaining sauce, uncovered, 5 MINUTES or until thickened. Spoon over pheasant.   2 Servings

   TIP: This recipe can easily be doubled. Cook orange sauce 2 minutes, 30 seconds. Cook pheasant in 2-quart (12 x 7) baking dish, 28 minutes, turning once.

Here is a simple way to prepare pheasant which would rate serving under glass.

PHEASANT IN MUSHROOM CREAM SAUCE

   1 pheasant (about 2 lb.), cut into pieces
  ¼ teaspoon salt
Dash pepper
   2 tablespoons chopped onion
  ½ cup sliced fresh or canned mushrooms
Half of 10½-oz. can condensed cream of mushroom soup
   1 tablespoon cornstarch
  ¼ cup sour cream
Parsley

In 2 or 3-quart casserole, arrange pheasant skin side down. Sprinkle with salt and pepper. Add onion, mushrooms and cornstarch mixed with cream of mushroom soup. COOK, covered, 20 MINUTES or until pheasant is done, turning pheasant once. Stir in sour cream and garnish with parsley.   2 Servings

   TIP: This recipe can easily be doubled. Cook, covered, in 2-quart (12 x 7) baking dish, 26 minutes, turning once.

Beef

We have given a wide variety of recipes for different cuts of beef: roasts, steaks, ground beef, some of the less tender cuts of beef and also a few frozen heat 'n serve meat products. The most successful and timesaving results are those that use the more tender cuts of meat. The less tender cuts of meat usually need more cooking time.

Roasts: When roasting beef in your microwave oven, use a rolled rib or standing rib roast for the most tender results. You may want to *undercook* a roast that has been cooked either conventionally or by microwave so you can place slices on each plate and finish cooking the meat in the microwave oven to suit individual preferences. You can also reheat any servings that have cooled.

Steaks: Recipes such as Sukiyaki and Beef Stroganoff use tender steak slices in a sauce; others, such as Citrus Steak use less tender steaks that have been marinated to increase tenderness and flavor. You wouldn't try to broil a steak in the microwave oven because it would not have a brown crust.* Some oven owners find the oven a great asset, though, when grilling or broiling because they can grill extra meat to be reheated later in the microwave oven. Only one cleaning of the grill and no waiting for a sunny day to have barbecued meat! Also, if everyone is not eating a meal at the same time, one doesn't have to keep the grill hot for latecomers. Steaks, hamburgers and other meat broiled indoors also can be completed in the oven to suit individual preferences.

Ground Beef: We have included several recipes using ground beef because it is a tender and economical meat that cooks well in your microwave oven. There is no need to pre-brown ground beef in any of the recipes in this chapter because the addition of sauces and gravy mixes has achieved similar browning. If you do decide to pre-brown ground beef, it will not alter the success of the recipes. Some people brown a large amount of ground beef at one time and then keep it on hand in several containers in their freezer. To give you even more flexibility in your meal planning, cooking times are given for some recipes that you can prepare ahead and then freeze to cook later.

To defrost Beef, see page 45.

*With Micro-Browner™ Steak Grill you may broil steak in microwave oven.

Gravy mix coating combines with meat juices during cooking to give meat patties a brown color and flavor. It's easy to have patties shaped and stored in refrigerator or freezer for quick meals.

GROUND BEEF PATTIES

1 to 1½ lbs. ground beef
Salt and pepper
1 package (⅝ oz.) brown gravy mix

Season ground beef with salt and pepper. Shape into ¼-lb. patties. Coat patties with gravy mix. Arrange in shallow baking dish. Cover with wax paper and cook:

    1 patty   — 2 minutes, 30 seconds
    2 patties — 3 minutes
    3 patties — 3 minutes, 30 seconds
    4 patties — 4 minutes
    5 patties — 4 minutes, 30 seconds
    6 patties — 5 minutes

                   4 to 6 Patties

TIPS: For additional seasoning, mix one of the following into ground beef:
    1 tablespoon Worcestershire sauce
    2 to 4 tablespoons chopped onion or
      1 tablespoon instant minced onion
    ½ teaspoon garlic salt
    1 tablespoon barbecue sauce
      or catsup
    1 teaspoon prepared mustard
    2 to 4 tablespoons pickle relish
    ¼ cup chopped canned mushrooms

• Patties can be topped with one of the following during last minute of cooking: Cheese, Sour cream, Onion dip, Cream of mushroom soup or Cheese sauce.

• Patties can be seasoned, shaped, coated with gravy mix and frozen. To cook frozen patties, cover with wax paper and cook:
    1 patty — Cook 2 minutes; rest 1 minute; cook 1 minute
    2 patties — Cook 2 minutes, 30 seconds; rest 1 minute; cook 2 minutes
    3 patties — Cook 3 minutes; rest 1 minute; cook 3 minutes
    4 patties — Cook 4 minutes; rest 1 minute; cook 3 minutes, 30 seconds

Meatballs, carrots and potatoes cook in a tomato sauce — very tasty, and colorful. Avoid substituting green vegetables for carrots because they become yellow in the acidic tomato sauce. Allow 30 minutes for cooking.

MEATBALL STEW

1 egg
1 lb. ground beef
½ cup (1 slice) soft bread cubes
¼ cup (1 small) chopped onion or
   1 tablespoon instant minced onion
1 teaspoon salt
½ teaspoon leaf marjoram or ¼ teaspoon ground marjoram
1 cube or teaspoon beef bouillon
1 large onion, sliced
2 large potatoes, peeled and cut into eighths
3 carrots, peeled and cut into 1-inch pieces
1 can (10¾ oz.) condensed tomato soup
1 soup can (1⅓ cups) water

In 3-quart casserole, beat egg with fork. Mix in ground beef, bread, onion, salt and marjoram; mix well. Shape into 20 meatballs and arrange in same dish. COOK, uncovered, 7 MINUTES, rearranging and turning about halfway. Drain off juices. Add bouillon, onion, potatoes, carrots, soup and water. Stir to mix evenly. COOK, covered, 20 TO 23 MINUTES or until vegetables are desired doneness, stirring occasionally. If desired, sprinkle with parsley.   4 to 6 Servings

Chili takes less than 20 minutes to prepare in the oven. Beans are added near the end of cooking time to avoid overcooking them.

CHILI

1 lb. ground beef
1 medium onion, sliced or chopped
2 to 3 teaspoons chili powder
2 cups (1 lb. can) undrained tomatoes
1½ teaspoons salt
1 teaspoon dry or prepared mustard
1 clove garlic, minced, or ⅛ teaspoon instant minced garlic
1 can (16 oz.) kidney beans, drained

In 2-quart casserole, crumble ground beef. Add onion and chili powder. COOK, uncovered, 5 MINUTES. Mix in remaining ingredients except beans, stirring to break up tomatoes. COOK, covered, 10 MINUTES. Add beans and COOK 3 MINUTES or until hot, stirring occasionally.   4 to 5 Servings

MENU

Saucy Oriental Meatballs
Rice* (132)
Pea Pods (117)
Baked Orange Bananas (137)

1. About 30 minutes before serving, cook rice* and let stand.
2. Cook meatballs and let stand.
3. Cook peas.
4. While preparing meal, assemble bananas; cook just before serving.

*It may be more convenient to cook Rice conventionally.

An unusual combination of ingredients for a new twist to the traditional meatball. Our taste panel especially liked the flavors.

SAUCY ORIENTAL MEATBALLS

1 lb. lean ground beef
½ cup (5-oz. can) chopped water chestnuts
½ teaspoon salt
1 tablespoon prepared horseradish
½ cup orange marmalade
⅛ teaspoon instant minced garlic or garlic powder
1½ tablespoons flour
2 tablespoons soy sauce
1 tablespoon lemon juice

In 1½-quart (8-inch round) baking dish, combine ground beef, water chestnuts, salt and horseradish. Form into 1-inch meatballs, arranging in same baking dish. Combine marmalade, garlic, flour, soy sauce and lemon juice. Spoon over meatballs. COOK, covered with wax paper, 7 MINUTES, rearranging and turning once. Serve with rice.   4 Servings

> **TIP:** These flavors would make tasty appetizers meatballs; serve on toothpicks from chafing dish.

SIMPLE CHILI

1 package (26 oz.) frozen Sloppy Joe sauce with beef
2 tablespoons chili powder
2 teaspoons ground cumin powder, if desired
⅛ teaspoon garlic powder or instant minced garlic
1 can (1 lb.) kidney beans, drained

Remove frozen Sloppy Joe mixture from foil pan and place in 2-quart casserole, breaking in half if necessary. COOK, covered, 7 TO 8 MINUTES or until thawed, turning over twice. Add remaining ingredients; stir to mix. COOK, covered, 5 TO 6 MINUTES or until hot.
4 Servings

An attractive and richly flavored meat loaf that uses very little filler. For a similar recipe, using 1½ lbs. ground beef, see page 32.

MEATY MEAT LOAF

  1 lb. ground beef
  ⅔ cup (5-oz. can) evaporated milk
  2 tablespoons onion soup mix
  ¼ teaspoon salt
  2 tablespoons brown sugar
  ½ teaspoon dry mustard
  2 tablespoons catsup

In 1 or 1½-quart (8 x 4) loaf dish, combine ground beef, milk, soup mix, and salt; mix well. (Mixture will be very moist.) Press evenly in pan. Combine brown sugar, mustard and catsup; spoon and spread over top of meat. **COOK,** covered with wax paper, **7 MINUTES** or until done. **LET STAND 5 MINUTES** before removing to serving platter and slicing.   3 to 4 Servings

> **TIPS:** Meat loaf can be made ahead and refrigerated 1 day or frozen 1 month. After refrigerating, cook as directed; after freezing, cook 8 minutes, rest 5 and cook 5 more minutes.
>
> • To eliminate having loaf dish in freezer, combine mixture in separate bowl. Then transfer to foil lined loaf dish. Freeze several hours, until firm. Remove meat loaf by lifting foil. Wrap separately and freeze. To cook, remove foil and return to loaf dish.
>
> • Meat loaf can be cooked in 1-quart casserole, by pushing meat away from center and inserting a small glass to form a tube. Reduce cooking time to 6 minutes. Remove glass and drain juices before inverting meat loaf onto serving plate.

SIMPLE STUFFED GREEN PEPPERS

  1 package (26 oz.) frozen Sloppy Joe sauce with beef
  1½ teaspoons leaf basil
  ½ cup quick-cooking rice, uncooked
  ½ cup water
  4 medium green peppers

Remove frozen Sloppy Joe mixture from foil pan. Place in 2-quart casserole, breaking mixture in half if necessary. **COOK,** covered, **6 TO 7 MINUTES** or until thawed, turning over twice. Add basil, uncooked rice and water; stir until mixed. Cut green peppers in half, lengthwise, removing core and seeds. Place in shallow casserole. Fill with Sloppy Joe mixture. **COOK,** covered with wax paper, **10 MINUTES. LET STAND 2 MINUTES** before serving.
8 Stuffed Pepper Halves

Meat loaf cooks quickly in just 10 minutes. Make an extra loaf and freeze it to cook later.

MEAT LOAF

  1½ lbs. ground beef
  1 egg
  ¼ cup dry bread crumbs or 1 slice bread, crumbled
  ¼ cup chopped onion or 1 tablespoon instant minced onion
  ¼ cup milk
  ½ teaspoon salt
  ½ teaspoon garlic salt or ⅛ teaspoon instant minced garlic
  ¼ teaspoon pepper
  1 tablespoon Worcestershire sauce

In large mixing bowl, combine all ingredients; mix well. Press evenly in 1½-quart (8 x 4) loaf dish. **COOK,** covered with wax paper, **10 MINUTES** or until done. **LET STAND 5 MINUTES** before slicing. If desired, top with catsup or barbecue sauce.   5 to 6 servings.

> **TIP:** Meat loaf can be frozen before cooking. Use within 1 month. Cook 8 minutes, rest about 5 minutes and cook 8 more minutes. Let stand 5 minutes before removing to serving platter.

We found we could cook stuffed peppers without first precooking peppers and rice. Easy to prepare and cook in 15 to 20 minutes.

STUFFED GREEN PEPPERS

  3 medium green peppers
  ¾ lb. ground beef
  ⅓ cup quick-cooking rice, uncooked
  1 teaspoon salt
  ¼ teaspoon pepper
  1 egg
  ⅓ cup water
  1 cup (8-oz. can) tomato sauce

Cut green peppers in half, removing core and seeds. Place peppers in 2-quart (12 x 7) baking dish. In medium mixing bowl, combine remaining ingredients, using only half of tomato sauce. Spoon mixture into pepper halves. Spoon remaining tomato sauce over the meat. **COOK,** covered with wax paper, **10 MINUTES** or until meat is done.   6 Stuffed Pepper Halves

> **TIPS:** Cooking the peppers for 10 minutes leaves them somewhat crunchy. For a softer texture, cook 12 to 13 minutes.
>
> • The peppers freeze well after being cooked for 10 minutes.
> Reheat frozen peppers:
>   3 peppers — 7 minutes
>   6 peppers — 10 minutes, 30 seconds

Because of their shape, lasagna noodles cook well in the baking dish which you will later use for assembling the complete lasagna. Start about 45 minutes before serving time.

LASAGNA

    8-oz. package lasagna noodles
    1 teaspoon salt
    1 lb. ground beef
    1 package (1 oz.) spaghetti sauce mix
    2 cups (16-oz. can) tomato sauce
    ½ cup (4-oz. can) drained mushroom
        stems and pieces
    1½ cups (12-oz. carton) creamed cottage
        cheese
    6 to 8-oz. package sliced Mozzarella
        cheese
    ½ cup grated Parmesan cheese

Place noodles in 2-quart (12 x 7) baking dish. Cover with water and sprinkle with salt. **COOK**, uncovered, **15 MINUTES**. Remove from oven and let noodles stand in cooking water while preparing meat sauce.

In 2-quart casserole or mixing bowl, crumble ground beef. **COOK**, uncovered, **5 MINUTES**, stirring occasionally to break beef into small pieces. Drain off juices. Stir in spaghetti sauce mix, tomato sauce and mushrooms. Drain noodles and rinse well to remove excess starch.

Assemble in 2-quart (12 x 7) baking dish by layering ⅓ of noodles, ⅓ of meat mixture, ½ of cottage cheese and ½ of Mozzarella cheese. Repeat with next layer of noodles. On last layer of noodles, spread last ⅓ of meat mixture and sprinkle with Parmesan cheese. Cover loosely with wax paper and **COOK 10 MINUTES** or until heated through. **LET STAND,** covered, about **5 MINUTES** for ease in cutting and serving. 6 to 8 Servings

> **TIPS:** Lasagna can be assembled ahead and refrigerated. If it has chilled completely, cook 12 minutes or until hot.
>
> • Recipe can be assembled in two 2-quart (8 x 8) or two 1½-quart (10 x 6) baking dishes. For these sizes it is easier to assemble in 2 layers and sprinkle Parmesan cheese on top of Mozzarella. You can freeze one dish for use at a later time. When ready to serve, just cook, covered with wax paper, 8 minutes, rest 5 minutes and then cook 6 more minutes or until hot.

Pictured clockwise: Make Ahead foods for your freezer — Meaty Meat Loaf, page 73, Ground Beef Patties, page 71, with Tater Tots, page 161, Stuffed Green Peppers, page 73, and Lasagna, above.

We have used the oven for cooking both the spaghetti noodles and the sauce; however, since there is no real time saving with cooking spaghetti in the oven, you may find it more convenient at times to cook it conventionally while the sauce cooks in the oven. If you have a favorite sauce recipe, use this as a timing guide for a similar amount of sauce.

SPAGHETTI WITH SAUCE

    6 cups water
    1 teaspoon salt
    7 oz. spaghetti
    1 lb. ground beef
    1 package (1 oz.) spaghetti sauce mix
    2 cups (1-lb. can) undrained tomatoes
    ¾ cup (6-oz. can) tomato paste
    ¾ cup water
    Parmesan cheese

In 2-quart (12 x 7) uncovered casserole heat water to about boiling (8 min.). Add salt and spaghetti. **COOK**, uncovered, **8 MINUTES**. Remove from oven and let spaghetti stand in cooking water while preparing sauce.

In 2-quart casserole or mixing bowl, crumble ground beef. **COOK**, uncovered, **5 MINUTES**, stirring occasionally to break ground beef into small pieces. Drain off juices. Stir in spaghetti sauce mix, tomatoes, tomato paste and water, breaking tomatoes into pieces. **COOK**, covered, **7 MINUTES**. Drain spaghetti and rinse well in water to remove excess starch. Place on platter; top with sauce and sprinkle with Parmesan cheese. If necessary, return platter to oven for 1 to 2 minutes to reheat spaghetti.

5 to 6 Servings

> **TIPS:** If you like a wine flavored sauce, use ¼ cup red wine for part of the water.
>
> • If desired, add a 4-oz. can mushroom stems and pieces, using the liquid for part of the water.

PIZZA CASSEROLE

    1 package (11½ oz.) frozen macaroni,
        beef and tomatoes
    ½ teaspoon leaf oregano
    ½ teaspoon leaf basil
    2 tablespoons grated Parmesan cheese
    2 slices Mozzarella cheese

Remove frozen macaroni from foil pan and place in 1-quart casserole. **COOK**, covered, **4 TO 5 MINUTES** or until thawed, turning once. Stir in oregano and basil. **COOK**, covered, **3 TO 4 MINUTES** or until hot. Sprinkle Parmesan cheese over top. Cut each slice Mozzarella cheese into 4 strips; lay criss-cross over casserole. **COOK**, covered, **1 TO 2 MINUTES** to partially melt cheese. 2 Servings

A speedy 10 minute Chow Mein made with ground beef. If you prefer, use chow mein meat (coarsely ground pork and veal) instead of ground beef.

GROUND BEEF CHOW MEIN

1 lb. ground beef
½ cup (4-oz. can) drained mushroom stems and pieces
½ teaspoon ground ginger
2 tablespoons soy sauce
1 package (⅝ oz.) brown gravy mix
1 medium onion, sliced, or 1 tablespoon instant minced onion
1 cup (2 stalks) sliced celery
2 cups (1-lb. can) undrained chow mein vegetables

In 1½ or 2-quart casserole, crumble ground beef. Stir in mushrooms, ginger and soy sauce. Sprinkle with gravy mix. **COOK**, covered, **5 MINUTES**. Stir in onion, celery and chow mein vegetables. **COOK**, covered, **5 MORE MINUTES** or until vegetables are desired doneness, stirring occasionally. Serve with rice or chow mein noodles. 4 to 5 Servings

TIP: If chow mein vegetables are drained, add 1 cup water.

SWEDISH MEATBALLS WITH GRAVY

1 egg, slightly beaten
1 lb. ground beef
1 slice bread, crumbled
¼ cup cream or milk
½ cup (1 med.) chopped onion or 2 tablespoons instant minced onion
½ teaspoon salt
¼ teaspoon pepper
¼ teaspoon mace or allspice, if desired
1 can (10¾ oz.) condensed beef gravy

In 1½-quart (8-inch round) baking dish, combine all ingredients except gravy. Shape into 8 to 10 meatballs, arranging in same dish. **COOK**, uncovered, **5 MINUTES**, turning and rearranging once. Drain fat. Spoon gravy over meatballs. **COOK**, covered, **3 MINUTES** or until heated through. 4 Servings

TIPS: Gravy mix can be used for canned gravy. Just sprinkle partially cooked meatballs with gravy mix and stir in ½ cup water (half red wine can be used) and cook as directed, stirring once.

● Canned soups can also be used for gravy. Meatballs are good with cream of chicken, mushroom or celery soup.

These meatballs can double as a main course with mashed potatoes or as hors d'oeuvres served with toothpicks. Keep some ready in the freezer for quick thawing and heating.

BURGUNDY BEEF BALLS

1 lb. ground beef
½ cup dry bread crumbs or cracker crumbs
⅓ cup burgundy or red wine
1 tablespoon instant minced onion or ¼ cup chopped onion
1 tablespoon parsley flakes or chopped parsley
1 teaspoon salt
⅛ teaspoon pepper
1 egg
1 package (⅝ oz.) brown gravy mix
¾ cup water

In 1½-quart (8-inch round) or 8 or 9-inch pie plate, combine all ingredients except gravy mix and water. Shape mixture into 1-inch balls, leaving them in same dish. Sprinkle meatballs with gravy mix. **COOK**, covered, **5 MINUTES**. Add water and **COOK**, covered, **3 MINUTES**. 4 Servings

TIP: We found our 2-quart casserole lid also fits the 8-inch round dish. If you do not have a cover that fits, use wax paper or a plate.

Ground beef, potatoes and mushroom soup cook together in an easy casserole that takes 17 minutes to cook. For another easy casserole, see One-Dish Macaroni and Beef, page 31.

MUSHROOM POTATOES AND BEEF

½ lb. ground beef
2 medium potatoes, thinly sliced
1 small (¼ cup) onion, chopped, or 1 tablespoon instant minced onion
1 can (7 oz.) undrained whole kernel corn
1 can (10½ oz.) condensed cream of mushroom soup
2 teaspoons soy sauce
¼ teaspoon salt
¼ teaspoon pepper
½ cup crumbled French-fried onion rings

In 1½-quart (8-inch round) baking dish, combine all ingredients except onion rings. **COOK**, covered, **17 MINUTES** or until potatoes are tender, stirring twice. Sprinkle onion rings on top. Serve immediately or for additional browning, place under broiler. 4 Servings

MENU

South-Of-The Border Special
Avocado and Pear Salad
Corn Muffins (128)
Crunchy Pudding Squares (141)

1. Early in day, prepare pudding squares and refrigerate.
2. About 20 minutes before serving, prepare and cook casserole; let stand.
3. Cook or reheat corn muffins.

A hearty chili and corn flavored casserole to serve a hungry family. It can be ready for dinner in about 20 minutes.

MEXICAN BEEF 'N DUMPLINGS

    2 lbs. ground beef
    2 to 3 teaspoons chili powder
1½ teaspoons salt
    1 small onion, chopped, or 2 tablespoons instant minced onion
    2 cups (16-oz. can) tomato sauce with onion, celery and green pepper
    2 cups (1-lb. can) undrained tomatoes
1½ cups (16-oz. can) drained whole kernel corn

Dumplings
    1 cup pancake mix
    ½ cup cornmeal
    ½ cup water
    2 tablespoons cooking oil
    1 egg

In 3-quart casserole, crumble ground beef. Sprinkle with chili powder. COOK, uncovered, 5 MINUTES, stirring once. Stir in salt, onion, tomato sauce, tomatoes and corn. COOK, covered, 5 MINUTES or until mixture boils. Meanwhile, prepare Dumplings by combining pancake mix, cornmeal, water, oil and egg; mix until well combined. When mixture boils, spoon dumplings on top of mixture. COOK, covered, 7 TO 8 MINUTES or until center dumpling is no longer doughy underneath. Let stand, covered, a couple minutes before serving.   8 Servings

> **TIPS:** For half a recipe, use 2-quart casserole, cook as directed and for Dumplings use 1 egg and 2 tablespoons water and cook 5 minutes.
>
> • Regular tomato sauce can be used, adding ½ cup chopped celery and ¼ cup chopped green pepper.

A Mexican flavored, easy main dish that cooks in just 10 minutes. If you like spicy, hot flavors, use the maximum chili powder.

SOUTH-OF-THE-BORDER SPECIAL

    1 lb. lean ground beef
    1 medium onion, sliced
    2 cups (1-lb. can) undrained tomatoes
    ½ cup sliced ripe olives
    1 to 1½ teaspoons chili powder
    1 package (⅝ oz.) brown gravy mix
    2 cups (about 4 oz.) coarsely crushed corn or taco chips

In 1½ or 2-quart casserole, crumble ground beef; stir in onion, tomatoes, olives and chili powder. Sprinkle with gravy mix. COOK, covered, 10 MINUTES, stirring occasionally after about 5 minutes. Top with corn chips just before serving. (If desired, about half of chips can be stirred into casserole and remainder sprinkled on top.)   4 to 5 Servings

This stroganoff that cooks in just 12 minutes is delicious served over rice. If cooking rice in the oven, cook first and then allow to stand while cooking the stroganoff. A vegetable can be cooked while adding the sour cream. If necessary, reheat the stroganoff and rice, about 45 seconds each.

GROUND BEEF STROGANOFF

    1 lb. ground beef
    1 package (⅝ oz.) brown gravy mix
    ¼ cup (1 small) chopped onion or
        1 tablespoon instant minced onion
    ½ cup (4-oz. can) drained mushroom stems and pieces (use liquid for part of water)
    ¾ cup water
    ½ cup sour cream

In 1 or 1½-quart casserole, crumble ground beef. COOK, uncovered, 5 MINUTES, stirring once; drain. Stir in gravy mix, onion, mushrooms and water. COOK, covered, 7 MINUTES. Stir in sour cream and LET STAND, covered, about 1 MINUTE to heat through. Serve over rice or noodles.   4 Servings

> **TIPS:** If desired, use ¼ cup red wine for part of water.
>
> • Stroganoff can be prepared ahead, except for adding sour cream and stored in refrigerator or freezer. To serve, heat until bubbly and stir in sour cream.

*This stroganoff recipe cooks in about
8 minutes. The meat will be very tender when
cooked to medium rare doneness; if
overcooked, it may become tough.*

BEEF STROGANOFF

    2 lbs. sirloin steak, cut into strips
    2 cups (1 pt. or 16 oz.) sliced fresh
      mushrooms
    2 medium onions, sliced
    4 teaspoons or cubes beef bouillon
    3 tablespoons flour
    2 tablespoons catsup
    1 teaspoon dry or prepared mustard
    ½ teaspoon salt
    ⅔ cup water (or ⅓ cup water and
      ⅓ cup red wine)
    ½ to 1 cup sour cream

In 2 or 2½-quart casserole, combine steak,
mushrooms, onions, bouillon and flour; mix
well. Stir in catsup, mustard, salt and water.
COOK, covered, 8 MINUTES or until meat is
desired doneness, stirring occasionally. Stir in
sour cream; serve over rice or noodles.,

6 Servings

> **TIP:** Stroganoff can be prepared, except
> for adding sour cream, then cooled and
> frozen. Allow to thaw before reheating to
> avoid overcooking meat. Stir sour cream
> into hot stroganoff.

*With the microwave oven, it is possible to
cook the sauce and still keep the meat
medium rare in this classic French dish.
About 12 minutes cooking time.*

BEEF BOURGUIGNONNE

    1½ to 2 lbs. sirloin steak, cut into 1½-inch
      cubes
    ¼ teaspoon salt
    2 tablespoons flour
    1 envelope onion soup mix
    ⅔ cup dry red wine
    1 cup (8 oz. or ½ pt.) sliced fresh
      mushrooms
    1 green pepper, cut into 1-inch pieces
    1⅔ cups (1-lb. can) drained, whole onions

In 2-quart casserole, combine steak, salt, flour,
soup and wine. COOK, covered, 7 MINUTES,
stirring once. Stir in mushrooms, green pepper
and onions. COOK, covered, 5 MINUTES or
until desired doneness.   6 Servings

> **TIPS:** If desired, 1 cup (two 4-oz. cans)
> drained mushroom stems and pieces can
> be used for fresh.
>
> • This can be frozen after cooking, but
> thaw before reheating to avoid overcooking
> meat.

MENU

**Beef Stroganoff
Buttered Noodles (132)
Broccoli (115)
Salad
Grasshopper Pie (155)**

1. Early in day, prepare pie and refrigerate.
2. About 30 minutes before serving, cook
   noodles.*
3. Cook stroganoff.
4. Cook broccoli.
5. Reheat noodles, if necessary.

*It may be more convenient to cook Noodles
conventionally.

*A traditional favorite made easy in the
microwave oven. Use a shallow dish that will
be attractive on the table. Prepare and
assemble ingredients in advance for quick
10 minute cooking.*

SUKIYAKI

    2 lbs. sirloin steak, cut into thin slices
    ½ cup soy sauce
    ½ cup sherry or water
    3 tablespoons sugar
    2 medium onions, thinly sliced
    1 cup (8 oz. or ½ pt.) sliced fresh or
      drained canned mushrooms
    1 cup (about 5) sliced green onion with
      tops
    ⅔ cup (5-oz. can) drained and sliced
      water chestnuts
    ¾ cup (5-oz. can) drained bamboo shoots
    2 cups (1-lb. can) drained bean sprouts

In 2-quart (12 x 7) baking dish, combine steak,
soy sauce, sherry and sugar. Allow to marinate
while preparing onions, mushrooms, green onion
and water chestnuts. (Can marinate several
hours). Add sliced onions, cover with wax paper,
and COOK 5 MINUTES*, stirring occasionally.
Push meat away from sides of dish and add
remaining ingredients, keeping each separate.
Tilt dish to spoon some of sauce over each
vegetable. COOK, covered with wax paper,
5 MINUTES or until vegetables are desired
doneness. Serve with rice.   4 to 6 Servings

> **TIP:** *This cooking time cooks steak to
> medium rare doneness; if you prefer your
> meat without a pink center, cook 6 minutes
> at this first stage of cooking.

Pictured, top: Rolled Rib Roast, page 80.

*Pictured, bottom: Beef Bourguignonne, left,
and Sukiyaki, above.*

A rolled rib roast will remain tender and juicy when cooked in your microwave oven. The fat around the outside of the meat and the seasoned salt will give you an attractively browned roast. For roasting beef in your microwave oven, use standing rib or rolled rib roast.

ROLLED RIB ROAST

**4 to 5-lb. rolled rib roast
1 clove garlic, if desired
Seasoned salt**

In bottom of 2-quart (8 x 8) baking dish, place an inverted saucer or small casserole cover to hold meat out of juices. Place thin slices of garlic under string holding meat together. Sprinkle roast with seasoned salt. Place roast, fat side down, on saucer and **COOK,** uncovered, for **HALF OF TIME.** Turn fat side up, baste, and **COOK,** covered with wax paper, for **REMAINDER OF TIME. LET STAND,** covered with foil, **20 MINUTES** before carving.

8 to 10 Servings

MINUTES PER POUND	INTERNAL TEMPERATURE
Rare — 5 minutes, 30 seconds	120° (Will increase to 140° during standing)
Medium — 6 minutes, 30 seconds	140° (Will increase to 160° during standing)
Well — 7 minutes, 30 seconds	160° (Will increase to 170° during standing)

TIPS: If meat has been at room temperature for an hour or more before cooking, reduce times 30 seconds per pound.

• A small custard or coffee cup can be used to hold the roast if it has a tendency to tip over.

• Do not use meat thermometer in oven when cooking.

STANDING RIB ROAST

Follow directions for rolled rib roast, pushing pieces of garlic into fat. Cook, fat side down with bone side up for first half of cooking time. (Cover the bone with a piece of foil during this first half of cooking time because the bone absorbs energy faster than the meat.) Remove foil; turn meat over and finish cooking.

MENU

**Beef Ragout
Mashed Potatoes (159)
Pineapple Cheese Salad (131)
Pickles
Cherry Crumble Squares (139)**

1. Early in day, prepare salad and allow to chill.
2. At least 1½ hours ahead, marinate meat for ragout.
3. About 1 hour before serving, cook cherry crumble squares.
4. Cook beef ragout.
5. Prepare instant mashed potatoes.*

*If preparing mashed potatoes from fresh potatoes, cook potatoes after first cooking of ragout. While ragout finishes cooking, let potatoes rest and then mash potatoes.

Beef stew with a special taste from red wine and cinnamon. We found the meat to be a little more tender when marinated as directed, but also thought it was good without the marinating. The cinnamon stick can be omitted if your family prefers a more basic stew flavor. After marinating, allow about 35 minutes for cooking.

BEEF RAGOUT

**2 lbs. beef stew meat
2 medium onions, sliced
1 cup red wine
1 package (⅝ oz.) brown gravy mix
2 tablespoons flour
1½ teaspoons salt
1 bay leaf
1 stick cinnamon
½ cup water
⅔ cup (4-oz. can) undrained mushroom stems and pieces
2 stalks celery, cut into 1-inch pieces
4 medium carrots, sliced ¼ inch thick**

In 2½ or 3-quart casserole, combine meat, onions, and red wine. Let stand at room temperature 1 hour or overnight in refrigerator, stirring once. Add gravy mix, flour, salt, bay leaf, cinnamon and water. **COOK,** covered, **20 MINUTES,** stirring twice. Add mushrooms, celery and carrots. **COOK,** covered, **10 TO 12 MINUTES** or until vegetables are desired doneness, stirring occasionally. Serve over noodles or potatoes or with hot biscuits.

6 Servings

TIPS: If you prefer to omit wine, use ¼ cup vinegar and ¾ cup water to marinate the meat; continue as directed.

• The celery cooks faster than the carrots, so it is cut into larger pieces. If you prefer to add potatoes, too, they should be cut fairly small and the cooking time increased 2 to 3 minutes.

Sauerbraten is one of the best uses of the less tender cuts of meat called for in this recipe because of the tenderizing effect of the long marinating. During the standing time of the meat, cook potatoes (or potato dumplings) and red cabbage in the oven to complete your meal. Cooking and resting time is about 1½ hours.

SAUERBRATEN

    3 to 3½-lb. boneless heel of round, rump
      or sirloin tip roast
    1 cup red wine vinegar
  1½ cups water
    1 onion, sliced
    5 whole cloves
    1 stalk celery, sliced
    2 bay leaves
    1 tablespoon salt
    4 peppercorns or ¼ teaspoon pepper
    2 tablespoons brown sugar
    6 gingersnaps, crushed

In 3 or 4-quart casserole, combine all ingredients except brown sugar and gingersnaps. Cover and marinate in refrigerator 24 to 48 hours, turning meat several times to season evenly.

Remove meat from marinade and strain marinade. Return meat to casserole along with strained marinade. **COOK**, covered tightly, **60 MINUTES** or until meat thermometer registers 150° (will increase to 160° during standing) turning meat over about halfway through cooking. **LET** meat **STAND** about **20 MINUTES** before slicing and serving. Remove meat to platter. Spoon fat from juices. Add brown sugar and gingersnaps to juice and **COOK**, uncovered, **5 MINUTES** or until bubbly. (If sauce is not desired thickness, add a few more crushed gingersnaps.) Slice meat and serve with sauce.

8 to 10 Servings

TIPS: The gingersnaps add a delicious flavor as well as thicken the sauce. If you do not have gingersnaps, you can use flour mixed with water to thicken juices. Add ¼ teaspoon ground ginger for flavor.

• Since it is important to keep moisture in the casserole, use a tight-fitting lid or a plate that will fit tightly.

• Do not use meat thermometer in oven when cooking.

This traditional corned beef dinner can be prepared in the oven in about 1½ hours. Leftovers can be sliced into thin slices for sandwiches because the corned beef becomes tender, but not fork tender.

NEW ENGLAND BOILED DINNER

    3-lb. corned beef
    4 cups water
    1 bay leaf
    1 teaspoon peppercorns
    6 whole cloves
    2 large potatoes, peeled and quartered
    3 carrots, sliced
    4 wedges cabbage

In 3-quart casserole, combine corned beef, water, bay leaf, peppercorns and cloves. **COOK**, tightly covered, **60 MINUTES**, turning meat once or twice. Drain off about 1½ cups water and turn corned beef. Add potatoes and carrots. **COOK**, covered, **15 MINUTES**; add cabbage wedges and **COOK**, covered, **10 MINUTES** longer or until vegetables are tender. To serve, slice meat across the grain. Serve some of cooking juices along with vegetables.   4 to 5 Servings*

TIPS: *There will be more corned beef than this, but this is as many vegetable servings that you can add to the corned beef and cook conveniently.

• If the corned beef has a packet of spices packaged with it, use these spices and omit the bay leaf, peppercorns and cloves.

• If casserole is larger than 3 quart, add enough water to half cover corned beef.

Pot roast can be cooked in the oven. We found it was most tender when cooked to the medium done stage. It will be tender, but not as fork tender as you get with long, slow conventional cooking.

POT ROAST

    4-lb. blade or chuck pot roast, 1½ inches
      thick
    1 package (⅝ oz.) brown gravy mix
    1 cup water

Place roast in 2-quart (12 x 7) baking dish. Sprinkle both sides of roast with gravy mix. **COOK**, uncovered, **10 MINUTES**. Add water and **COOK**, covered with wax paper, **25 MINUTES** or until meat thermometer registers 150° (will increase to 160° during standing). **LET STAND 20 MINUTES** before serving. If desired, thicken juices by adding 1 to 2 tablespoons flour dissolved in ¼ cup water. Bring to boil.

4 to 6 Servings

TIP: Do not use meat thermometer in oven when cooking.

We found that a less tender steak, such as round, was best with marinating. This citrus flavored steak marinates 1 hour and then cooks 40 minutes.

CITRUS STEAK

　　1 medium onion, sliced
　　2 tablespoons barbecue sauce or catsup
　　¼ cup lemon juice
　　¼ cup soy sauce
　　⅛ teaspoon powdered thyme, if desired
　　2 lbs. round steak, cut into serving pieces
　　1 cup water
　　2 teaspoons cornstarch
　　½ orange, sliced, if desired

In 2-quart (12 x 7) baking dish, combine onion, barbecue sauce, lemon juice, soy sauce and thyme. Add meat, dipping in sauce and turning sauce side up. Marinate 1 hour, turning once. COOK, uncovered, 10 MINUTES. Add water and COOK, covered with wax paper, 30 MINUTES, turning once. Remove meat to serving platter. Mix cornstarch with 1 tablespoon water; stir into juices. Return to oven and bring to boil (2 min.). Add orange slices and pour over meat.

4 to 6 Servings

Scoring and sprinkling with tenderizer helps tenderize this flank steak before it is cooked in the oven. Overcooking will toughen steak.

STUFFED FLANK ROLL UP

　　1 flank steak (1 to 1½ lbs.)
　Meat tenderizer
　　1½ cups soft bread cubes
　　¼ cup chopped onion or 1 tablespoon
　　　instant minced onion
　　½ cup chopped celery
　　1 tablespoon parsley flakes
　　½ teaspoon powdered sage or thyme
　Dash pepper
　　2 tablespoons water or red wine
　　1 cup water
　　1 teaspoon or cube beef bouillon

Score both sides of steak diagonally, about 1 inch apart. Sprinkle both sides with meat tenderizer. Combine bread cubes, onion, celery, parsley, sage, pepper and 2 tablespoons water. Place stuffing down center of steak, lengthwise. Roll and tie steak with string. Place seam side down in 1½-quart (8 x 4) loaf dish. Pour water and bouillon in dish. COOK, covered with wax paper, 15 MINUTES. Slice and serve with juices.

4 to 6 Servings

MENU

**Swiss Steak
Tater Tots (161)
Peas (117)
Salad
Apple Pudding Cake (138)**

1. Night before, marinate steak.
2. About 1 hour before serving, prepare and cook apple pudding cake.
3. Cook swiss steak.
4. Cook peas.
5. Thaw and heat tater tots.

For more tender meat, begin marinating the steak the night before serving. Then, just start cooking about 30 minutes before meal time. Kitchen shears are handy for cutting meat into serving pieces.

SWISS STEAK

　　2 lbs. round steak, cut into serving pieces
　　1 can (10¾ oz.) condensed tomato soup
　　⅔ cup (4-oz. can) undrained mushroom
　　　stems and pieces
　　1 medium onion, sliced
　　⅛ teaspoon pepper

Combine all ingredients except meat in 2-quart (12 x 7) baking dish. Add meat, dipping in sauce and turning sauce side up. Cover and refrigerate overnight, turning once or twice. (Can be cooked now, following directions below, but meat will not be as tender.) COOK, covered with wax paper, 30 MINUTES, turning meat once.

4 to 6 Servings

Wine, tomato, and additional seasonings give these ready-to-eat frozen ribs an Italian touch in about 15 minutes. With a foil pan this deep, remove the ribs to speed thawing and heating.

SHORTRIBS OF BEEF ITALIENNE

　　1 package (11½ oz.) frozen shortribs of
　　　beef
　　¼ cup dry white wine
　　1 small fresh tomato, diced
　　1 small clove garlic, crushed, or
　　　⅛ teaspoon instant minced garlic
　　1½ tablespoons parsley flakes
　　¼ bay leaf
　　½ teaspoon leaf basil
　　⅛ teaspoon leaf thyme

Remove frozen shortribs from foil pan and place in 1½-quart casserole. COOK, covered, 4 TO 5 MINUTES or until thawed, turning once. Add remaining ingredients. COOK, covered, 5 TO 6 MINUTES or until hot. LET STAND 3 MINUTES before serving. 2 Servings

Ham and Pork

Ham: A tender meat, ham is also very versatile. Whether you choose half a ham, slices, cubes or Canadian bacon, they will be successfully cooked in a microwave oven and need no browning. Pick a new idea to become a recipe favorite such as Scalloped Ham 'n Cabbage or the easy but elegant Ham-Asparagus Hollandaise. The shorter time for cooking ham is because it is pre-cooked and also because the high sugar content of ham attracts microwave energy.

Pork: In your microwave oven all cuts of pork will cook thoroughly and completely; loin roasts, chops, ribs and cubes. You will notice that pork quality affects the tenderness of the meat when cooked in a microwave oven as it does when cooked conventionally. We have included recipes for both family and special occasions . . . from Country Barbecued Ribs to Stuffed Pork Chops.

An attractive way to serve cooked, ready-to-eat or leftover ham. Make extras and refrigerate for easy, individual main dishes.

HAM 'N YAM STACKS

    4 to 6 medium yams or sweet potatoes
    2 tablespoons brown sugar
    ½ tablespoon cornstarch
    ⅛ teaspoon cinnamon
    1 cup (8-oz. can) undrained crushed pineapple
    1 tablespoon lemon juice
    6 slices (1 serving each) cooked ham

Cook yams as directed on page 118. Meanwhile, prepare sauce by combining in 2-cup measure, brown sugar, cornstarch, cinnamon, pineapple and lemon juice. **COOK, uncovered, 3 MINUTES**, stirring occasionally until mixture boils and thickens.

Arrange ham on serving platter; cool yams enough to handle. Peel yams, slice or leave whole and arrange on top of ham. Spoon sauce over each serving. **COOK, uncovered, 4 MINUTES** or until heated through.

6 Servings

TIPS: For individual servings, heat 1 minute if room temperature; 2 minutes if refrigerated temperature.

• If desired, use canned yams or sweet potatoes and omit step of cooking yams.

An especially colorful and tasty dress up for ham. You can serve a ham slice more economically by buying a ready-to-eat boneless ham, cutting a slice and then using the remainder for other recipes.

FESTIVE HAM SLICE

    1 ham slice, cut 1 inch thick (2¼ lbs.)
    ½ cup whole cranberry sauce
    ½ orange, sliced and quartered
    Whole cloves

Place ham slice in shallow baking dish or platter. **COOK, covered loosely with wax paper, 5 MINUTES.** Spoon cranberry sauce over top of ham. Insert a clove in each orange piece and arrange on cranberry sauce. **COOK, uncovered, 1 MINUTE, 30 SECONDS.** 6 to 8 Servings

TIPS: Cherry pie filling can be used for cranberry sauce.

• For other ham slice thicknesses cook:
½ inch thick — 3 minutes, 30 seconds; then, 1 minute
1½ inch thick — 9 minutes; then 2 minutes
Increase or decrease sauce as desired.

An easy supper dish that is made in one step. For variety, try with chicken, turkey, shrimp or tuna.

HAM ROMANOFF

    1 package (6¼ oz.) noodles Romanoff mix
  1½ cups water
    ½ cup milk
    3 cups (1 lb.) cubed cooked ham
    ½ cup (4-oz. can) drained chopped mushrooms

In 2-quart casserole, combine contents from uncooked noodle mix with remaining ingredients; mix well. **COOK, covered, 10 MINUTES** or until noodles are tender, stirring occasionally.

4 Servings

TIPS: When using a 5.5 oz. package noodles Romanoff, use 1¼ cups water and allow to stand several minutes after cooking to allow to thicken.

• If desired, use ¼ cup sherry for part of water.

This recipe calls for the popular, ready-to-eat ham. Since this ham is already cooked, time to reach serving temperature is all that is necessary. Allow 6 minutes per pound as a timing guide with ham.

BAKED HAM

**1 small ready-to-eat ham or ham half
   (2 to 3 lbs.)
Glaze, if desired**

In 2-quart (8 x 8) baking dish, place inverted saucer or small casserole cover to keep ham out of juices. Place ham on saucer. **COOK,** uncovered, **FIRST HALF OF COOKING TIME.** Turn ham, bottom side up, and **COOK,** covered loosely with wax paper, **SECOND HALF OF COOKING TIME** or until meat thermometer registers 115° (will increase to 130° during standing). **LET STAND,** covered with foil, **20 MINUTES** to finish heating.   6 to 8 Servings

TIPS: If one end of ham is smaller, cover with foil during first half of cooking time.

• When cooking a whole ham (over 5 lb.), increase cooking time 1 minute per pound.

• For an easy glaze, try brushing the ham with apple or currant jelly, orange marmalade, or a combination of ⅓ cup brown sugar and ⅓ cup drained crushed pineapple.

Cabbage is a favorite because of its delicious flavor and attractive color when cooked in a microware oven.

SCALLOPED HAM 'N CABBAGE

**4 cups (½ med. head) shredded cabbage
2 tablespoons flour
½ teaspoon caraway seed or ¼ teaspoon
   nutmeg
1 cup milk
3 cups (1 lb.) cubed cooked ham
French-fried onion rings, if desired**

In 2-quart casserole, mix cabbage with flour and caraway seed. Stir in milk and ham. **COOK,** covered, **11 MINUTES** or until cabbage is desired doneness. Top with onion rings just before serving.   4 to 5 Servings

Pictured, top to bottom: Country Barbecued Ribs, page 88 (combination of microwave cooking and grilling), Stuffed Pork Chops, page 87, Sweet and Sour Pork, page 89, Baked Ham with Apple Jelly Glaze, above, and Stuffed Pork Tenderloin, page 89 (garnished with kumquats).

HAM LOAF

**3 eggs, slightly beaten
1½ lbs. ground cooked ham
½ cup (½ slice) soft bread cubes
¼ cup firmly packed brown sugar
1 tablespoon chopped onion or
   1 teaspoon instant minced onion
2 tablespoons chopped green pepper,
   if desired
1½ tablespoons prepared mustard
¼ cup milk**

In mixing bowl, combine all ingredients. Press mixture into 1½-quart (8 x 4) loaf dish. **COOK,** covered with wax paper, **12 MINUTES** or until done. Let stand a few minutes before slicing and serving.   4 to 6 Servings

TIPS: For individual ham loaves, place ½ cup mixture in about nine 5 or 6-oz. custard cups. Cook, uncovered:

1 cup	— 2 minutes
2 cups	— 3 minutes
3 cups	— 4 minutes
4 cups	— 5 minutes

Invert onto serving plate.

• Loaf can be topped before cooking with mixture of ¾ cup drained crushed pineapple and 2 tablespoons brown sugar. For individual loaves, place 1 tablespoon of this mixture in bottom of each custard cup.

A drop of oil in cooking water will keep noodles from boiling over the casserole dish.

HAM 'N NOODLE BAKE

**1½ cups water
1 cup noodles, uncooked
1 cup cubed cooked ham
1 cup cooked or canned cut green beans
1 can (10½ oz.) condensed cream of
   celery soup
¼ teaspoon dry mustard
⅛ teaspoon pepper
⅓ to ½ cup milk
Buttered bread crumbs or French-fried
   onion rings**

In 2-quart casserole, bring water to boil (3 min.). Add noodles and **COOK,** uncovered, **9 MINUTES. LET STAND,** covered, **5 MINUTES** and drain.

Add ham, green beans, soup, mustard, pepper and milk. **COOK,** covered, **3 TO 4 MINUTES** or until hot, stirring once. Top with crumbs just before serving.   4 Servings

TIP: Casserole can be made ahead by cooking noodles and adding remaining ingredients. Refrigerate. Just before serving, cook, covered, 6 minutes or until hot, stirring once.

These will heat most evenly if rolls are placed in spoke fashion on a round plate, with the larger stalk ends of asparagus toward outer edge.

HAM-ASPARAGUS HOLLANDAISE

**1 package (1⅝ oz.) hollandaise sauce mix
or ⅔ cup prepared hollandaise sauce
3 tablespoons (half of 3-oz. pkg.) cream
cheese
¼ cup mayonnaise or salad dressing
1 package (10 oz.) frozen asparagus
spears
8 slices (two 4-oz. pkgs.) boiled ham
Slivered, toasted almonds, if desired**

In 2-cup measure, prepare hollandaise sauce mix according to package directions. COOK 2 MINUTES, 30 SECONDS or until mixture boils, stirring 3 times. In small bowl, soften cream cheese (10 sec.); blend in mayonnaise. Remove wax or foil overwrap from asparagus and place package in oven and COOK 2 MINUTES. Open package and rearrange asparagus. Close package and COOK 4 MINUTES. Spread cream cheese mixture on ham slices. Divide asparagus spears among ham slices. Roll up, securing with toothpick. Place rolls on serving platter and COOK, uncovered, 1 MINUTE. Pour sauce over rolls and COOK another 2 MINUTES or until hot. Garnish with almonds.   4 to 5 Servings

> **TIP:** To heat 1 roll that has been refrigerated, cook 45 seconds; 2 rolls, cook 1 minute.

This recipe is very easy to double for larger amounts. One of our consumer testers wrapped these in foil after cooking the roll-ups and took them on a picnic. She found them to be a nice change from sandwiches.

SWISS HAM ROLL-UPS

**15 frozen tater tots
4 slices (4-oz. pkg.) boiled ham
2 slices (half 8-oz. pkg.) Swiss cheese
¼ cup sour cream**

COOK tater tots on paper plate or towel, uncovered, 1 MINUTE, 30 SECONDS or until thawed. Place ½ slice of cheese on each ham slice. Spread each cheese slice with sour cream. Place 3 tater tots inside each ham-cheese slice and roll-up, fastening with toothpick. Place on serving platter and COOK, uncovered, 2 MINUTES or until hot.   4 Roll-ups (2 Servings)

> **TIPS:** To heat 1 roll, cook 45 seconds; 2 rolls, cook 1 minute, 15 seconds.
>
> ● Sliced bologna and American cheese can be used for ham and Swiss cheese.

Orange marmalade makes a quick glaze on Canadian bacon. This is already pre-cooked, so only reheat time is necessary. For heating plain Canadian bacon slices, see page 15.

ORANGE GLAZED CANADIAN BACON

**1½ lbs. Canadian-style bacon
¼ cup orange marmalade
Dash dry mustard**

Cut bacon into 8 slices (about ½ inch thick). Place in 2-quart (12 x 7) baking dish. Spread about 1 teaspoon marmalade on each slice. Sprinkle with dry mustard. COOK, covered with wax paper, 6 MINUTES or until heated through.
4 Servings

This tangy glazed Canadian bacon can be served for brunch or dinner.

GLAZED CANADIAN BACON

**1½ lbs. Canadian-style bacon
½ cup drained pickle relish
2 tablespoons honey
¼ teaspoon dry or prepared mustard**

Place meat in 1½-quart (10 x 6) baking dish. Cut meat, halfway through, into 6 slices. Combine relish, honey and mustard; spoon between slices of meat. COOK, loosely covered with wax paper, 12 MINUTES or until heated through, occasionally spooning sauce over meat.
6 Servings

A spicy, colorful sauce coats these pork chops that are ready within 15 minutes. Good with potato salad and corn on the cob.

BARBECUED PORK CHOPS

**4 loin or rib pork chops, cut ½ inch thick
¾ cup barbecue sauce
½ cup (1 med.) chopped onion or
2 tablespoons instant minced onion
1 clove garlic, minced or ⅛ teaspoon
instant minced garlic
½ teaspoon salt
⅛ teaspoon pepper**

Arrange chops in single layer in 2-quart (8 x 8) or 1½-quart (10 x 6) baking dish. Combine remaining ingredients and pour over chops. COOK, covered with wax paper, 12 MINUTES or until done, occasionally spooning sauce over chops.   4 Servings

> **TIP:** For 6 chops, use 2-quart (12 x 7) baking dish, increase barbecue sauce to 1 cup and increase cooking time to 15 minutes.

This stuffing is easily layered between two thin pork chops. Gravy mix adds a rich brown color and flavor to the meat.

STUFFED PORK CHOPS

½ cup milk
¼ cup butter or margarine
2 cups dry seasoned bread stuffing
1 package (⅝ oz.) brown gravy mix
8 thin rib or loin pork chops
(about 1½ lbs.)

In mixing bowl, heat milk and butter together, about 1 minute, 30 seconds or until butter melts. Add bread stuffing and stir until moistened. (For ease in sprinkling gravy mix, pour into a salt shaker.) Sprinkle one side of 4 chops with gravy mix, placing that side down in shallow pie plate or baking dish. Spoon ½ cup stuffing on each chop. Top with other four chops, sprinkling top side with remaining gravy mix. **COOK,** uncovered, **12 MINUTES** or until done.

4 Servings

Rice and pork chops cook together in just 16 minutes. Serve with spinach (cook in oven after cooking chops) and sliced tomato salad.

RICE 'N HONEY CHOPS

1⅓ cups quick-cooking rice, uncooked
1⅓ cups orange juice
½ cup raisins
1 teaspoon salt
4 rib or loin pork chops, cut ½ inch thick
2 tablespoons honey

In 2-quart (8 x 8) baking dish, combine rice, orange juice, raisins and salt. Stir to mix. Arrange chops on top, pressing into rice mixture. Drizzle honey over top. **COOK,** covered with wax paper, **16 MINUTES** or until chops are done. If desired, remove paper the last 2 minutes and spoon some rice over chops; or, after cooking, place pan under broiler a few minutes to brown chops. 4 Servings

TIP: For 3 chops, cook about 13 minutes.

SMOKED PORK CHOPS

Arrange chops in shallow baking dish or platter. If desired, brush with honey or orange marmalade. Cook, covered loosely with wax paper, until edges of meat begin to sizzle:

3 chops — 4 minutes
4 chops — 5 minutes
5 chops — 6 minutes

MENU

**German Style Smoked Chops
Boiled Potatoes (117)
Onion-Topped Broccoli (121)
Tapioca Pudding (140)**

1. About 1 hour before serving, cook pudding.
2. Cook first cooking of broccoli.
3. Cook potatoes*, drain and let stand covered.
4. Cook chops.
5. Finish broccoli.
6. Reheat potatoes.
*It may be more convenient to cook Potatoes conventionally.

The smokey flavor of smoked chops goes nicely with the flavors of tart sauerkraut and sweet apples.

GERMAN-STYLE SMOKED CHOPS

2 cups (1-lb. can) drained sauerkraut
1 small onion, chopped or 1 tablespoon instant minced onion
2 medium apples, chopped
1 tablespoon sugar
4 smoked pork chops
½ cup water

In 2-quart (8 x 8) baking dish, mix together half of sauerkraut, onion, apple, and sugar. Top with chops; layer remaining sauerkraut, onion, apple and sugar over chops. Mix this layer lightly to distribute ingredients. Pour water over mixture and **COOK,** covered with wax paper, **8 TO 10 MINUTES** or until apple is tender.

4 Servings

TIP: If you want juices to serve over boiled potatoes or potato dumplings, increase water to 1 cup.

Pork chops take on golden brown color from mushroom soup.

GOLDEN PORK CHOPS

4 loin or rib pork chops, cut ½ inch thick
1 medium onion, sliced
½ teaspoon salt
1 can (10½ oz.) condensed golden mushroom soup

In 2-quart (8 x 8) baking dish, arrange chops. Top with onion and sprinkle with salt. Spoon soup over top. **COOK,** covered with wax paper, **15 MINUTES** or until pork chops are done. If desired, place under broiler a few minutes to brown. 4 Servings

A pork roast will be thoroughly done when cooked 10 minutes per pound. It will also be nicely browned because of its top layer of fat.

PORK LOIN ROAST

4-lb. pork loin roast

In 2-quart (12 x 7) baking dish, place an inverted saucer or small casserole cover. Cover bone section with foil during first half of cooking. Place roast, fat side down in baking dish. COOK, uncovered, **20 MINUTES** (half of cooking time). Remove foil, turn roast fat side up and COOK, loosely covered with wax paper, **20 MINUTES** or until meat thermometer registers 165° (will increase to 185° during standing). LET STAND, covered with foil, about **20 MINUTES**.

6 to 8 Servings

> **TIP:** To prevent overcooking, place foil over small ends of pork roasts during first half of cooking.

Cubes of pork and bits of pineapple cook in a tangy barbecue sauce. The flavors are especially good served with rice. One of our consumer testers said her children liked it served in a bun. If preparing rice in oven, cook rice after cooking pork and gravy mix. While rice stands, finish cooking pork. If necessary, reheat rice about one minute.

TANGY PORK BARBECUE

1½ lbs. cubed pork
1 package (⅝ oz.) brown gravy mix
2 stalks celery, sliced
1 small onion, sliced
1½ cups (13¼-oz. can) undrained
    pineapple tidbits
¾ cup catsup
1 tablespoon prepared mustard
1 tablespoon Worcestershire sauce
1 green pepper, sliced

In 2-quart casserole, sprinkle gravy mix over pork cubes, tossing to coat. COOK, covered with wax paper, **5 MINUTES**. Stir in remaining ingredients except green pepper. COOK, covered, **15 MINUTES** or until pork is done, stirring occasionally. Add green pepper and COOK **1 MINUTE** or until of desired doneness.

5 to 6 Servings

> **TIP:** This is especially good reheated because the flavors blend while standing.

MENU

French Onion Soup (108)
Pork Loin Roast
Acorn Squash 'N Apples (125)
Pickled Beets (120)
Garlic French Bread (129)
Streusel Rhubarb Cake (152)

1. Early in day, cook cake, beets and cook soup ready for final cooking.
2. About 1 hour before serving, cook roast and let stand.
3. Cook squash first cooking and let stand. Then prepare for final cooking.
4. Reheat soup and serve.
5. Finish squash while removing soup bowls from table.
6. Reheat sliced roast if necessary.
7. Heat bread.

Ribs begin cooking in the microware oven and then are quickly finished on the grill. This idea can be used with other meats that normally need long grilling times.

COUNTRY BARBECUED RIBS

1½ to 2 lbs. country-style ribs
Sauce
¼ cup catsup
¼ cup chili sauce or tomato sauce
1 tablespoon brown sugar
2 tablespoons chopped onion or
    1½ teaspoons instant minced onion
½ teaspoon salt
⅛ teaspoon garlic powder or instant
    minced garlic
1 teaspoon dry or prepared mustard
½ tablespoon Worcestershire sauce
Dash Tabasco sauce
1 slice lemon or 1 teaspoon lemon juice

Cut ribs into one-rib pieces. Arrange in 2-quart (8 x 8) baking dish (place larger pieces around edge). COOK, covered with wax paper, **12 MINUTES** or until partially cooked, rearranging halfway through cooking time. Meanwhile, in 1-cup measure, combine ingredients for sauce; mix well. Remove ribs from oven; drain. COOK sauce, uncovered, **1 MINUTE** or until mixture boils, stirring once. Pour over ribs, turning to coat or dip each rib into sauce to coat. Cool and refrigerate until ready to grill or grill immediately.

Grill over hot coals for 15 to 20 minutes, turning occasionally until ribs are browned and heated through.

3 to 4 Servings

> **TIPS:** Ribs can be broiled as well as grilled.
>
> • For larger amounts, use 2-quart (12 x 7) baking dish or a dish large enough to arrange the ribs in single layer. Add 5 minutes additional cooking time for each additional pound of ribs; increase sauce proportionately.

Pork tenderloin is often quite economical because there is no bone or waste. This recipe has a tasty sesame seed stuffing that goes well with pork. Start preparing about 1 hour before serving time to allow for cooking and resting times.

STUFFED PORK TENDERLOIN

¼ **cup butter or margarine**
¼ **cup sesame seed**
½ **cup (1 stalk) chopped celery**
2 **tablespoons chopped onion or**
  2 **teaspoons instant minced onion**
3 **slices bread, cubed**
1 **teaspoon salt**
½ **teaspoon poultry seasoning or thyme**
1 **teaspoon Worcestershire sauce**
2 **pork tenderloins, about 1¼ lbs. each**

In mixing bowl, combine butter, sesame seed, celery and onion. COOK, uncovered, 3 MINUTES, stirring occasionally. Mix in bread, salt, poultry seasoning and Worcestershire sauce.

Cut each pork tenderloin almost through lengthwise, flatten slightly. To keep meat out of juices, invert a saucer in bottom of 2-quart (12 x 7) baking dish. Lay one of flattened tenderloins, cut-side up, in baking dish. (For ease in tying, place about 4 pieces of string at intervals under tenderloin.) Spoon bread stuffing onto tenderloin. Top with other tenderloin, cut-side down with wide end over narrow end of bottom piece. Bring string around tenderloins, tying to hold together. COOK, uncovered, 15 MINUTES, LET REST, covered, 10 MINUTES and then COOK, uncovered, an additional 10 MINUTES. For easier slicing, cover loosely with foil and LET STAND 10 TO 15 MINUTES.

6 Servings

> **TIPS:** If desired, use 2 cups seasoned bread cubes for bread, salt and poultry seasoning.
>
> • For other size tenderloins, cook about 10 minutes per pound with a rest period halfway through cooking time.

> **MENU**
>
> **Sherry Glazed Spareribs**
> **Savory Potatoes (124)**
> **Corn Relish (122)**
> **Coleslaw Salad**
> **Ice Cream with French Chocolate Syrup (153)**
>
> 1. Early in day, cook corn relish.
> 2. About 45 minutes before serving, cook and prepare potatoes ready for final heating.
> 3. Cook spareribs.
> 4. Finish potatoes.
> 5. While clearing table and placing ice cream in bowls, cook chocolate sauce.

Serve these ribs for dinner or as an appetizer. Ribs take on a rich brown color during the 30 minutes of cooking.

SHERRY GLAZED SPARERIBS

2 **lbs. spareribs, cut into 1-inch pieces**
¼ **cup firmly packed brown sugar**
1 **tablespoon cornstarch**
3 **tablespoons soy sauce**
¼ **cup sherry**
¼ **cup orange juice**

Arrange ribs in 2-quart (12 x 7) baking dish. COOK, covered with wax paper, 5 MINUTES. Drain juices and rearrange ribs. Combine brown sugar and cornstarch; mix in remaining ingredients. Pour over ribs. COOK, covered with wax paper, 25 MINUTES or until done, occasionally turning and rearranging ribs in pan. Pour off excess fat before serving. If desired, garnish with orange slices, cut in half.

4 Servings

All ingredients, except green pepper, are cooked together in this main dish or appetizer. Green pepper keeps its crunch and color when added toward the end of cooking time.

SWEET AND SOUR PORK

1½ **lbs. cubed pork**
2 **tablespoons cornstarch**
3 **tablespoons soy sauce**
¼ **cup firmly packed brown sugar**
¼ **teaspoon ginger**
¼ **cup vinegar**
½ **cup water**
1½ **cups (13¼-oz. can) undrained pineapple tidbits**
1 **small onion, sliced**
2 **medium green peppers, cut into strips**

In 2-quart casserole, toss pork with cornstarch; mix in remaining ingredients except green pepper. COOK, covered, 12 MINUTES or until pork is done, stirring once. Stir in green pepper and COOK, covered, 1 MINUTE. 4 to 6 Servings

Sausage and Luncheon Meats

Luncheon meats and sausages (except fresh pork sausage) are already cooked so you are just bringing them to a serving temperature with your oven. To avoid overcooking the meat, it is sometimes added toward the end of the cooking time when it is part of a longer cooking casserole. It is not necessary to score the outer edge of sausage before cooking it. Sausage combinations are good make aheads for individual servings that can be kept on hand in the refrigerator as a quickly heated meal or snack.

Here is a quick and tasty way to make German potato salad using dehydrated hash brown potatoes. Do not use a paper towel under the bacon because you need the bacon drippings for the salad. You can mix it together early in the day and then cook just before serving to heat the salad and bologna.

BOLOGNA AND GERMAN POTATO SALAD

4 slices bacon
1⅓ cups hash brown potatoes
1⅔ cups water
1 teaspoon parsley flakes
¼ teaspoon salt
2 teaspoons instant minced onion or
  3 green onions, sliced
2 tablespoons sugar
1 tablespoon flour
¼ cup water
¼ cup white vinegar
1 ring (12 oz.) bologna

Place bacon in 2-quart casserole. COOK, covered with one or two paper towels, 2½ TO 3 MINUTES or until crisp. Remove paper towel and bacon, leaving extra drippings in casserole. Add potatoes and 1⅔ cups water. COOK, covered, 6 MINUTES. Stir in crumbled bacon and remaining ingredients except bologna, mixing well. Arrange evenly in casserole. Top with ring of bologna. COOK, covered, 4 MINUTES, 30 SECONDS or until hot.

3 to 4 Servings

> **TIP:** If desired, use 12 oz. (¾ lb.) wieners for bologna. For best heating, arrange spoke fashion around edge of casserole, cutting in half crosswise if necessary. Since wieners are smaller than bologna, reduce final cooking period to 3 minutes.

BOLOGNA ROLL UPS

Sliced bologna
Onion dip, cream cheese or sour cream
Strips of cheese or pickle

Spread about ½ tablespoon dip down center of each slice of bologna. Top with a cheese or pickle strip. Roll up, fastening with toothpicks. Place on serving platter. COOK 8 roll ups, uncovered, 2 MINUTES or until hot.

8 Roll Ups

> **TIPS:** For 4 roll ups, cook 1 minute. If desired, place roll ups (before heating) in wiener buns. Heat 1 roll up, in a bun, 25 seconds or until hot.
>
> • Bologna can be spread with mustard and filled with leftover mashed potato or other thick casserole mixtures. Heat 2 minutes, 30 seconds or until hot. The potato mixture in Crunchy Topped Luncheon Slices, page 94, would be good with sliced bologna or ham.

Select the foods your family likes and thread them on wooden or metal skewers (be sure the length will fit in the oven without touching the walls) keeping the larger foods toward the ends and the smaller foods toward the center. They can be assembled early or just provide the various foods and let everyone thread their own skewer.

BOLOGNA KABOBS

1 ring (12 oz.) bologna
1 small can pineapple chunks, drained
1 can (16 oz.) whole potatoes, drained
1 green pepper, cut into 1-inch pieces
Pitted ripe olives
¼ cup orange marmalade or Russian
  salad dressing
Cherry tomatoes, if desired

Cut bologna into ¾-inch slices and if desired remove skin. Alternate bologna, pineapple, potatoes, green pepper and olives on wooden or metal skewers. Arrange on shallow platter or baking dish. Brush with marmalade. COOK, uncovered, 4 MINUTES. Add tomatoes at ends of skewers. COOK 1 MINUTE or until tomatoes are heated.

4 Servings

> **TIPS:** Cooked sweet potatoes can be used for canned whole potatoes.
>
> • Cooked ham, cut into 1-inch cubes, can be used for bologna.
>
> • Popsicle sticks make handy skewers for using in the oven.

CABBAGE ROLLS

- **½ lb. fresh pork sausage**
- **1 medium head green cabbage***
- **½ lb. ground beef**
- **2 eggs, beaten**
- **¼ cup milk**
- **⅓ cup quick-cooking rice**
- **¾ teaspoon salt**
- **¼ teaspoon pepper**
- **¼ teaspoon mace or nutmeg**
- **1 medium onion, finely chopped**
- **2 cups (16-oz. can) tomato sauce**

In 2-quart casserole or bowl, crumble pork sausage; COOK, uncovered, **3 MINUTES** or until no longer pink, breaking up with fork once. Drain. Wrap head of cabbage in wax paper and **COOK 8 MINUTES** or until leaves are softened. Meanwhile, add remaining ingredients, except tomato sauce, to pork sausage; mix well. Remove 12 cabbage leaves (save partially cooked center and complete cooking at another meal). Place ¼ cup meat mixture on each leaf and roll to enclose meat mixture, securing with toothpicks. Place rolls, seam-side down in 2-quart (12 x 7) baking dish.

Pour tomato sauce over rolls. COOK, covered with wax paper, **16 MINUTES** or until cabbage is tender. 12 Rolls (3 to 4 Servings)

TIPS: *The 12 cabbage leaves can be removed from head of cabbage before cooking and cooked separately in covered casserole, using times as directed.

- To remove excess fat from ground beef, add beef to sausage for initial cooking; increase cooking time to 5 minutes.

- For half a recipe, use 1½ quart (10 x 6) baking dish and cooking times of 2 minutes, 6 minutes and 10 minutes.

Pictured: Bologna Kabobs, page 90, (see recipe for use of metal skewers), served on Rice, page 132, and Cabbage Rolls, above.

These times are based on a 1-lb. package of wieners that contains about 10 wieners. For directions on heating wieners in a bun, see page 18.

WIENERS

Place wieners on serving plate. Cook, uncovered, until wieners are hot:

> 1 wiener — 30 seconds
> 2 wieners — 45 seconds
> 3 wieners — 1 minute
> 4 wieners — 1 minute, 30 seconds
> 6 wieners — 2 minutes
> 10 wieners — 3 minutes

MENU

Corn 'N Wieners
Casserole Bread (130)
Sliced Tomatoes with Creamy Wilted Salad Dressing (27)
Fruit Crunch (138)

1. Night before, start bread.
2. About 30 minutes before serving, cook bread.
3. Cook Fruit Crunch.
4. Cook Corn 'N Wieners.
5. Cook dressing for tomatoes.

This supper dish needs only 10 minutes cooking time. The basic ingredients will probably be on hand without special shopping needed.

CORN 'N WIENERS

⅓ cup chopped onion or 1 tablespoon instant minced onion
⅓ cup sliced green pepper
2 tablespoons butter or margarine
2 cans (12 oz. each) whole kernel corn, drained
⅔ cup pitted black olives, cut in half
⅓ cup shredded Swiss cheese
6 wieners, cut into ½-inch slices
2 to 3 tablespoons catsup
Grated Parmesan cheese

In 2-quart casserole, combine onion, green pepper and butter. COOK, covered, 3 MINUTES or until tender, stirring once. Stir in corn, olives, Swiss cheese and wieners. COOK, covered, 5 MINUTES, stirring once. Spoon catsup over casserole and sprinkle with Parmesan cheese. COOK, covered, 2 MINUTES or until cheese is melted. 6 Servings

Bratwurst will cook in the oven, but will lack browning. Unless serving bratwurst in a bun, you will probably prefer to place them on the grill or under the broiler for browning.

BRATWURST IN BEER

¾ to 1 lb. bratwurst
1 medium onion, sliced
1 to 1½ cups beer

Arrange bratwurst in single layer in shallow casserole. Top with onion and beer. COOK, covered, 5 MINUTES, rearranging and turning once. Let stand in beer until ready to grill or broil. Grill or broil until desired brownness. If desired, serve with the onions (to brown onions, drain and fry in small amount of butter). 3 to 4 Servings

> **TIPS:** These can be cooked and left to marinate in beer up to 12 hours.
>
> • Try this same idea with equal amounts of Knackwurst or Metwurst.

The smokie links in this dish accent the mildly flavored ingredients. Cheese is added near the end of the cooking time to avoid stringiness.

SMOKIE MUSHROOM SUPPER

1 medium onion (½ cup), chopped
1 can (10½ oz.) condensed cream of mushroom soup
⅔ cup (4-oz. can) undrained mushroom stems and pieces
1½ cups (12-oz. can) undrained corn with red and green peppers
1 cup quick-cooking rice, uncooked
2 eggs, beaten
¼ cup milk
1 package (10 oz.) smokie links
1 cup (4 oz.) shredded Monterey Jack cheese

In 2-quart casserole, COOK onion, covered, 2 MINUTES or until tender. Add soup, mushrooms, corn, rice, eggs and milk. Reserve 4 smokie links and cut remaining links into ½-inch slices; stir into casserole mixture. COOK, covered, 12 MINUTES or until rice is tender, stirring once. Stir in cheese until melted. Cut reserved smokie links in half and arrange spoke fashion on top of casserole. COOK, covered, 2 MINUTES or until links are hot. 6 to 8 Servings

SAUCY WIENERS

1 lb. wieners, cut into ¼-inch slices
½ green pepper, sliced
1 medium onion, sliced
½ cup (4-oz. can) drained mushroom stems and pieces
2 cups (16-oz. can or jar) prepared spaghetti sauce

In 1½ or 2-quart casserole, combine all ingredients. COOK, covered, **8 MINUTES** or until hot, stirring occasionally. Serve with potatoes, noodles or rice; or spoon on toast or sandwich buns.   4 to 6 Servings

> **TIP:** The green pepper and onion will still be crunchy with these times. If you prefer soft vegetables, cook vegetables along with spaghetti sauce until desired doneness; then add wieners and mushrooms and heat through, about 4 minutes.

Here's a hot potato salad turned into a main dish with sauerkraut and cocktail franks.

FRANK 'N POTATO SALAD

4 cups (2 lbs.) prepared potato salad
1 cup (8-oz. can) drained sauerkraut
½ lb. cocktail franks
½ teaspoon salt
½ teaspoon caraway seed
Paprika

In 1½ or 2-quart casserole, combine all ingredients except paprika. COOK, covered, **7 MINUTES** or until hot, stirring once. Sprinkle with paprika before serving.   6 Servings

Beans, Kraut and Wieners

We found those who normally don't care for sauerkraut were pleasantly surprised with this dish. This is good served with baked potatoes. Start cooking the sauerkraut first, then cook potatoes before the final heating of wieners.

SAVORY KRAUT 'N WIENERS

¼ cup butter or margarine
1 stalk celery, sliced
1 small onion, sliced
¼ cup sugar
1 cube or teaspoon beef bouillon
¼ teaspoon ground ginger
1½ tablespoons cornstarch
1 tablespoon chopped pimiento, if desired
2 tablespoons vinegar
1½ cups water
2 cups (1-lb. can) sauerkraut (drain, using liquid for part of water)
4 to 8 wieners

In 2-quart casserole, combine butter, celery and onion. COOK, uncovered, **2 MINUTES**, stirring after butter melts. Stir in sugar, bouillon, ginger and cornstarch. Add pimiento, vinegar, water and sauerkraut; mix well. COOK, covered, **5 MINUTES**, stirring occasionally. Arrange wieners on top and COOK, covered, **2 MINUTES** or until heated through.
                         4 to 5 Servings

> **TIP:** For 2 servings, cook half of ingredients in 1-quart casserole. Cook sauerkraut about 3 minutes and then after adding wieners, cook 1 minute, 30 seconds.

The slightly sweet beans and tart sauerkraut combine to give an interesting sweet-sour flavor. A good last minute dish using foods that can easily be kept in the freezer and cupboard. Ready to serve in about 15 minutes.

BEANS, KRAUT AND WIENERS

1 lb. wieners
1 can (1 lb. 15 oz.) pork and beans
¼ cup chili sauce or catsup
2 cups (1-lb. can) drained sauerkraut
1 teaspoon caraway seed

In 2-quart casserole, slice half of wieners into ¼-inch slices. Stir in pork and beans and chili sauce. Top with sauerkraut; sprinkle with caraway seed. COOK, covered, **8 MINUTES**. Cut remaining wieners in half crosswise and arrange in spoke fashion around outside edge of dish. COOK, covered, **4 MINUTES** or until wieners are hot.   5 to 6 Servings

> **TIP:** The same size can of baked beans can be used for pork and beans. Or, use about 2 cups homemade baked beans.

These wieners can be served over buns as a sandwich or on toothpicks as an appetizer.

BARBECUED WIENERS

    1 package (⅝ oz.) home-style gravy mix
    1 cup water
    1 tablespoon instant minced onion or
        ¼ cup chopped onion
    1 cup catsup
    1 tablespoon prepared mustard
    10 wieners, cut into ½-inch slices

In 1-quart casserole, combine gravy mix, water and onion. COOK, uncovered, **3 MINUTES,** stirring twice. Add catsup, mustard and wieners. COOK, covered, **6 MINUTES** or until hot, stirring once.   5 Servings

> **TIP:** This dish can be refrigerated and reheated. Cook, covered, 7 minutes or until hot, stirring twice.

MENU

Crunchy Topped Luncheon Slices
Hot Bean Compote (119)
Coleslaw
Vanilla Pudding (23)

1. About 30 minutes before serving, cook pudding.
2. Cook bacon for bean compote.
3. Prepare potatoes for Crunchy Topped Luncheon Slices.
4. Cook Hot Bean Compote.
5. Cook Crunchy Topped Luncheon Slices.

Slices of luncheon meat are topped with onion flavored potatoes and crunchy onion rings. Wait until just before heating to add onions to potatoes because the onion rings will become soggy upon standing.

CRUNCHY TOPPED LUNCHEON SLICES

    4-Serving recipe mashed potato flakes
    ½ cup creamed cottage cheese
    1 can (3½ oz.) French-fried onion rings
    1 can (12 oz.) luncheon meat

Prepare 4-servings mashed potatoes as directed on package, adding ½ cup additional potato flakes. (Water, salt and butter for preparing potatoes can be cooked in microwave oven in covered 1-quart casserole for about 4 to 5 minutes or until mixture boils.) To prepared potatoes, stir in cottage cheese and about ⅔ can onion rings. Slice luncheon meat into 4 to 6 slices. Arrange slices on serving platter. Mound spoonfuls of potato mixture on each slice. COOK, uncovered, **3 TO 4 MINUTES** or until hot. Top with remaining onion rings, pressing into potato mixture. Serve immediately.   4 to 6 Servings

Currant jelly and horseradish combine to make an unusual sounding (but delightfully tasty) glaze for luncheon meat. Easily prepared and cooked in about 10 minutes.

ZESTY LUNCHEON SLICES

    ¼ cup firmly packed brown sugar
    ¼ cup currant or apple jelly
    1 tablespoon prepared horseradish
    1 can (12 oz.) luncheon meat
    1 can (1 lb.) pear halves, peach halves or pineapple slices

In 1½-quart (10 x 6) or 2-quart (12 x 7) baking dish, combine brown sugar, jelly and horseradish. Slice meat into 4 to 6 slices. Dip in glaze mixture, turning to coat both sides and arrange in baking dish. Arrange fruit along side or on top of meat slices. Spoon glaze over each. COOK, uncovered, **4 MINUTES** or until hot, occasionally spooning glaze over meat and fruit.   4 to 5 Servings

This is an attractive and tasty way to dress up canned luncheon meat. The glaze is cooked in the measuring cup which eliminates using an extra dish.

ORANGE GLAZED LUNCHEON LOAF

    1 can (12 oz.) luncheon meat
    4 thin orange slices, cut in half
    8 whole cloves
    ¼ cup orange marmalade
    1 teaspoon flour
    ⅛ teaspoon dry mustard or ¼ teaspoon prepared mustard

Place meat in 2-quart (8 x 8) or 1½-quart (8-inch round) baking dish. Cut half way through meat into 8 slices. Insert orange slice between each slice and clove in top of each slice. In 1-cup measure, combine orange marmalade, flour and mustard. COOK, uncovered, **1 MINUTE.** Stir and spread over meat. COOK, loosely covered with wax paper, **5 MINUTES** or until glaze begins to bubble around edges.   4 Servings

> **TIP:** Pineapple slices, cut in half may be used for orange slices.

Other Meats

Veal and Lamb: Both of these are young and tender meats and both cook well in your microwave oven. We have included recipes for roasts, cutlets and cubes and also ground lamb and lamb stew meat.

Variety Meats: Although the majority of variety meats such as heart or tongue need long, slow cooking, you can use the microwave oven for recipes that start with the meat already cooked conventionally. A more tender variety meat, however, such as calf liver, cooks easily and quickly in a microwave oven.

Game: See the Beef section as a guide for cooking similar cuts of game. You can tenderize game by grinding it and using it in a recipe such as Burgundy Beef Balls or by using a commercial tenderizer as in the Stuffed Flank Roll Up recipe. You can also marinate game the same way beef is marinated in the recipes for Sauerbraten, Beef Ragout or Swiss Steak. Buttermilk can be used as a simple marinade that both tenderizes the meat and removes some of the wild taste of game. Cooked game sausage can be used in the wiener or bologna recipes such as Savory Kraut 'N Wieners.

To defrost Other Meats, see page 45.

This recipe can be prepared with either riblets or stew meat. The riblets have bones which will not affect cooking time but will affect the number of servings that should be planned for each pound of meat. For riblets, allow about ½ lb. per serving of meat; for boneless stew meat, allow about ¼ lb. meat.

LAMB RIBLETS IN TOMATO SAUCE

   2 lbs. lamb riblets or stew meat
   1 package (⅝ oz.) brown gravy mix
  ¼ teaspoon salt
  ⅛ teaspoon pepper
   1 tablespoon brown sugar
   1 medium onion, sliced
   1 stalk celery, sliced
   1 can (10¾ oz.) condensed tomato soup

In 2 or 2½-quart casserole, combine lamb and gravy mix. **COOK**, uncovered, **5 MINUTES**. Add remaining ingredients, stirring to combine. **COOK**, covered, **24 MINUTES** or until tender, stirring occasionally. Serve over rice or potatoes.   4 to 6 Servings

Since lamb is young tender meat, it does not need long cooking to tenderize. The meat is cooked for a short time with gravy mix to aid in browning the meat and sauce.

EASY LAMB STEW

   1 lb. boneless lamb stew meat
   1 package (⅝ oz.) brown gravy mix
  ½ teaspoon sugar
   2 tablespoons flour
   1 teaspoon salt
  ⅛ teaspoon pepper
  ⅛ teaspoon instant minced garlic or
     1 clove garlic, minced
   1 teaspoon Worcestershire sauce
   1 cup water
  ½ cup red wine
   3 medium carrots, cut into ½-inch pieces
   2 stalks celery, cut into 1-inch pieces
   2 medium potatoes, cut into 1-inch cubes

In 2 or 3-quart casserole, combine lamb, gravy mix and sugar. **COOK**, uncovered, **5 MINUTES**. Stir in remaining ingredients, mixing well. **COOK**, covered, **20 MINUTES** or until vegetables and meat are desired doneness, stirring occasionally.   4 Servings

> **TIPS:** If desired, omit wine and use 1½ cups water.
>
> • Other tender meats such as cubed veal or cubed chicken breast meat can be used for lamb. Prepare as directed.

Lamb shanks make hearty, tasty servings for guests or family. This recipe features a flavorful sauce that cooks with the shanks. The 15 minutes rest time makes it convenient to cook a vegetable or dessert in the oven, too.

LAMB SHANKS IN WINE SAUCE

   4 lamb shanks (about 2¾ lbs.)
   1 medium onion, sliced
   1 teaspoon salt
  ½ to 1 bay leaf
   2 tablespoons flour
  ½ cup water
  ½ cup red wine
   4 carrots, sliced into ¼-inch slices
   1 stalk celery, chopped

[handwritten: Cook 40 min — Leave 15 add B.V. Pepper Rosemary]

In 2½ or 3-quart casserole, combine lamb shanks, onion, salt and bay leaf. Mix flour with water to dissolve. Add to lamb along with remaining ingredients. **COOK**, covered, **28 MINUTES** or until lamb is done, turning lamb about 3 times to coat with sauce. **LET STAND**, covered, **15 MINUTES** to finish cooking. Serve with potatoes or noodles.   4 Large Servings

CURRIED LAMB MEATBALLS

1 lb. ground lamb
1 clove garlic, minced, or ⅛ teaspoon instant minced garlic
1 medium onion, sliced
1 stalk celery, sliced
2 tablespoons flour
1½ to 2 teaspoons curry powder
1 teaspoon salt
2 cubes or teaspoons chicken bouillon (crush cubes)
¼ cup chutney
1 teaspoon prepared mustard
¾ cup water

In 1½-quart (8-inch round) baking dish, combine ground lamb and garlic. Push meat to one side and form meat into 1-inch balls, arranging in same dish. Add onion and celery; COOK, uncovered, **5 MINUTES**, rearranging and turning once. Drain off fat. Sprinkle meatballs with flour, curry powder, salt and bouillon. Stir in chutney, mustard and water. COOK, uncovered, **4 MINUTES** or until done, stirring once.   4 Servings

PLUM GLAZED LAMB ROAST

1 can (1 lb. 1 oz.) plums, drain and reserve ¼ cup syrup
2 tablespoons lemon juice
1 tablespoon soy sauce
1 teaspoon Worcestershire sauce
1 teaspoon leaf basil
⅛ teaspoon instant minced onion or 1 teaspoon minced onion
4-lb. boned leg of lamb roast

In 4-cup measure or in blender, combine plums, ¼ cup plum syrup and seasonings. Purée sauce by mashing with fork and forcing through sieve or processing on medium speed in blender. Place roast on inverted saucer or small casserole cover in 2-quart (8 x 8) baking dish. Baste roast with plum sauce. COOK, uncovered, **20 MINUTES**. Turn roast and baste with additional plum sauce. COOK, uncovered, **20 MINUTES** or until meat thermometer registers 160° (will increase to 180° during standing), basting several times with sauce. LET STAND, covered with foil, **20 MINUTES** before carving.   6 to 8 Servings

Pictured, top to bottom: Garlic Glazed Lamb Roast, right, Veal Parmigiana, page 98, Liver, Bacon and Onions, page 99, and Curried Lamb Meatballs, above, with condiments of raisins, pickle relish and chopped peanuts.

MENU

Bouillon Sipper (43)
Garlic Glazed Lamb Roast
Rice Pilaf (132)
Tangy Mustard Cauliflower (121)
Relishes
Snow-Capped Custard (143)

1. Early in day, prepare custard for Snow-Capped Custard.
2. About 1 hour before serving, cook roast for half of time.
3. Cook Rice Pilaf.
4. Finish cooking roast.
5. Heat Bouillon Sipper.
6. Cook cauliflower.
7. Reheat rice if necessary.
8. While clearing table, cook meringues on custards.

A garlic glaze enhances the flavor of lamb. The roast will be a very pleasing brown color when done. For cooking other size lamb roasts, use 10 minutes per pound cooking time.

GARLIC GLAZED LAMB ROAST

⅓ cup dry sherry
1 tablespoon paprika
½ teaspoon leaf basil
2 tablespoons soy sauce
2 tablespoons oil
3 cloves garlic, minced, or ⅜ teaspoon instant minced garlic
4-lb. boned leg of lamb roast

In 1-cup measure, combine all ingredients except roast. COOK, uncovered, **45 SECONDS** or until mixture is warm. Place roast on inverted saucer or small casserole cover in 2-quart (8 x 8) baking dish. Baste roast with garlic glaze. COOK, uncovered, **20 MINUTES**. Turn roast and baste with additional garlic glaze. COOK, uncovered, **20 MINUTES** or until meat thermometer registers 160° (will increase to 180° during standing), basting several times with garlic glaze. LET STAND, covered with foil, **20 MINUTES** before carving.   6 to 8 Servings

LAMB PATTIES WITH PLUM SAUCE

1 lb. ground lamb
½ teaspoon salt
⅛ teaspoon pepper
½ cup plum preserves
2 teaspoons lemon juice

In 2-quart (8 x 8) baking dish, combine lamb, salt and pepper. Shape into 4 patties and arrange in same baking dish. COOK, uncovered, **3 MINUTES**. Drain and turn patties; top with plum preserves and sprinkle with lemon juice. COOK, uncovered, **2 MINUTES** or until lamb is no longer pink. Spoon sauce from baking dish over patties before serving.   4 Servings

This makes a convenient dish for company, because it is easy to assemble ahead for quick finishing in the microwave oven just before serving. Since the tomato sauce is very flavorful, serve with a mild vegetable such as corn or green beans.

VEAL PARMIGIANA

　　1 egg, slightly beaten
　¼ teaspoon salt
　　2 tablespoons cornflake crumbs
　⅓ cup grated Parmesan cheese
　　1 lb. veal cutlets or boneless round steak
　　2 tablespoons oil
　　1 medium onion, chopped
　　4 oz. (1 cup) sliced or shredded
　　　Mozzarella cheese
　　1 cup (8-oz. can) tomato sauce
Pepper
　⅛ teaspoon leaf oregano or Italian
　　　seasoning
Parmesan cheese

In shallow dish, beat egg with salt. Combine crumbs and ⅓ cup Parmesan cheese on shallow plate or wax paper. Cut veal into 4 serving pieces and pound to make ¼ inch thick. Dip veal in egg, then in crumb mixture, coating well. Brown over medium high heat in oil in fry pan until golden brown, turning to brown both sides. Arrange in 1½-quart (10 x 6) baking dish, adding drippings from fry pan. While meat is browning, **COOK** onion in small sauce dish, covered with saucer, **2 MINUTES** or until tender. Sprinkle onion over meat in baking dish. Top with cheese slices, then spoon tomato sauce over top. Sprinkle with pepper and oregano. **COOK**, covered with wax paper, **6 MINUTES** or until bubbly. Sprinkle with Parmesan cheese and **COOK**, covered, **30 SECONDS** to melt cheese.　　4 Servings

　　TIPS: To make ahead, assemble in baking dish and refrigerate. Since mixture is cold, increase cooking time to 8 minutes.

　　● Beef round steak, cut ¼ inch thick, can be used for veal.

A veal dish that has everything cooked together in one step.

VEAL WILD RICE

　　2 lbs. boneless veal cubes
　　1 medium onion, chopped
　　1 package (6 oz.) wild and white rice mix
　　1 can (10½ oz.) condensed golden
　　　mushroom soup
　　1 cup (2 stalks) chopped celery
　　1 can (8½ oz.) water chestnuts,
　　　undrained and sliced
　⅓ cup (2½-oz. jar) undrained mushrooms
　　1 tablespoon soy sauce
　1½ cups water

In 2-quart casserole, combine all ingredients; mix well. **COOK**, covered, **30 MINUTES** or until wild rice is tender, stirring once.　　6 Servings

　　TIP: If quick-cooking rice is used, cook, covered, 20 minutes or until rice is tender. Add 1 teaspoon salt to replace seasoning in wild rice mix.

Veal is tender young beef so it will cook quickly in this rich brown sauce. Noodles can be cooked conventionally. To complete your meal, cook buttered carrots in the oven after veal has cooked. If desired, serve with a fruit salad.

VEAL GOULASH

　　1 lb. boneless veal cubes
　　1 package (⅝ oz.) brown gravy mix
　　1 medium onion (½ cup), chopped
　　2 stalks celery, chopped
　　2 tablespoons flour
　1½ cups water
　¼ cup sherry
　　1 teaspoon paprika
　½ teaspoon salt
　⅛ teaspoon instant minced garlic or
　　　1 clove garlic, minced
　　1 teaspoon Worcestershire sauce

In 1½ or 2-quart casserole, combine veal, gravy mix, onion and celery. **COOK**, uncovered, **5 MINUTES**. Stir in remaining ingredients, mixing well. **COOK**, covered, **9 MINUTES** or until veal is done, stirring occasionally. Let stand a few minutes before serving over noodles or potatoes.　　3 to 4 Servings

　　TIP: Sherry can be omitted, increasing water to 1¾ cups.

Golden mushroom soup adds a rich brown color and flavor to this simple veal roast. Either a rump or shoulder roast can be used. If cooking other sizes of roast, use 9 minutes per pound as a guide for timing.

VEAL ROAST

3-lb. veal shoulder or rump roast
½ teaspoon salt
½ teaspoon leaf marjoram or ¼ teaspoon powdered marjoram
1 can (10½ oz.) condensed golden mushroom soup

In 3 or 4-quart casserole, place meat bone side down. Sprinkle with salt and marjoram. Spoon soup over top. COOK, covered, **27 MINUTES** or until meat thermometer registers 150° (will increase to 170° during standing), turning meat twice. LET STAND, covered, **20 MINUTES** to finish cooking.   6 Servings

Chicken livers cook in a creamy sauce highlighted by tangy green grapes. The grapes add a refreshing color and flavor to the chicken livers. Serve over brown rice or in patty shells.

SAUCY CHICKEN LIVERS

¼ cup butter or margarine
¼ cup (1 small) chopped onion or 1 tablespoon instant minced onion
1 lb. chicken livers
½ tablespoon cornstarch
1 teaspoon sugar
½ teaspoon salt
⅛ teaspoon pepper
1 teaspoon Worcestershire sauce
¼ cup water
¼ cup sherry
1 cube or teaspoon chicken bouillon
1 cup seedless green grapes
Parsley

In 1 or 1½-quart casserole, combine butter and onion; COOK, uncovered, **4 MINUTES** or until golden brown. Add livers, coating well. Stir in remaining ingredients except grapes and . parsley. COOK, covered, **6 MINUTES** or until livers are done, stirring occasionally. Stir in grapes and COOK, covered, **1 MINUTE** to heat through. Garnish with parsley.   4 Servings

> **TIP:** To defrost chicken livers place packages in oven and cook 1 minute, rest, cook 1 minute, open packages and separate livers, cook 30 seconds.

When cooking liver in the oven, tender liver such as baby beef liver cooks best. With beef liver there is some connective tissue that may take long, slow cooking to tenderize. For best tenderness and juiciness, cook liver just until it loses its pinkness on the inside.

LIVER, BACON AND ONIONS

4 slices bacon
2 medium onions, sliced
1 lb. baby beef liver, sliced
Salt and pepper

In 9-inch pie plate or 1½-quart (10 x 6) baking dish, arrange bacon in layers, cutting in half if necessary. Cover with layer of paper towel to prevent spatters. COOK **2 MINUTES, 30 SECONDS** or until crisp. Remove bacon, leaving drippings in baking dish. Add onions, stirring to coat with drippings. COOK, uncovered, **5 MINUTES** or until light brown, stirring twice. Push onions to side of dish and add liver, turning to coat with drippings. Sprinkle with salt and pepper. Top with onions and crumbled bacon. COOK, covered with wax paper, **3 MINUTES** or just until inside is no longer pink, turning and rearranging once.
4 Servings

This dish that uses tongue you cook conventionally is good served over rice. If you prepare the rice in the oven, cook it first while you assemble this; then let rice stand while you cook a vegetable and heat the tongue and pineapple sauce.

TONGUE IN PINEAPPLE SAUCE

2 tablespoons butter or margarine
2 cubes or 2 teaspoons chicken bouillon
1 tablespoon brown sugar
2 tablespoons cornstarch
1 tablespoon soy sauce
1½ cups water
1 cup (8½-oz. can) undrained crushed pineapple
8 to 12 slices cooked tongue

In 1½ or 2-quart casserole, melt butter (about 20 sec.). Stir in bouillon, brown sugar, cornstarch, soy sauce, water and pineapple. Add tongue slices. COOK, covered, **8 MINUTES** or until mixture boils and thickens, stirring twice.   4 Servings

> **TIPS:** If desired, add sliced water chestnuts before heating or toasted almonds after heating.
>
> • For 2 servings, prepare in 1-quart casserole, use half of all ingredients and cook 5 minutes.

Eggs and Cheese

Both eggs and cheese require careful watching; the timings given in the recipes are quite exact. Cooking occurs in such a short time that seconds *do* make a difference. Once you have mastered cooking eggs in your microwave oven, it will be the easiest and most convenient way you can imagine to prepare them.

Eggs: Yolk has a high fat content which tends to make it cook faster than egg white. Covering the dish with plastic wrap for a fried egg holds in the heat to finish cooking the white without overcooking the yolk during the standing time. It is easiest to cook scrambled eggs because the yolk and white are mixed together before cooking. Stirring while cooking scrambled eggs prevents overcooking on the outside edges.

Eggs cooked in your oven will give you far more flexible breakfasts. One or two servings can be fixed at a time or you can undercook a larger amount and then reheat as needed. We have not included directions for hard boiled eggs because eggs cooked in the shell might explode, due to pressure created within the shell by such rapid cooking. This could possibly happen even after eggs are removed from the oven.

When developing recipes, we have used extra large eggs from the refrigerator. If you use smaller eggs or ones at room temperature, you may need to decrease the time very slightly. It is quite normal to hear a popping noise while eggs are cooking.

Cheese: Different types of cheese often can be interchanged, according to personal tastes. Cheese is overcooked if it has become rubbery.

The Fondue and Rarebit recipes are especially easy with all the ingredients stirred and cooked together in one step.

MENU

Glazed Grapefruit (16)
Egg Foo Yong Scramble
Peachy Chicken Rice Salad (131)
English Muffin Bread (130)

1. Day before, prepare and cook bread and prepare salad.
2. About 15 minutes ahead, cook eggs.
3. Heat grapefruit while toasting bread.

This elegant brunch or luncheon dish can be made with ease in the oven. You'll especially notice the green color retained in the asparagus and the moistness of the ham. Prepare the Hollandaise sauce before the rest of this recipe and simply reheat 30 to 45 seconds.

EGGS BENEDICT

1 package (10 oz.) frozen asparagus spears
4 English muffins, split and toasted
4 slices ham, ⅛ to ¼ inch thick
4 poached eggs
1 recipe (⅔ cup) Hollandaise sauce (page 133)

Remove wax or foil overwrap and place package of frozen asparagus in oven; **COOK 3 MINUTES.** Open carton and rearrange, moving center spears to outside. Close carton and **COOK 2 MINUTES.** Drain on paper towel. Using 4 luncheon plates, arrange one English muffin and one ham slice on each plate; divide asparagus evenly and arrange on ham. **COOK** 2 plates at a time, uncovered, **1 MINUTE, 30 SECONDS** or until ham is hot. Carefully place poached eggs on asparagus and top with hot Hollandaise sauce. Serve immediately.
4 Servings

TIP: You may find it easier to poach the eggs conventionally because you'll have less egg breakage when placing on asparagus. This will also free the oven for preparation of asparagus and Hollandaise sauce.

This supper or brunch dish contains crunchy bean sprouts. Any leftovers will make interesting sandwiches for lunch boxes.

EGG FOO YONG SCRAMBLE

6 eggs
1 can (16 oz.) bean sprouts, drained
½ cup chopped onion or 2 tablespoons instant minced onion
¼ cup chopped green pepper
2 tablespoons soy sauce
2 tablespoons butter or margarine

In 1½ or 2-quart casserole, beat eggs. Stir in remaining ingredients. **COOK,** covered, **5 MINUTES, 30 SECONDS** or until eggs are almost set, stirring twice during last half of cooking time. **LET STAND,** covered, **1 TO 2 MINUTES** before serving. 4 to 5 Servings

As with conventional cooking, egg dishes may be difficult to wash after standing. We found using a vegetable spray-on coating on the dish before cooking made cleaning easier. If you wish to omit melting butter, just cut it in pieces and add along with milk.

SCRAMBLED EGGS

EGGS	BUTTER OR MARGARINE	MILK	COOKING TIME		
			COOK	STIR	COOK
1	1 tsp.	1 tbsp.	30 sec.	Stir	15 sec.
2	2 tsp.	2 tbsp.	45 sec.	Stir	30 sec.
3	1 tbsp.	3 tbsp.	1 min., 10 sec.	Stir	45 sec.
4	4 tsp.	4 tbsp.	1 min., 45 sec.	Stir	50 sec.
5	5 tsp.	5 tbsp.	2 min.	Stir	1 min., 15 sec.
6	2 tbsp.	6 tbsp.	2 min., 25 sec.	Stir	1 min., 25 sec.

In soup bowl or 20-oz. casserole (use 1-quart casserole for 4, 5 or 6 eggs), melt butter (25 to 30 sec.). Add eggs and milk; mix with fork to scramble. Cook, covered, stirring after ⅔ cooked. Stir again when done. Season to taste.

TIPS: The eggs don't need stirring until ⅔ cooked because little coagulation of the egg has taken place before that time.

• To reheat refrigerated eggs on serving plate, cook, covered with bowl:

1 egg — 30 seconds
2 eggs — 45 seconds
3 eggs — 1 minute, 10 seconds
4 eggs (2 eggs/plate) — 1 minute, 45 seconds

For these times, we used extra large eggs that were at refrigerator temperature. The cooking time is especially critical when preparing eggs that do not have the white and yolk mixed together (see Tip).

Eggs may cook at slightly different rates because of their size or age. It is easiest to poach eggs in individual dishes so that an egg that cooks at a different rate can be removed early or left in the oven a few seconds longer.

FRIED EGGS

Melt ¼ teaspoon butter (25 sec.) in the bottom of 10-oz. custard cup or soup or sauce dish with 4 to 4½-inch bottom diameter. Break 1 egg in each dish, and cook, covered with a saucer or plastic wrap:

1 egg — 30 to 35 seconds
2 eggs — 1 minute to 1 minute, 5 seconds
3 eggs — 1 minute, 30 seconds to 1 minute, 35 seconds
4 eggs — 2 minutes to 2 minutes, 5 seconds

LET STAND, covered, **1 MINUTE** before serving. This will give you an egg with a soft yolk and cooked white.

TIPS: The composition of egg is such that the yolk has the highest fat content. Microwave energy tends to cook the yolk before the white. By covering the egg during cooking, the egg can be taken out before the white is completely set; the trapped steam will finish cooking the white during standing.

• An overcooked fried egg can be cut up and used as a hard-cooked egg in salads or sauces.

POACHED EGGS

In 10-oz. custard cup or soup bowl, heat ¼ cup water and ¼ teaspoon white vinegar to boiling (about 1 min.). Carefully break an egg into dish. **COOK**, covered tightly with plastic wrap, **25 SECONDS. LET STAND,** covered, **1 MINUTE** before serving.

TIPS: For 2 eggs, each cooked in individual dishes, cook 1 minute; for 3 eggs in individual dishes, cook 1 minute, 30 seconds.

• For poaching in bouillon, omit vinegar and use ½ cup water and 1 cube or teaspoon chicken bouillon, stirring after first heating to dissolve bouillon.

This is a good brunch or luncheon dish to serve family or guests. Allow about 20 minutes to prepare, or assemble bacon, eggs and sauce ahead of time and then just heat about 5 minutes before serving.

BACON AND EGG CASSEROLE

6 hard-cooked eggs
6 slices bacon
2 tablespoons butter or margarine
2 tablespoons flour
½ teaspoon salt
1 cup milk
¼ teaspoon pepper
⅛ teaspoon dry or prepared mustard
Half of 3½-oz. can French-fried onion rings

Cook eggs conventionally. In 2-quart casserole or baking dish, **COOK** bacon between layers of paper towel until crisp, about **3 MINUTES, 15 SECONDS**. Remove bacon, paper towels and excess drippings from dish. Melt butter in same baking dish (20 sec.). Stir in flour and salt until smooth. Gradually add milk, stirring constantly. **COOK**, uncovered, about **3 MINUTES** or until thickened, stirring occasionally. Stir in pepper and mustard. Peel and quarter hard cooked eggs; arrange in the sauce. Crumble bacon and sprinkle over eggs. **COOK**, uncovered, **2 MINUTES** or until hot. Add onion rings and **COOK**, uncovered, **1 MINUTE**.   4 Servings

> **TIP:** If desired, use bacon drippings for butter.

A delicious blend of Denver sandwich flavors. Serve for lunch or brunch with toast or rolls and fresh fruit. The stirring during cooking is necessary to cook the center without overcooking the edges. The total cooking time is 5½ minutes, plus time to cook bacon.

DENVER BRUNCH SANDWICH

8 slices bacon
6 eggs
⅓ cup milk
½ cup salad dressing or mayonnaise
¼ cup chopped pimiento
¼ cup chopped green pepper
¼ teaspoon salt
6 tomato slices (1 large or 2 medium)

In 1½-quart (10 x 6) baking dish, **COOK** bacon between layers of paper towel until crisp, about **4 MINUTES**. Remove bacon, paper towels and excess drippings from dish; crumble bacon. Meanwhile beat eggs, milk and salad dressing until well mixed. Stir in pimiento, green pepper, salt and bacon. Pour into baking dish. Cover tightly with plastic wrap. **COOK 3 MINUTES**; stir, moving cooked portion to center. Cover again and **COOK 2 MINUTES** or until center is almost set. Arrange tomato slices on top and **COOK 30 SECONDS. LET STAND**, covered, **2 MINUTES** to finish cooking. 5 to 6 Servings

The timing of an omelet is very short. We do not suggest using more than 4 eggs for an omelet because it is easy to overcook the outside before the center is set. The tight fitting plastic covering is necessary to hold in the heat for even cooking.

OMELET

3 eggs
3 tablespoons milk
⅛ teaspoon salt
Dash pepper
1 tablespoon butter or margarine

In mixing bowl, combine eggs, milk, salt and pepper; beat until well mixed. Melt butter in 9-inch pie plate (30 sec.). Pour in egg mixture. Cover tightly with plastic wrap. **COOK 1 MINUTE, 15 SECONDS**; stir to move cooked edges toward center. Cover again with plastic wrap and **COOK 1 MINUTE. LET STAND**, covered, at least **1 MINUTE** before loosening with rubber scraper, folding over and sliding onto serving plate. If underside is softer than you prefer, return omelet on serving plate to oven for an additional 30 to 60 seconds.   2 Servings

> **TIPS:** For 2 egg omelet, use ½ tablespoon butter, 2 eggs, 2 tablespoons milk, ⅛ teaspoon salt and dash pepper. Cook in 8-inch pie pan 45 seconds; stir; cook 1 minute.
>
> • For 4 egg omelet, use 1 tablespoon butter, 4 eggs, 4 tablespoons milk, ¼ teaspoon salt, dash pepper. Cook in 10-inch pie pan 1 minute, 30 seconds; stir; cook 1 minute, 15 seconds.
>
> • For bacon omelet, cook bacon as directed on page 15, before cooking egg. Crumble bacon and add to top of omelet after cooking.
>
> • For cheese omelet, sprinkle with ¼ to ½ cup shredded cheese just before turning out of dish. Return to oven 30 seconds to melt cheese.

Pictured, top to bottom: Brunch Special, page 103, Denver Brunch Sandwich, left, and Welsh Rarebit, page 104, served over toast and garnished with nutmeg.

Potatoes, Canadian bacon and eggs all cook together in just one dish. Add a tart, colorful fruit cup and a few sweet rolls for a hearty, tasty brunch.

BRUNCH SPECIAL

1⅓ cups dehydrated hash brown potatoes
1 package (1½ oz.) sour cream sauce mix
2¼ cups water
1 tablespoon chives, if desired
4 slices (4 oz.) Canadian-style bacon
4 eggs
Salt and pepper

In 2-quart (8 x 8) baking dish, combine dry potatoes, sauce mix, water and chives. Stir to mix (mixture will be lumpy). **COOK, uncovered, 8 MINUTES.** Stir, then arrange bacon slices down center of dish. **COOK, covered, 2 MINUTES.** Make 2 indentations along each side of bacon. Break egg into each. Sprinkle with salt and pepper. Cover with plastic wrap and **COOK 2 MINUTES, 30 SECONDS** or until eggs are almost set. **LET STAND,** covered, **2 MINUTES** to finish cooking eggs.   4 Servings

This basic Swiss fondue can now be made without the slow, gradual stirring in of the cheese. Just heat all ingredients together until warm enough to melt the cheese, then blend together.

SWISS FONDUE

4 cups (16 oz.) shredded Swiss cheese
¼ cup flour
¼ teaspoon salt
¼ teaspoon nutmeg
Dash pepper
2 cups white wine
1 to 2 tablespoons Kirsch, if desired

In 1½-quart dish or casserole, combine cheese, flour, salt, nutmeg and pepper. Add wine and mix well. **COOK, covered, 6 MINUTES,** stirring several times during the last 2 minutes. Stir well after removing from oven to finish melting cheese. If all is not melted, heat 30 to 60 more seconds. Stir in Kirsch. Serve immediately by spearing squares of French bread with fork and dipping into the fondue.   6 Servings

TIPS: Most of the earthenware fondue pots can be used in the oven. Just cover with plastic wrap or tight fitting cover to hold in the heat. To be sure your dish is useable, check it using the test on page 6.

• For half a recipe use 1-quart casserole and reduce cooking time to 4 minutes.

• Leftover fondue is good served hot over vegetables like a cheese sauce or as a sauce for open-faced ham sandwich.

Serve this as rarebit over toast, or use in a fondue dish for dipping cubes of bread. It reheats easily in the oven.

WELSH RAREBIT

2 eggs
1 cup beer
2 cups (10 oz.) cubed American cheese
2 tablespoons butter or margarine
1 teaspoon dry or prepared mustard
1 teaspoon Worcestershire sauce
4 drops Tabasco sauce

In 1-quart bowl or casserole, beat eggs. Stir in remaining ingredients. **COOK**, uncovered, **5 MINUTES** or until cheese is melted and mixture thickened, stirring about once every minute. Beat with beater or wire whip to make smooth. Serve over toast. 4 Servings

> **TIPS:** For heartier servings, top toast with slices of turkey or chicken before adding sauce.
>
> • Other types of processed cheese can be used.

This cheese-custard pie is good for brunch, supper or an evening snack.

CHEESE AND BACON PIE

9-inch Baked Pastry Shell
4 slices bacon
3 eggs, slightly beaten
1 cup milk
2 cups (8 oz.) shredded Swiss cheese
Half of 3½-oz. can French-fried onion rings, slightly crushed

Prepare and cook pastry shell as directed on page 155 and set aside to cool. Place bacon between paper towels on paper or glass plate and **COOK** about **2 MINUTES, 30 SECONDS** or until crisp. Beat together eggs and milk. Add cheese, onion rings and crumbled bacon. Pour into pastry shell. **COOK**, uncovered, **8 MINUTES** or until almost set. **LET STAND 10 MINUTES** to finish cooking. Cut into wedges and serve. 6 Servings

TOMATO MACARONI AND CHEESE

1 can (10¾ oz.) condensed tomato soup
1⅓ cups (1 soup can) water
¼ cup butter or margarine
1 teaspoon parsley flakes
1 package (7¼ oz.) macaroni and cheese sauce mix

In 2-quart casserole, combine all ingredients. **COOK**, covered, **10 MINUTES** or until macaroni is just about tender, stirring occasionally. **LET STAND**, covered, **5 MINUTES** to finish cooking. 3 to 4 Servings

A tuna-macaroni casserole that starts with frozen macaroni and cheese. Stirring the frozen macaroni prevents overcooking the outside before the center has thawed.

NEPTUNE'S MACARONI AND CHEESE

1 package (12 oz.) frozen macaroni and cheese
2 tablespoons chopped celery
1 tablespoon chopped onion or
1 teaspoon instant minced onion
1 tablespoon water
1 can (6½ oz.) tuna fish, drained
2 tablespoons chopped ripe olives
½ cup seasoned croutons, slightly crushed

Remove frozen macaroni and cheese from foil pan and place in 1-quart casserole. **COOK**, covered, **5 MINUTES**, stirring twice; set aside. Place celery, onion and water in small soup bowl; cover with saucer and **COOK 2 MINUTES**. Add to macaroni mixture along with tuna fish and olives. **COOK**, covered, **4 MINUTES** or until heated through. Top with crushed croutons before serving. 2 to 3 Servings

> **TIP:** For 4 to 5 Servings, double amounts and cook in 2-quart casserole for cook periods of 8 minutes; 2 minutes and 5 minutes. Use 1 to 2 cans tuna depending on personal taste and number of people to be served.

When starting with uncooked macaroni, you can have macaroni and cheese in just 15 minutes.

SIMPLE MACARONI AND CHEESE

1 cup uncooked macaroni
2 tablespoons flour
¼ cup chopped onion or 1 tablespoon instant minced onion
1 teaspoon salt
Dash Tabasco sauce
1 cup milk
1 cup water
2 tablespoons butter or margarine
1 cup (4 oz.) cubed or shredded cheese

In 2-quart casserole, combine macaroni, flour, onion, salt and Tabasco sauce. Stir in milk and water; dot with butter. **COOK**, covered, **10 TO 12 MINUTES** or until macaroni is just about tender, stirring occasionally. Stir in cheese. **LET STAND 3 TO 5 MINUTES** to finish cooking and melt cheese. 3 to 4 Servings

> **TIP:** For additional color and flavor, add 2 tablespoons chopped pimiento, 2 tablespoons chopped parsley or 1 teaspoon dry mustard.

Fruit Cup
Cheese and Shrimp Bake
Oriental Asparagus (119)
Chilled Lemon Soufflé (142)

1. Day before, prepare soufflé and assemble Cheese and Shrimp Bake.
2. About 30 minutes before serving, cook Cheese and Shrimp Bake.
3. Cook Asparagus.

This cheese and shrimp dish is assembled several hours ahead to allow the custard-milk mixture to soak into the bread. Try it for brunch or lunch — just put it in the oven about 18 minutes before serving time.

CHEESE AND SHRIMP BAKE

 8 slices bread
 2 cans (4½ oz. each) shrimp, drained
 ½ cup (1 stalk) chopped celery
 2 tablespoons chopped onion or
  ½ tablespoon instant minced onion
 1 can (10½ oz.) condensed cream of
  mushroom soup
 2 tablespoons lemon juice
 ½ teaspoon Worcestershire sauce
 4 oz. (1 cup) shredded or sliced American
  or Cheddar cheese
 ¾ cup milk
 3 eggs
 ¼ cup butter or margarine

Trim crusts from bread (use for dressing or croutons). Arrange 4 slices of bread on bottom of 2-quart (8 x 8) baking dish. Top with shrimp, celery, and onion. Combine soup with lemon juice and Worcestershire sauce; spoon over shrimp. Top with cheese and remaining 4 slices of bread. Beat together milk and eggs; pour over sandwich mixture. Cut butter into pieces and place over top. Cover with plastic wrap and refrigerate 6 to 12 hours or overnight.

To cook, loosen plastic wrap slightly and COOK 12 MINUTES or until mixture is bubbly near center. LET STAND, covered, 5 MINUTES before serving.   4 Servings

 TIP: A 6½-oz. can tuna fish, drained and flaked can be used for shrimp.

The taste of quiche without the crust. A good recipe for a hearty brunch or light supper, served with rolls and fruit.

CRUSTLESS QUICHE

 3 eggs
 1 cup half and half or evaporated milk
 ½ teaspoon salt
 ¼ teaspoon nutmeg
 1 tablespoon parsley flakes
 2 cups (8 oz.) shredded Swiss cheese
 ½ cup grated Parmesan cheese
 ⅔ cup (4 oz.) cubed Canadian-style bacon
  or cooked ham

In mixing bowl, beat eggs, half and half, salt and nutmeg until well mixed. Stir in parsley, cheeses and Canadian bacon. Pour into six 6-oz. custard cups. COOK, uncovered, 10 MINUTES (stir after 3 to 5 minutes to move cooked edges to center) or until knife inserted in center comes out clean. LET STAND 2 MINUTES to finish cooking. If desired, unmold on toasted English muffin halves or tomato slices to serve.   6 Servings

CHEDDAR CHICKEN CASSEROLE

 2 pouches (6½ oz. each) frozen creamed
  chicken
 1 package (12 oz.) frozen macaroni and
  cheese
 2 teaspoons chopped green onion tops
  or chives
 ½ cup chopped celery and tops
 ½ cup coarsely chopped cashew nuts or
  almonds

Remove frozen creamed chicken and macaroni from containers and place in 1½-quart casserole. COOK, covered, 8 MINUTES, turning twice. Stir in green onion, celery and nuts. COOK, covered, 6 MINUTES, stirring occasionally. If desired, just before serving top with buttered bread crumbs or crushed corn chips.   4 Servings

OVEN MACARONI AND CHEESE

 ¼ cup chopped onion or 1 tablespoon
  instant minced onion
 1 tablespoon butter or margarine
 1 can (10¾ oz.) condensed Cheddar
  cheese soup
 ½ cup milk
 1¼ cups water
 2 cups uncooked macaroni

In 2-quart casserole, combine all ingredients. COOK, covered, 10 MINUTES or until macaroni is just about tender, stirring occasionally. LET STAND, covered, 3 TO 5 MINUTES to finish cooking.   3 to 4 Servings

 TIP: For additional color and flavor, add 2 tablespoons chopped pimiento, 2 tablespoons chopped parsley or 1 teaspoon dry mustard.

Soup and Sandwiches

What could go together better than soup and a sandwich, either for lunch or a light dinner? Or, start your day off right with a breakfast mug of clear soup. Add soup as your first course for dinner . . . fix it ahead and then reheat it in bowls just before serving.

Soups: Recipes include both those made from quick home recipes and those that begin with a can of soup and take off from there. You can cook soup in a pitcher or you can often save dishes by heating prepared soup right in the serving bowls. To heat canned soup, see Lunch section page 20. You will save the most time when cooking a smaller amount of soup and one without a soup bone.

Sandwiches: Choose any sandwich form: open faced, bun, whole loaf or regular sandwiches of two bread slices. Firmly textured bread works best in the oven. The bread is usually toasted for more body and flavor and to prevent the filling from making the bread soggy. Sandwiches are placed on a paper towel or napkin in the oven to absorb any excess moisture.

Sandwich fillings are one of the best ways to utilize leftovers. Fillings can often be prepared ahead and the bread toasted; when ready to serve, just assemble the sandwiches and heat. The times do not differ between open faced and regular sandwiches because it is the filling, rather than the extra slice of bread, that determines the cooking time. Bread should be only warm when the filling is hot. If a filling is frozen, thaw first before combining with bread so the bread will not overcook in the time it takes to heat the filling. A meat sandwich such as roast beef or pastrami heats most evenly if the meat is thinly sliced. We have given cooking times for a range of individual servings with the recipes for occasions when you may need only one or a few sandwiches.

Since lentils cook relatively quickly for a dried pea or bean, they can be cooked with the microwave oven in the same time it takes to cook a ham hock. The lentils and ham will be tender and tasty, but some of the tissue around the ham meat may still be tough. This can easily be removed when removing the meat from the bone. This homemade soup can be ready to serve in an hour.

HAM AND LENTIL SOUP

> **1 cup (½ lb.) dry lentils**
> **1¼ to 1½-lb. ham hock**
> **1 medium onion, sliced**
> **1 carrot, sliced**
> **6 peppercorns or ¼ teaspoon pepper**
> **1 tablespoon Worcestershire sauce**
> **1 teaspoon salt**
> **6 cups water**

Sort and wash lentils. In 3 or 4-quart casserole, combine lentils, ham hock, onion, carrot, peppercorns, Worcestershire sauce, salt and 4 cups of the water. **COOK,** covered, **28 MINUTES,** stirring occasionally. Add remaining 2 cups water and **COOK,** covered, **14 MINUTES,** stirring occasionally. **LET STAND 10 MINUTES;** remove ham hock and cut meat from bone. Return meat to soup; if necessary, reheat.   **3 to 4 Servings**

TIPS: The water is added in two steps to reduce the chance of boiling over. If added all at once, be sure your container is large enough to handle boiling.

• Split peas will cook in about the same time as lentils. For split pea and ham soup, just substitute the same amount of split peas for lentils. The whole peas (not split) need longer cooking time and are cooked just as fast conventionally.

MENU

Potato Soup
Tuna Salad Buns (113)
Pickles and Relishes
Warm Cookie (22)

1. About 20 minutes before serving, cook soup.
2. Heat Tuna Salad Buns.
3. When ready, warm cookie.

Because of the large quantity of this soup, you will not save a lot of cooking time, but there are times when it may be convenient to just put it in the oven and stir it occasionally for even cooking. If you have a soup bone that you have cooked conventionally, these times would apply for adding vegetables and then cooking in your microwave oven.

GROUND BEEF-VEGETABLE SOUP

1 lb. ground beef
1 package (⅝ oz.) brown gravy mix
2 cups (1-lb. can) undrained tomatoes
1 medium onion, chopped or sliced
2 medium carrots, chopped
1 stalk celery, chopped
1 medium potato or rutabaga, cubed
3 cups water
1 tablespoon salt
⅛ teaspoon pepper
1 tablespoon Worcestershire sauce
1 bay leaf

In 3 or 4-quart casserole, crumble ground beef; sprinkle with gravy mix. COOK, uncovered, 5 MINUTES, stirring once. Add remaining ingredients; COOK, covered, 28 TO 30 MINUTES or until vegetables are desired doneness, stirring occasionally.   5 to 6 Servings

> **TIPS:** To use leftover cooked beef for soup, use about 3 cups cubed beef for ground beef and add 2 to 3 beef bouillon cubes. Follow directions above, eliminating first cooking period.
>
> • If desired, ½ cup uncooked rice or macaroni can be used for potato.

This very basic potato soup will be a family favorite. Soup and a sandwich will make a complete lunch.

POTATO SOUP

3 cups (4 med.) diced potatoes
¼ cup chopped onion or 1 tablespoon instant minced onion
½ teaspoon salt
1½ cups water
2 tablespoons flour
2 cups milk

In 2-quart casserole, combine potatoes, onion, salt and water. COOK, covered, 12 MINUTES or until potatoes are almost tender. Dissolve flour in a small amount of the milk. Stir flour mixture and remaining milk into potatoes; COOK, uncovered, 3 MINUTES or until mixture boils.   4 Servings

This delicately colored and flavored soup would be excellent for the first course of a meal.

SHRIMP BISQUE

2 tablespoons chopped onion
1 tablespoon butter or margarine
1 cup milk
1 teaspoon or cube chicken bouillon (crumble cube)
¼ teaspoon Tabasco sauce
1 teaspoon chopped chives
Half of 10¾-oz. can condensed tomato soup
1 tablespoon lemon juice
1 can (4½ oz.) shrimp, drained and coarsely chopped
1 cup light cream

In 1 or 1½-quart casserole or 4-cup measure, combine onion and butter. COOK, uncovered, 2 MINUTES or until onion is tender. Stir in milk, bouillon, Tabasco and chives. COOK, uncovered, 2 MINUTES. Stir in tomato soup and lemon juice; COOK, uncovered, 2 MINUTES, stirring once. Stir in shrimp and cream and COOK, uncovered, 1 MINUTE or until hot, but not boiling.   3 to 4 Servings

> **TIP:** After tomato soup is added to milk, it may appear curdled. Further cooking and the addition of cream result in a smooth soup.

CLAM CHOWDER

2 slices bacon
1 can (8 oz.) minced clams
1 large potato, peeled and cubed
¼ cup chopped onion or 1 tablespoon instant minced onion
1 medium carrot, sliced
2 tablespoons flour
1⅓ cups milk
1 teaspoon salt
Dash pepper

In 2-quart casserole, place bacon in layer. Cover with paper towel and COOK about 1 MINUTE, 30 SECONDS or until crisp. Remove towel and bacon, leaving extra drippings in pan. To drippings, add liquid from clams, potato, onion and carrot. COOK, covered, 8 MINUTES or until tender, stirring occasionally. Mix flour with small amount of milk to dissolve. Add to cooked mixture along with remaining milk, salt, pepper and minced clams. COOK, covered, 3 MINUTES or until mixture boils, stirring occasionally. LET STAND about 3 MINUTES before serving. Garnish with crumbled bacon and parsley.   3 to 4 Servings

> **TIP:** For Manhattan Chowder, add 1 cup (8 oz.) undrained tomatoes with clams; increase final cooking time to 4 minutes.

After filling serving dishes, you can heat soup until it is piping hot before placing on the table. This is especially handy for guest dinners where the soup sometimes cools before everyone is at the table and ready to eat.

FRENCH ONION SOUP

2 large or 3 medium onions, sliced
¼ cup butter or margarine
4 cups water
6 cubes or teaspoons beef bouillon
½ teaspoon paprika
1 teaspoon Worcestershire sauce
Dash pepper
4 to 6 slices French bread, toasted
Grated Parmesan cheese

In 4-quart casserole or Dutch oven, combine onions and butter. COOK, uncovered, 7 MINUTES or until onions are limp, stirring occasionally. Add water, bouillon, paprika, Worcestershire sauce and pepper. COOK, covered, 7 MINUTES or until hot and bubbly. Place in 4 to 6 individual soup bowls. Top with toasted bread and sprinkle generously with cheese. COOK 2 bowls at a time, uncovered, 30 SECONDS to melt cheese.   4 to 6 Servings

> **TIPS:** For a rich, wine flavor, use ½ cup white wine or sherry for part of water.
>
> • To make several hours ahead, cook onion and add remaining ingredients except bread. Let stand at room temperature. About 10 minutes before serving, cook 7 minutes or until hot and bubbly and continue as directed.

Add a sandwich with this soup for a complete meal. Leftovers can be added easily to make an even heartier soup (see Tip).

CHEESY CLAM CHOWDER

1½ cups (10-oz. pkg.) frozen mixed
    vegetables
1 can (10¾ oz.) condensed clam chowder
1 soup can milk (1¼ cups)
1 cup (4 oz.) shredded Cheddar cheese

In 1½ or 2-quart casserole, COOK mixed vegetables, covered, 6 MINUTES, stirring once. Add clam chowder, milk and cheese. COOK, covered, 3 MINUTES or until hot, stirring once.
4 to 6 Servings

> **TIP:** For a heartier soup, cubes of cooked meat or other vegetables can be added. Increase cooking time 30 seconds for each ½ cup of additional ingredients.

A chowder that can be prepared with common ingredients from the cupboard shelf and refrigerator.

CORNY WIENER CHOWDER

1 tablespoon butter or margarine
1 cup (2 stalks) sliced celery
1 lb. wieners, cut up
2 cups (1-lb. can) cream-style corn
1 can (10½ oz.) condensed cream of
    celery or potato soup
1 cup milk
1 to 1½ tablespoons Worcestershire sauce
½ teaspoon salt

In 2 or 3-quart casserole, combine butter and celery. COOK, covered, 5 MINUTES or until tender. Stir in remaining ingredients and COOK, covered, 6 MINUTES or until hot, stirring once.
6 Servings

> **TIP:** If desired, 2 cups cubed ham, luncheon meat or bologna can be used for wieners.

OYSTER VEGETABLE CHOWDER

2 tablespoons butter or margarine
¼ cup chopped onion or 1 tablespoon
    instant minced onion
1 medium carrot, sliced
1 stalk celery, sliced
½ teaspoon salt
⅛ teaspoon pepper
1 cup water
1 can (8 oz.) oysters, undrained
½ cup uncooked shell or elbow macaroni
1 cup milk

In 2-quart casserole, combine butter, onion, carrot, celery, salt and pepper. COOK, covered, 5 MINUTES or until carrots are tender. Add water, liquid from oysters and macaroni. COOK, covered, 8 MINUTES or until macaroni is tender, stirring once. Stir in milk and oysters; COOK, covered, 3 MINUTES or until hot.   4 Servings

Dry soup mixes need time to rehydrate after coming to a boil. We do not suggest using individual soup bowls because the soup may boil over the edge.

DEHYDRATED SOUP MIX

Prepare 1 envelope of soup mix in 4-cup measure or 1 or 2-quart casserole, using amount of liquid called for on package. COOK, covered, 2 TO 3 MINUTES or until mixture comes to a boil, stirring twice. LET STAND, covered, at least 5 MINUTES to allow food pieces to rehydrate. If necessary, reheat to serving temperature.

Crunchy almonds make this turkey salad filling something special.

HOT TURKEY SALAD BUNS

 2 cups chopped cooked turkey
 1 cup (4 oz.) shredded Cheddar cheese
 ¼ cup chopped celery
 ¼ cup diced roasted almonds
 ½ cup mayonnaise or salad dressing
 ¼ teaspoon salt
 2 tablespoons pickle relish or chopped
  sweet pickle
 6 hamburger buns

In mixing bowl, combine all ingredients except buns; mix well. Split buns and place bottom half on paper napkins or plate; spread with turkey mixture. Top with top of buns. COOK, uncovered, 3 MINUTES or until filling steams when top of bun is lifted.   6 Sandwiches

   TIPS: If buns are toasted, these could be assembled ahead for last minute heating.

   • Chopped peanuts or toasted sesame seeds can be used for almonds.

This recipe is ideal for using the leftovers from a turkey dinner. The vegetables could be leftovers also and a little leftover gravy could be used instead of the soup.

DAY AFTER TURKEY SANDWICHES

 4 slices bread, toasted
 4 slices turkey
 Half of 10½ -oz. can condensed cream of
  mushroom soup
 1 cup (8-oz. can) drained mixed vegetables
 4 slices processed cheese

Toast bread and arrange on serving plates. Arrange turkey on bread. Spoon soup on turkey, spreading evenly; top with vegetables and cheese slices. COOK 2 at a time, uncovered, 1 MINUTE, 30 SECONDS or until cheese is melted.   4 Sandwiches

   TIPS: Natural cheese could also be used, but the creamy consistency of the processed cheese makes it ideal for melting and shaping around the vegetables.

   • Other favorite canned or cooked vegetables can be used for mixed vegetables.

This is an easy way to have the flavors of turkey dinner . . . turkey, dressing and gravy all in a bun. They are good for assembling ahead, too.

TURKEY BUNS

 3 tablespoons butter or margarine
 1½ cups cubed cooked turkey
 ¼ cup chopped celery
 2 tablespoons chopped onion or
  ½ tablespoon instant minced onion
 ¼ teaspoon salt
 ¾ teaspoon poultry seasoning or sage
 4 hamburger buns
 1 package (⅝ oz.) brown gravy mix

In mixing bowl, melt butter (20 sec.). Add turkey, celery, onion, salt and sage. Leaving buns unsplit, hollow out top of buns, leaving ½ inch thick ring around edge. Crumble this extra bread into turkey mixture; mix well. Fill buns with turkey mixture. Place buns on paper napkin lined platter or tray; set aside. In 2-cup measure or gravy bowl, combine gravy mix with water as directed on package. COOK, uncovered, 2 MINUTES or until mixture boils, stirring occasionally. Cover and set aside. Heat buns by COOKING, uncovered, 2 MINUTES or until inside of filling feels warm. To serve, place buns on serving plates and spoon gravy over each.   4 Sandwiches

   TIPS: This can be assembled ahead for quick heating of buns and cooking of gravy just before serving.

   • Other types of buns can also be used.

This recipe uses the leftover small pieces of a turkey.

HOT TURKEY SANDWICHES

 1 cup chopped cooked turkey
 ¼ cup chopped onion or 1 tablespoon
  instant minced onion
 ⅓ cup mayonnaise or salad dressing
 2 teaspoons prepared mustard
 6 slices bread, toasted
 6 slices American cheese

In small bowl, combine turkey, onion, mayonnaise and mustard. Place toasted bread on 2 paper towel lined plates; spread evenly with filling. Top each with cheese slice. COOK 1 plate at a time, uncovered, 1 MINUTE or until cheese is melted.   6 Sandwiches

   TIP: If tray or platter is used, cook 6 sandwiches at a time, uncovered, 2 minutes.

A tasty mixture of corned beef, sauerkraut, apple and Swiss cheese, piled into pumpernickel buns and heated. They would be good to make ahead for quick reheating after a ball game.

REUBEN SALAD BUNS

1 can (15 oz.) corned beef or 8 oz. thin sliced corned beef
¾ cup (8-oz. can) drained sauerkraut
1 small apple, cored and shredded
1 cup (4 oz.) shredded Swiss cheese
2 tablespoons thousand island dressing
1 teaspoon dill weed
2 teaspoons prepared mustard
8 pumpernickel rolls or hamburger buns

In mixing bowl, break up canned corned beef with fork or cut fresh corned beef into shreds. Add remaining ingredients except buns; mix to combine. Cut buns in half horizontally and scoop out part of inside bread (can be saved and used for bread crumbs), leaving about ½ inch edge on crust of roll. Spoon corned beef into bottom half of rolls, pressing into cavity. Top with top half of roll. Heat on paper plates or napkins by cooking, uncovered, until steam appears when top of bun is lifted:

    8 rolls — 4 minutes
    4 rolls — 2 minutes, 30 seconds
    2 rolls — 1 minute, 30 seconds
    1 roll   — 1 minute

        8 Buns

Leftover cooked meats such as beef, ham, pastrami or corned beef can be heated for sandwiches. Several thin slices of meat heat more quickly than one thick slice.

SLICED MEAT SANDWICHES

Place bottom half of bun on paper plate or napkin. Arrange thinly sliced meat on bun until filling is ½-inch thick. Top with other half of bun. **COOK**, uncovered, until filling is hot:

    1 sandwich   — 30 seconds
    2 sandwiches — 45 seconds
    3 sandwiches — 1 minute
    4 sandwiches — 1 minute, 15 seconds

MENU

Reuben Sandwiches
Canned Soup (20)
Fruit
Brownies (147)

1. About 20 minutes before serving, cook brownies.
2. Heat soup in soup dishes.
3. Heat sandwiches.

Reuben sandwiches can be easily prepared in the oven. We especially liked them because there were few dirty dishes and we could reduce calories by not frying the sandwiches.

REUBEN SANDWICHES

8 slices pumpernickel or other dark bread
½ lb. thinly sliced corned beef
¾ cup (8-oz. can) well drained sauerkraut
2 to 3 tablespoons thousand island dressing
4 slices Swiss cheese (about 4 oz.)

Toast bread and arrange 4 slices on paper towels, napkins or small paper plates. Top each slice with corned beef, then drained sauerkraut, salad dressing and cheese. Top with other slices of toasted bread. **COOK**, uncovered, **3 TO 3½ MINUTES** or until cheese is melted in center. Serve immediately.   4 Sandwiches

TIPS: For 2 sandwiches, cook 1½ to 2 minutes; for 1 sandwich, cook 1 to 1¼ minutes.

• Leftover sandwiches can be reheated. If they have been refrigerated, cut each sandwich in half and separate halves, leaving about an inch between for ease in heating the centers.

• For ease in placing sandwiches in oven and removing, assemble on napkins or paper towels on plastic serving tray that will fit in the oven.

• To quickly and easily drain sauerkraut, drain excess liquid and then place sauerkraut in several layers of paper towel and squeeze out excess liquid.

Pictured, left to right: Sliced Meat Sandwich, left, using roast beef in small French loaf, Reuben Salad Buns (pumpernickel), left, Fishwich in hot dog bun, page 113, and Hot Tuna Sandwich Loaf, page 112.

A tangy barbecue sauce turns strips of canned luncheon meat into a new sandwich taste. Keep extra prepared filling on hand for quick sandwiches. Heat sandwiches directly on serving plates because the sauce may run onto the plates.

BARBECUED LUNCHEON SANDWICHES

1 tablespoon butter or margarine
½ cup (½ pepper) chopped green pepper
1 can (12 oz.) luncheon meat
¾ cup barbecue sauce
6 hamburger buns, split and toasted
6 slices cheese

In 1-quart casserole, combine butter and green pepper. **COOK**, uncovered, **2 MINUTES**, stirring once. Cut luncheon meat into strips or cubes and add to pepper along with barbecue sauce, mixing to combine. **COOK**, covered, **4 MINUTES** or until mixture is bubbly, stirring twice. Spoon mixture onto toasted buns, topping with cheese slice and top half of bun. Return to oven and **COOK**, uncovered, about **1 MINUTE** to melt cheese.   6 Sandwiches

> **TIPS:** The various seasoned luncheon meats are good used in this recipe, too.
>
> ● This idea would also be good with sliced bologna, cut into thin strips.
>
> ● To use leftover filling, spoon refrigerated filling into toasted bun; top with cheese and heat 1 bun about 1 minute or until cheese is melted.

A can of chili, slices of bread and cheese combine to make a sandwich with the flavor of lasagna. Some leftover casserole with a thick consistency could be used in place of the canned chili.

OPEN-FACED LASAGNA SANDWICHES

4 slices bread, toasted
1 can (15½ oz.) chili without beans
1 cup cottage cheese
4 slices American or Mozzarella cheese
Parmesan cheese

Toast bread and arrange on serving plates. Top with chili, spreading to edges. Spoon cottage cheese on chili and spread evenly. Top with cheese slices; sprinkle with Parmesan cheese. **COOK** 2 sandwiches at a time, uncovered, **1 MINUTE, 30 SECONDS** or until cheese is melted.   4 Sandwiches

HOT TUNA SANDWICH LOAF

3 hard-cooked eggs, chopped
1 can (6½ oz.) tuna fish, drained
¼ cup chopped onion or 1 tablespoon instant minced onion
1 teaspoon salt
¼ to ½ teaspoon pepper
½ teaspoon prepared mustard
½ cup mayonnaise or salad dressing
1 lb. loaf French bread (about 15 inches long)
3 slices (¾ oz. each) American cheese

In mixing bowl, combine eggs, tuna, onion, salt, pepper, mustard and mayonnaise; mix well. Cut off lengthwise top ⅓ of French bread. With a fork, hollow out bottom ⅔ of loaf. (Save unused bread for bread crumbs.) Fill loaf with tuna filling. Cut cheese slices in half and place over tuna mixture; replace top of loaf. **COOK**, uncovered, on paper towel, **3 MINUTES** or until cheese is melted. Slice 1 to 2 inches thick for serving.   6 Servings

> **TIP:** If French bread is longer than 15 inches, place in oven diagonally. If still too long, cut off one end to fit oven.

These burgers cook right in the teriyaki marinade, thus eliminating the need to marinate. They make good sandwiches with the tasty addition of a pineapple slice.

TERIYAKI BURGERS

½ cup soy sauce
3 tablespoons sugar
3 green onions, sliced
½ teaspoon ground ginger
⅛ teaspoon instant minced garlic or 1 clove garlic, minced
1 lb. ground beef
4 slices (8¼-oz. can) pineapple
4 hamburger buns, split and toasted

In 2-quart (8 x 8) baking dish, combine soy sauce, sugar, onions, ginger and garlic; mix well. Shape beef into 4 patties. Add to soy sauce mixture, turning over to coat. **COOK**, uncovered, **6 MINUTES** or until done, turning once during last half of cooking time. Top with pineapple slice and **COOK**, uncovered, **30 SECONDS** to warm pineapple. Serve on toasted buns.   4 Sandwiches

> **TIP:** If desired, make open-faced sandwiches by topping slices of French bread with meat patties and pineapple and spooning remaining teriyaki sauce over bread.

A tuna salad filling gives a new twist to hot dog buns. If the buns are toasted, they can be assembled in advance for last minute heating as needed.

TUNA SALAD BUNS

**1 can (6½ oz.) tuna fish, drained
1 cup (4 oz.) cubed cheese
2 tablespoons chopped onion or
  ½ teaspoon instant minced onion
2 tablespoons chopped green pepper
2 tablespoons pickle relish
¼ cup sliced stuffed green olives
⅓ cup mayonnaise or salad dressing
6 hot dog buns, split and if desired toasted**

In mixing bowl, combine all ingredients except buns. Place bottom half of buns on paper napkin lined tray or platter. Pile filling on buns; top with top half of buns. COOK, uncovered, **2 MINUTES, 15 SECONDS** or until filling steams when top of bun is lifted.   6 Sandwiches

> **TIP:** When heating one or two buns, wrap buns loosely in paper napkins and cook: 1 bun for 1 minute; 2 buns for 1 minute, 30 seconds.

Frozen fish sticks are easily thawed in the oven and then popped between split hot dog buns and heated. Try some with sliced dill pickles or pickle relish for added flavor.

FISHWICHES

**1 package (8 oz.) frozen precooked and
  breaded fish sticks (8 sticks)
Tartar sauce
4 hot dog buns, split**

Place fish sticks on paper lined plate in spoke fashion. To thaw, cook 1 minute; rest 1 minute; cook 30 seconds. If desired, toast buns; place on paper napkin or plate. Spread buns with tartar sauce. Place 2 fish sticks in each bun. COOK, uncovered, **1 MINUTE, 30 SECONDS** or until fish is hot.   4 Sandwiches

> **TIPS:** A thin sliced piece of American cheese, cut the shape of the bun, can be placed on top of fish sticks in buns. Increase cooking time to 1 minute, 40 seconds or until cheese melts.
>
> • Fishwiches are good served with coleslaw or add some to filling after heating.

Here's a good way to use leftover cooked beef or pork. Thinly sliced meat will assure the center of the sandwich being thoroughly hot.

BARBECUE WRAP-UPS

**4 hamburger buns, split
½ lb. cooked roast beef or pork,
  thinly sliced
¼ cup barbecue sauce
4 slices cheese**

Place bottom half of buns on paper plate or towel lined plate. Top with roast beef, barbecue sauce, cheese, and top half of bun. COOK, uncovered, **2 MINUTES, 30 SECONDS** or until hot.   4 Sandwiches

> **TIP:** Toasting the buns gives the sandwiches more flavor and prevents the bread from becoming soggy.

Tomato-rice soup makes these burgers quick and easy.

SPOON BURGERS

**1 lb. ground beef
½ teaspoon salt
⅛ teaspoon pepper
¼ teaspoon chili powder
Dash Tabasco sauce
½ cup chopped onion or 2 tablespoons
  instant minced onion
1 can (10½ oz.) condensed tomato-rice
  soup
6 to 8 hamburger buns, split and toasted**

In 1½-quart (8-inch round) baking dish, crumble ground beef. COOK, uncovered, **4 MINUTES,** stirring once. Drain. Add seasonings, onion and soup. COOK, covered with wax paper, **4 MINUTES,** stirring once. To serve, spoon on toasted buns.   6 to 8 Servings

An easy deviled ham spread makes hot open-faced sandwiches. The recipe calls for split hot dog buns but other types of rolls or toasted bread could be used as a base.

DEVILISH HAMWICHES

**1 can (2¼ oz.) deviled ham
1 cup (4 oz.) shredded Swiss cheese
1 tablespoon pickle relish
2 teaspoons prepared mustard
2 hot dog buns, split and toasted**

Combine all ingredients except buns in small mixing bowl. Place buns on paper napkins or plates spread with ham mixture. COOK, uncovered, **1 MINUTE, 10 SECONDS** or until cheese is melted.   4 Small Sandwiches

> **TIP:** Other types of shredded cheese can be used for Swiss. The time for melting may vary 5 to 10 seconds.

Vegetables

The color and flavor of vegetables cooked in the oven are superior to most other methods of cooking vegetables. You use very little water so there is no need to drain vegetables before serving and, therefore, less chance of losing nutrients.

All vegetables are cooked covered to completely utilize this small amount of water. When vegetables such as squash or potatoes are cooked whole, the shell or skin acts as the vegetable's own cover to keep in the heat during cooking.

Vegetables should still be a little firm when they are removed from the oven because they will continue to cook. The recipes in this book insure a crispness to your vegetable dishes; if you prefer vegetables with a softer texture, increase the cooking time slightly. You may want to look at the section on Sauces (pages 133, 134) for a sauce to accompany a particular vegetable.

Vegetable recipes cooked with a conventional oven are fairly adaptable to microwave cooking. However, with microwave cooking, salt is usually added near the end or after the cooking period to avoid drying out the vegetables. Even when leftover vegetables are reheated, they will come close to their original flavor and color.

You can cook frozen vegetables in their paper carton, rearranging or stirring the contents halfway through the cooking time. Also, individual servings can be removed from the economical large plastic bags of frozen vegetables and then cooked in a serving dish.

Canned vegetables take less time to cook than fresh or frozen vegetables because they are already cooked and just need heating. When you want to combine vegetables, remember to use all canned vegetables or combine fresh or frozen vegetables that have similar cooking times.

See page 28 for Simple Scalloped Potatoes recipe.

VEGETABLE	AMOUNT	COOKING DISH	METHOD	STIR OR RE-ARRANGE	TIME	SEASONINGS
Artichokes						
Fresh (3½ inches in diameter)	1	Wax paper or 2-quart covered casserole	Wrap in wax paper or place in casserole	None	4-4½ min.	Butter, Cream sauce, Hollandaise sauce, Lemon juice, Mornay sauce, Nutmeg
	2				6-7 min.	
	3				8-9 min.	
	4				10-11 min.	
Frozen (hearts)	10 oz. pkg.	1 qt. covered	Add 2 tbsp. water	Once	4-5 min.	
Asparagus						
Fresh (spears or cut)	¾ lb. (15 stalks)	1 qt. covered	Add ¼ cup water	Once	4-4½ min.	Bechamel sauce, Butter, Cheese Sauce, with Corn, Cream, Creamed egg sauce, Creamy dill sauce, Hollandaise sauce, Lemon butter, Sour cream sauce, Toasted almonds
	1½ lbs. (30 stalks)	2 qt. covered	Add ¼ cup water	Once	8-9 min.	
Frozen (spears or cut)	10 oz. pkg. (1½ cups)	1 qt. covered	Place icy side up	Once	7-8 min.	
	9 oz. pouch	——	Make slit in pouch	Once	5-6 min.	
Beans, green or wax						
Fresh	1 lb. (3 cups)	1½ qt. covered	Add ⅓ cup water	Once	10-12 min.	Butter, Cheese sauce, Chives, Cream sauce, Creamy mustard sauce, Crumbled bacon, Mushrooms, Nutmeg, Onions, Quick and easy tomato sauce, Toasted almonds, Water chestnuts
	2 lbs. (6 cups)	2 qt. covered	Add ⅓ cup water	Once	14-16 min.	
Frozen (French or cut)	10 oz. pkg. (1½ cups)	1 qt. covered	Add 2 tbsp. water Place icy side up	Once	6-7 min.	
	10 oz. pouch	——	Make slit in pouch	Once	6-7 min.	

VEGETABLE	AMOUNT	COOKING DISH	METHOD	STIR OR RE-ARRANGE	TIME	SEASONINGS
Beans, Lima						
Fresh	1 lb. (2 cups shelled)	1 qt. covered	Add ½ cup water	Once	8-10 min.	Butter, Cheese sauce, Chopped ham, with Corn, Crumbled bacon, Quick and easy tomato sauce, Sour cream sauce, Toasted almonds
	2 lbs. (4 cups shelled)	1½ qt. covered	Add ½ cup water	Once	12-14 min.	
Frozen (Ford-hook or baby)	10 oz. pkg.	1 qt. covered	Add ½ cup water	Once	9-10 min.	
	10 oz. pouch	——	Make slit in pouch	Once	6-7 min.	
Beets						
Fresh (Whole)	4 medium	2 qt. covered	Cover with water	None	15-17 min.	Butter, Orange juice concentrate, Orange marmalade, Pickled
Broccoli						
Fresh	1½ lbs.	1½ qt. covered Arrange stems toward outside of dish.	Split stems for uniform size. Add ¼ cup water	None	7-9 min.	Butter, Buttered bread crumbs, Cheese sauce, Creamed egg sauce, Creamy mustard sauce, Crumbled bacon, Hollandaise sauce, Mornay sauce, Parmesan cheese, Sour cream sauce, Speedy shrimp sauce, Toasted almonds
Frozen (spears or chopped)	10 oz. pkg.	1 qt. covered	Place icy side up	Once	7-8 min.	
	10 oz. pouch	——	Make slit in pouch	Once	6-7 min.	
Brussels Sprouts						
Fresh	½ lb. (2 cups)	1 qt. covered	Add 2 tbsp. water	Once	4-5 min.	Butter, with Carrots, Cream cheese, Cream sauce, Creamy mustard sauce, Hollandaise sauce
	1 lb. (4 cups)	1½ qt. covered	Add 2 tbsp. water	Once	6-7 min.	
Frozen	10 oz. pkg. (1½ cups)	1 qt. covered	Add 2 tbsp. water	Once	8-9 min.	
	10 oz. pouch	——	Make slit in pouch	Once	5-6 min.	
Cabbage						
Fresh	½ medium head (4 cups)	1½ qt. covered	Add 2 tbsp. water	Once	5-6 min.	Butter, Cheese sauce, Cream, Cream cheese, Creamy mustard sauce, Crumbled bacon, Nutmeg
	1 medium head (8 cups)	2½ qt. covered	Add 2 tbsp. water	Once	8-9 min.	
Carrots						
Fresh (Sliced or Slivered)*	2 medium	1 qt. covered	Add 2 tbsp. water	Once	4-5 min.	With Brussels sprouts, Butter, with Cauliflower, Cinnamon, Cloves, Cream, Cream cheese, Crumbled bacon, Ginger, Glazed, Mashed, Nutmeg, Parsley, with Peas
	4 medium	1 qt. covered	Add 2 tbsp. water	Once	7-8 min.	
	6 medium	1½ qt. covered	Add 2 tbsp. water	Once	9-10 min.	

*Diced — Cook 1-2 minutes less.

[handwritten note in left margin near Broccoli row: "I A 4 P. Bunch Not done After 9½ M."]

VEGETABLE	AMOUNT	COOKING DISH	METHOD	STIR OR RE-ARRANGE	TIME	SEASONINGS
Carrots — continued						
Frozen	10 oz. pkg.	1 qt. covered	Place icy side up	Once	7-8 min.	
	10 oz. pouch	——	Make slit in pouch	Once	6-7 min.	
*Diced — Cook 1-2 minutes less.						
Whole — Cook 1-2 minutes more; increase water to ¼ cup.						
Cauliflower						
Fresh	1 medium head (flowerets)	1½ qt. covered	Add 2 tbsp. water	Once	6-7 min.	Butter, Cheese sauce, Chives, Cream, Cream sauce, Hollandaise sauce, Nutmeg, Speedy shrimp sauce, Thousand island dressing
	1 medium head (whole)	1½ qt. covered	Add 2 tbsp. water	None	7-8 min.	
	1 large head (whole)	2½ qt. covered	Add 2 tbsp. water	None	12-14 min.	
Frozen	10 oz. pkg.	1 qt. covered	Place icy side up	Once	8-9 min.	
	10 oz. pouch	——	Make slit in pouch	Once	6-7 min.	
Celery						
Fresh	6 stalks (4 cups, sliced)	1½ qt. covered	Add 2 tbsp. water	Once	8-10 min.	Bouillon, Brown gravy mix, Butter, Cheese sauce, Cream sauce
Corn						
Fresh (cut from cob)	1½ cups (3 ears)	1 qt. covered	Add 2 tbsp. water or cream	Once	5-6 min.	Butter, Celery, Chive butter, Cream, Cream cheese, Crumbled bacon, Green pepper and pimiento, Onion dip, Parmesan cheese, Quick and easy tomato sauce
	3 cups (6 ears)	1 qt. covered	Add 2 tbsp. water or cream	Once	6-7 min.	
Frozen	10 oz. pkg. (1½ cups)	1 qt. covered	Add 2 tbsp. water or cream	Once	5-6 min.	
	10 oz. pouch	——	Make slit in pouch	Once	4-5 min.	
Corn on the Cob						
Fresh	1 ear	Wrap in wax paper or place in covered casserole	If desired, butter	None	2-2½ min.	Butter, Chive butter, Onion butter (onion soup mix and butter)
	2 ears	,,	,,	None	3-4 min.	
	3 ears	,,	,,	None	5-6 min.	
	4 ears	,,	,,	None	6-7 min.	
	6 ears	,,	,,	None	8-9 min.	
Frozen	2 ears	,,	,,	None	6-8 min.	
	4 ears	,,	,,	None	10-12 min.	
Onions						
Fresh (quartered)	8 small or 2 large	1 qt. covered	No water	None	6-7 min.	Butter, Cream, Cream cheese, Currant jelly, Nutmeg, Sour cream sauce
	4 large	1½ qt. covered	No water	None	8-9 min.	

VEGETABLE	AMOUNT	COOKING DISH	METHOD	STIR OR RE-ARRANGE	TIME	SEASONINGS
Onions — continued						
Frozen (In Cream Sauce)	10 oz. pkg.	1 qt. covered	No water	Once	5-6 min.	
	10 oz. pouch	1 qt. covered	Make slit in pouch	Once	5-6 min.	
Parsnips						
Fresh (quartered)	4 medium	1½ qt. covered	Add ¼ cup water	Once	7-8 min.	Bacon drippings, Bechamel sauce, Brown sugar glaze, Butter
Peas, Green						
Fresh (shelled)	2 lbs. (2 cups)	1 qt. covered	Add 2 tbsp. water	Once	7-8 min.	Butter, Carrots, Chives, Corn, Cream, Cream cheese, Creamed, Green onions, Mint, Mushrooms, Onion dip, Orange marmalade
	3 lbs. (3 cups)	1½ qt. covered	Add 2 tbsp. water	Once	9-10 min.	
Frozen	10 oz. pkg. (1½ cups)	1 qt. covered	Place icy side up	Once	5-6 min.	
	10 oz. pouch	1 qt. covered	Make slit in pouch	Once	5-6 min.	
Pods (frozen)	6 oz. pouch	——	Make slit in pouch	Once	2-3 min.	
Peas and Carrots						
Frozen	10 oz. pkg. (1½ cups)	1 qt. covered	Place icy side up	Once	6-7 min.	Butter, Chives, Cream, Crumbled bacon,
Peas, Black-Eyed						
Frozen	10 oz. pkg.	1 qt. covered	Add ¼ cup water	Once	10-11 min.	Bacon drippings, Butter, Corn, Cream, Ham
Potatoes, Baked						
Fresh	1 medium	Place on paper towel	——	None	3½-4 min.	Butter, Cheese, Chives, Crumbled bacon, Deep fried parsley, Green onions, Onion soup dip, Paprika, Sour cream, Toasted almonds, Whipped cream cheese
	2 medium	Place on paper towel	Leave 1-inch space between	None	6½-7 min.	
	3 medium	,,	,,	None	8½-9 min.	
	4 medium	,,	,,	None	10-11 min.	
	5 medium	,,	,,	None	13-14 min.	
	6 medium	,,	,,	None	15-16 min.	
	7 medium	,,	,,	None	18-19 min.	
	8 medium	,,	,,	None	21-22 min.	
Potatoes, Boiled						
Fresh (peeled and quartered)	2 medium	1½ qt. covered	Cover with water. Add ½ tsp. salt	None	8-10 min.	Bouillon, Butter, Cheese sauce, Chives, Creamed onions, Green onions, Onion soup mix, Paprika, Parsley
	4 medium	1½ qt. covered	Cover with water. Add ½ tsp. salt	None	15-18 min.	

VEGETABLE	AMOUNT	COOKING DISH	METHOD	STIR OR RE-ARRANGE	TIME	SEASONINGS
Potatoes, Sweet or Yams						
Fresh	1 medium	Place on paper towel		None	3-4 min.	Brown sugar glaze, Buttered, Cherry glaze, Crumbled bacon, Maple syrup glaze, Mashed, Miniature marshmallows, Pineapple glaze
	2 medium	Place on paper towel	Leave 1-inch space between	None	5-6 min.	
	4 medium	″	″	None	7-8 min.	
	6 medium	″	″	None	9-10 min.	
Spinach						
Fresh	1 lb. (4 cups)	2 qt. covered	Cook in water that clings to leaves	Once	5-6 min.	Butter, Cheese sauce, Cream cheese, Creamed egg sauce, Crumbled bacon, Lemon juice, Mushroom soup, Nutmeg, Onion dip, Sliced raw onion
Frozen (Leaf or chopped)	10 oz. pkg.	1 qt. covered	Place icy side up	Once	6-7 min.	
	10 oz. pouch	——	Make slit in pouch	Once	6-7 min.	
Squash, Acorn or Butternut						
Fresh (whole)	1 medium	None	Cook whole. Cut in half, remove seeds and season	None	6-8 min.	Brown sugar or honey glaze, Buttered, Cinnamon or nutmeg, Cooked apples or other fruit, Cranberry sauce, Maple syrup, Sausage
	2 medium	None	″	None	12-14 min.	
Squash, Hubbard						
Fresh	6″ x 6″ piece	1½ qt. covered or wrap in wax paper	Add ¼ cup water to casserole	Once	7-8 min.	Brown sugar glaze, Buttered, Maple syrup, Mashed with ginger or nutmeg, Orange marmalade, Pineapple
Frozen	10 oz. pkg.	1 qt. covered	Add butter, if desired	Once	5-6 min.	
Squash, Zucchini						
Fresh (sliced)	2 medium (3 cups)	1 qt. covered	Add ¼ cup water	Once	6-7 min.	Butter, Chive sour cream, Creamed egg sauce, Parmesan cheese
Turnips						
Fresh (cut in eighths)	4 medium	1½ qt. covered	Add ¼ cup water	Once	10-12 min.	Butter, Chives, Cream, Lemon juice, Mashed
Vegetables, Mixed						
Frozen	10 oz. pkg. (1½ cups)	1 qt. covered	Add 2 tbsp. water	Once	5-6 min.	Bechamel sauce, Buttered, Cheese sauce, Cream, Cream cheese, Crumbled bacon
	10 oz. pouch	——	Make slit in pouch	Once	5-6 min.	

*Toasted almonds, crunchy celery, asparagus
and water chestnuts cook together in a soy
flavored butter.*

ORIENTAL ASPARAGUS

  2 tablespoons butter or margarine
  2 tablespoons slivered almonds
  1½ cups (10-oz. pkg.) frozen cut asparagus
  ½ cup (1 stalk) sliced celery
  **½ cup (5-oz. can) sliced and drained
     water chestnuts**
  1 tablespoon soy sauce

In 1-quart casserole, combine butter and
almonds. COOK, uncovered, **3 MINUTES** or
until golden brown, stirring occasionally.
Remove almonds, leaving butter in casserole.
To butter, add asparagus, celery and water
chestnuts. COOK, covered, **7 MINUTES** or until
desired doneness, stirring occasionally during
last half of cooking time. Stir in soy sauce and
almonds and let stand, covered, a few minutes
to heat through.   4 Servings

> **TIP:** To eliminate an extra dish, place
> toasted almonds in water chestnut can
> until ready to use.

*A combination that tastes like a version of
bean salad but is served warm. This would be
a good dish for a buffet supper or picnic.*

HOT BEAN COMPOTE

  4 slices bacon
  ⅓ cup sugar
  1 tablespoon cornstarch
  1 teaspoon salt
  ⅛ teaspoon pepper
  ½ cup vinegar
  1 medium onion, sliced
  1½ cups (1-lb. can) drained cut green beans
  1½ cups (1-lb. can) drained cut wax beans
  1½ cups (1-lb. can) drained red kidney beans

In 2-quart casserole, arrange bacon in single
layer. Cover with paper towel and COOK
2½ TO 2¾ MINUTES or until crisp. Remove
paper towel and bacon, leaving drippings in
casserole. To drippings, add sugar, cornstarch,
salt and pepper; blend well. Stir in vinegar, then
remaining ingredients; mixing well. COOK,
covered, **10 MINUTES** or until sauce has boiled
and thickened slightly, stirring occasionally.
Crumble bacon over top.   8 to 10 Servings

*Pictured, top to bottom: Tangy Mustard Cauliflower, page
121, Oriental Asparagus, above, Corn on the Cob, page
116 (cooked in husks rather than wax paper), Baked
Lentils, page 120, and Double Onion Bake, page 123.*

BAKED BEANS

2 cups (1-lb. can) baked beans or beans
    and pork in tomato sauce
1 small (¼ cup) onion, chopped, or
    1 tablespoon instant minced onion
¼ cup catsup
½ teaspoon dry or prepared mustard
2 tablespoons brown sugar
4 slices bacon, cut into pieces

In 1-quart casserole, combine all ingredients
except bacon; mix well. Top with bacon.
COOK, covered, 10 MINUTES or until hot and
bacon is cooked.   4 Servings

*Lentils cook fairly quickly for a dry pea or
bean. Here they are flavored like baked beans,
but prepared with just 35 minutes cooking. A
large casserole is used because of boiling
during first cooking period.*

BAKED LENTILS

1 cup (½ lb.) dry lentils
3 cups water
2 slices bacon, cut into small pieces
¼ cup firmly packed brown sugar
¼ cup (1 small) chopped onion or
    1 tablespoon instant minced onion
¼ cup chili sauce
¼ cup molasses
1 cup water
1 teaspoon salt
1 teaspoon dry or prepared mustard

Wash and sort lentils. In 3 or 4-quart casserole,
combine lentils and 3 cups water. COOK,
covered, 20 MINUTES, stirring occasionally.
Stir in remaining ingredients and COOK,
covered, 15 MINUTES or until lentils are just
about tender, stirring occasionally. LET STAND
at least 5 MINUTES before serving.

5 to 6 Servings

TIP: If lentils become dry, just add
additional water.

HARVARD BEETS

¼ cup sugar
1 tablespoon cornstarch
½ teaspoon salt
Dash pepper
¼ cup vinegar
1 cup beet liquid plus water
1 can (1 lb.) diced beets, drain and
    reserve liquid

In 1-quart casserole, combine sugar, cornstarch,
salt, and pepper. Stir in vinegar, liquid and
beets. COOK, covered, 6 MINUTES or until
mixture boils and thickens slightly, stirring
occasionally during last half of cooking time.

4 to 5 Servings

*Although we've used canned beets here, the
same technique can be used with freshly
cooked beets.*

PICKLED BEETS

2 cups (1-lb. can) drained sliced or whole
    beets (Reserve ⅓ cup liquid)
⅓ cup sugar
⅓ cup beet liquid or water
⅓ cup vinegar
1 teaspoon pickling spice, if desired

In 3 or 4-cup serving dish, combine drained
beets, sugar, liquid and vinegar. Tie pickling
spice in piece of cheesecloth or nylon reinforced
paper towel. Add to beets. COOK, covered,
4 MINUTES or until mixture boils, stirring once.
Cool and remove pickling spices before serving.
Leftovers will keep several weeks in refrigerator.

2 Cups Pickles

TIP: If desired, use 3 whole cloves, 2 whole
allspice and ½ stick cinnamon for pickling
spice.

*This company dish has a very mild flavored
lemon sauce poured over the broccoli.
Almonds are toasted in the oven and
sprinkled over the sauce.*

BROCCOLI WITH LEMON SAUCE

½ cup slivered almonds
1 tablespoon butter or margarine
2 packages (10 oz.) frozen broccoli spears
2 packages (3 oz.) cream cheese
⅓ cup milk
1 teaspoon grated lemon peel
1 tablespoon lemon juice
½ teaspoon ground ginger
¼ teaspoon salt

In small bowl, combine almonds and butter.
COOK, uncovered, 3 MINUTES, stirring twice.
Set aside. Remove wax or foil overwrap, place
packages of frozen broccoli in oven and
COOK 5 MINUTES. Open packages and
rearrange broccoli. Close packages and COOK
5 MINUTES or until broccoli is just about
tender. Let stand while preparing sauce. In
2-cup measure, soften cream cheese (30 sec.).
Cream until smooth. Add milk, lemon peel,
lemon juice, ginger and salt. COOK,
uncovered, 1 MINUTE, 30 SECONDS or until
hot. Place broccoli spears on serving platter,
pour on sauce and sprinkle with almonds.

6 to 8 Servings

TIPS: If necessary, the broccoli with sauce
can be returned to oven about 1 minute
or until hot.

• Fresh broccoli can be used, cooking in
    covered casserole as directed in
    cooking chart.

ONION-TOPPED BROCCOLI

**2 packages (10 oz. each) frozen broccoli
spears**
1 can (5 oz.) water chestnuts, sliced
**1 to 2 cans (10½ oz. each) condensed
cream of celery or mushroom soup**
**Half of 3½-oz. can French-fried onion
rings**

In 2-quart (12 x 7) baking dish, place frozen
broccoli, icy side up. **COOK,** covered with wax
paper, **8 MINUTES** or until broccoli is just about
tender, rearranging once. Sprinkle water
chestnuts over broccoli; top with soup.
Arrange onion rings on top. **COOK,** uncovered,
4 MINUTES or until hot. 6 to 8 Servings

> **TIPS:** Leftovers are good reheated in the
> microwave oven.
>
> • These flavors are good with celery or
> green beans. Use 3 cups of fresh celery or
> 2 packages French-cut green beans. Cook
> as directed in cooking chart, page 114.
> A 1½-quart (10 x 6) or 2-quart (8 x 8)
> baking dish can be used.

*The oven helps make this attractive casserole
easy by cooking the broccoli and the
cheese sauce.*

CHEESY BROCCOLI

**2 packages (10 oz. each) frozen broccoli
spears**
2 tablespoons butter or margarine
2 tablespoons flour
½ teaspoon salt
1 cup milk
½ to 1 cup shredded Cheddar cheese
1 fresh tomato, sliced

Remove wax or foil overwrap, place packages of
frozen broccoli in oven and **COOK**
6 MINUTES. Open packages and rearrange
broccoli. Close packages and **COOK**
2 MINUTES or until broccoli is just about tender.
After broccoli cooks, prepare cheese sauce by
melting butter in 2-cup measure (30 sec.).
Blend in flour and salt. Stir in milk. **COOK,**
uncovered, **2 MINUTES** or until mixture boils
and thickens, stirring occasionally during last
half of cooking time. Stir in cheese until melted.
Arrange broccoli on serving plate. Sprinkle with
salt to taste. Top with cheese sauce; arrange
sliced tomatoes on cheese sauce. **COOK,**
uncovered, **2 MINUTES** to heat tomatoes.
6 to 8 Servings

> **TIP:** Fresh broccoli can be used, cooking
> in covered casserole as directed in
> cooking chart.

*Nutmeg enhances the flavor of this recipe.
Cabbage retains a fresh green color, even
when cooked.*

CHEESY CABBAGE

4 cups (½ med. head) cabbage, shredded
½ teaspoon salt
¼ cup milk
**¼ cup chopped onion or 1 tablespoon
instant minced onion**
2 tablespoons butter or margarine
Dash nutmeg, if desired
½ cup shredded cheese

In 2-quart casserole, combine cabbage, salt,
milk, onion, butter and nutmeg. **COOK,** covered,
6 MINUTES or until just about tender, stirring
once. Stir in cheese and **LET STAND**
2 MINUTES before serving. 4 Servings

*Cauliflower has a delicious taste when cooked
in the microwave oven. This idea for serving
is very simple, but special looking.*

TANGY MUSTARD CAULIFLOWER

1 medium head cauliflower
½ cup mayonnaise or salad dressing
**¼ teaspoon instant minced onion or
½ tablespoon minced onion**
1 teaspoon prepared mustard
½ cup shredded Cheddar cheese

Place cauliflower in 1½-quart casserole or other
casserole with cover that holds cauliflower. Add
2 tablespoons water. **COOK,** covered, **7 TO
8 MINUTES** or until just about tender. Combine
mayonnaise, onion and mustard, mixing well.
Place cooked cauliflower on serving plate.
Spread mayonnaise mixture over top and about
halfway down sides. Sprinkle with cheese.
COOK, uncovered, **1 MINUTE** to heat topping
and melt cheese. 6 to 8 Servings

> **TIP:** The topping can be spooned over
> cooked cauliflower floweretes. For 10-oz.
> package, use half the topping amounts.

*Carrots team with apple and brown sugar for
this tasty combination.*

GLAZED CARROTS

4 to 5 medium carrots, sliced
1 tart cooking apple, peeled and chopped
2 tablespoons brown sugar
2 tablespoons butter or margarine
2 tablespoons water
¼ teaspoon salt

In 1-quart casserole, combine all ingredients
except salt. **COOK,** covered, **7 TO 8 MINUTES**
or until carrots are just about tender. Sprinkle
with salt. 5 to 6 Servings

A glaze of honey and butter coats these carrots as they cook.

HONEY GLAZED CARROTS

4 medium carrots, sliced or cut into strips
2 tablespoons butter or margarine
2 tablespoons honey
2 tablespoons water
¼ teaspoon salt

In 1-quart casserole, combine carrots, butter, honey and water. COOK, covered, 7 TO 8 MINUTES or until carrots are just about tender, stirring occasionally. Stir in salt.   4 Servings

> **TIP:** If desired, add ¼ teaspoon ground ginger or 1 teaspoon chopped candied ginger with honey.

This family vegetable dish is stirred once during cooking and then allowed to finish cooking without being stirred so it will set like a custard.

CORN PUDDING

2 tablespoons butter or margarine
2 eggs, slightly beaten
1 cup milk
2 cups (17-oz. can) cream-style corn
2 tablespoons flour
1 teaspoon salt
½ teaspoon pepper

In 1-quart casserole, melt butter (20 sec.). Add remaining ingredients, mixing well. COOK, covered, 9 MINUTES or until pudding is just slightly soft in the center, stirring once. LET STAND 2 MINUTES before serving.
4 to 6 Servings

Corn relish can be made any time of year with canned corn. Make several jars and keep in refrigerator for 2 to 3 weeks.

CORN RELISH

2 cups (1-lb. can) drained whole kernel corn (Reserve 2 tablespoons liquid)
⅓ cup pickle relish
⅓ cup chopped pimiento
⅓ cup chopped green pepper
¼ cup sugar
¼ cup (1 small) chopped onion or 1 tablespoon instant minced onion
¼ cup vinegar
2 teaspoons cornstarch
½ teaspoon celery seed
1 tablespoon prepared mustard

In 4-cup serving dish, combine all ingredients, mixing well. COOK, covered, 6 MINUTES or until mixture boils and thickens slightly, stirring twice. Cool before serving. Store in refrigerator.
2½ Cups Relish

DOUBLE ONION BAKE

¼ cup slivered or chopped almonds
1 teaspoon butter or margarine
1 package (10 oz.) frozen creamed onions
¼ cup shredded Cheddar cheese
1 tablespoon parsley flakes
One-fourth of 3½-oz. can French-fried
**   onion rings**

In 1-quart casserole, combine almonds and
butter. COOK, uncovered, 3 MINUTES, stirring
twice. Add frozen onions, cheese and parsley.
COOK, covered, 5 MINUTES or until onions are
tender, stirring once. Sprinkle with onion rings.
2 to 3 Servings

TIPS: If using creamed onions in a pouch,
place pouch in oven and cook 2 minutes
for ease in removing from pouch. Reduce
remaining cooking time to 3 minutes.

• For 4 to 6 servings, use 1½-quart
casserole, double ingredient amounts and
increase onion cooking time to 8 to
9 minutes.

• Prepare this recipe and use to fill whole
tomatoes. See Corn Filled Tomatoes,
page 125.

GLAZED ONIONS

8 small whole onions, peeled
2 tablespoons butter or margarine
½ cup apple jelly

In 1-quart casserole, COOK onions, covered,
6 MINUTES or until onions are tender. Drain.
Stir in butter and jelly. COOK, uncovered,
1 MINUTE or until jelly melts.   3 to 4 Servings

*This very colorful dish uses frozen peas that,
in this recipe, taste as if they were fresh.*

PEAS WITH ONIONS AND MUSHROOMS

2 tablespoons butter or margarine
¼ cup chopped onion or 1 tablespoon
**   instant minced onion**
½ cup (4-oz. can) drained mushroom
**   stems and pieces**
1½ cups (10-oz. pkg.) frozen peas
Dash pepper
Dash allspice
¼ teaspoon salt

In 1-quart casserole, combine butter and onion.
COOK, covered, 2 MINUTES or until onion is
tender. Add mushrooms, frozen peas, pepper
and allspice. COOK, covered, 5 MINUTES,
30 SECONDS or until peas are just about
tender, stirring once. Stir in salt.   4 Servings

*Pictured, top to bottom: Acorn Squash 'N Apples, page
125, Pickled Beets, page 120, Stuffed Baked Potatoes, right,
and Cheesy Broccoli, page 121.*

*Fresh from the garden or the market, tiny
potatoes and fresh peas can be easily cooked
in your microwave oven. Since potatoes, peas
and sauce are cooked in the oven, plan to
cook the main dish conventionally or serve
with a roast that has a long resting period
before serving.*

CREAMED GARDEN POTATOES AND PEAS

1 lb. small early red skin potatoes
1½ lbs. fresh peas in pod (1½ cups shelled)
2 tablespoons butter or margarine
1 tablespoon chopped onion or 1 teaspoon
**   instant minced onion**
2 tablespoons flour
1¼ teaspoons salt
¼ teaspoon dill weed
⅛ teaspoon pepper
1½ cups milk

Cook potatoes on layer of paper towel in oven,
first pricking skin of each at least once with a
fork to prevent bursting during cooking. COOK
8 TO 9 MINUTES or until potatoes begin to
soften when pressed. Remove and set aside.
Shell peas and wash. Place in serving dish, add
2 tablespoons water and COOK, covered with
plate or plastic wrap, 5 MINUTES. Set aside.
In 4-cup measure, combine butter and onion.
COOK, uncovered, 1 MINUTE, stirring once.
Blend in flour, salt, dill and pepper. Stir in milk,
mixing well. COOK, uncovered, 3 MINUTES,
30 SECONDS or until mixture boils. Meanwhile
peel potatoes and arrange in serving dish with
peas. Pour sauce over vegetables. If necessary,
reheat by COOKING, uncovered, 1 TO
2 MINUTES or until hot.   4 to 5 Servings

STUFFED BAKED POTATOES

4 medium potatoes
2 tablespoons butter or margarine
½ to ¾ cup milk
Salt and pepper to taste
½ cup shredded American or Cheddar
**   cheese**

Bake potatoes as directed on page 117. LET
STAND, uncovered, 5 MINUTES. Cut potatoes
in half. Scoop out potato into mixing bowl,
being careful not to break or tear shell.
(A paper towel will protect hand from heat of
potato.) Mash potato; add butter, milk, salt and
pepper; mixing well. Fill potato shells, placing
on serving plate. Top with cheese. COOK,
uncovered, 3 MINUTES or until hot.
4 Large or 8 Small Servings

TIPS: If made ahead and refrigerated,
increase cooking time to 5 minutes.

• Potatoes can be stuffed and frozen.
Thaw and heat by cooking, uncovered,
15 minutes or until hot.

Sour cream and cheese turn mashed potatoes into something special. The timing and method for preparing the potatoes can be used as a guide for preparing mashed potato flakes in the oven.

SAVORY POTATOES

    1½ cups water
    ½ teaspoon salt
     2 tablespoons butter or margarine
    ½ cup milk
    1½ cups mashed potato flakes
    ½ cup sour cream
    ½ teaspoon onion salt
     1 egg
    Shredded cheese

In 1½ or 2-quart casserole, combine water, salt and butter. COOK, covered, **2 MINUTES, 30 SECONDS** or until mixture boils. Add milk and with fork stir in potato flakes. Stir in sour cream, onion salt and egg; mix well. Arrange in casserole; sprinkle with cheese. COOK, covered, **4 MINUTES** or until hot.   4 to 5 Servings

> **TIPS:** To make ahead, prepare through sprinkling with cheese. When ready to serve, complete final cooking, adding 1 minute if potatoes have been refrigerated.
>
> • If desired, 3 cups mashed potatoes can be used, adding sour cream, onion salt, egg and cheese as directed.
>
> • For 2 servings, prepare in 1-quart casserole and use half of ingredient amounts except use 1 egg. Cook 1 minute, 30 seconds to heat water and 2 minutes, 30 seconds to heat finished potatoes.

For holiday dinners, prepare this, as well as the mashed potatoes, early in the day and reheat just before serving. This will free the oven for cooking a fresh or frozen vegetable and last minute reheating of a platter of sliced turkey.

GLAZED SWEET POTATOES

    4 medium sweet potatoes
    ½ cup firmly packed brown sugar
    ¼ cup butter or margarine

Cook potatoes as directed on page 118. Peel and slice, arranging in 1½-quart casserole. Sprinkle with brown sugar and dot with butter. COOK, covered, **6 MINUTES** or until heated through, occasionally spooning glaze over potatoes.   6 to 8 Servings

MASHED POTATOES

Cook potatoes as directed for baked or boiled potatoes in cooking chart on page 117. Peel or drain; mash, adding milk, butter and seasoning as desired.

These yam-topped peach halves would make an attractive garnish on a platter of sliced turkey, fried chicken or pork roast.

PEACHY YAMS

     1 can (1 lb. 13 oz.) peach halves
    2½ cups (1 lb. 1-oz. can) mashed cooked
        sweet potatoes or yams
     2 tablespoons brown sugar
     2 tablespoons butter or margarine
     2 tablespoons brandy
    ½ tablespoon grated orange peel
    ¼ teaspoon salt

Drain peach halves, placing 4 tablespoons syrup in mixing bowl. Arrange peach halves cut-side up on serving plate. (To make peaches stand upright, cut thin slice from bottom, placing this piece in the hollow on upper side.) To peach syrup, add remaining ingredients, mixing well. Spoon mixture onto peach halves. Sprinkle with additional brown sugar. COOK, uncovered, **4 MINUTES** or until hot.   6 to 7 Servings

> **TIPS:** These can be assembled ahead and then heated when ready to serve.
>
> • Additional peach syrup can be substituted for brandy.
>
> • The amount of peach syrup needed may vary with the type of potatoes used. We used vacuum packed potatoes which have no liquid. If using ones with liquid, drain the liquid and add only enough peach syrup to moisten.

Brown sugar and nuts make a caramel topping on these sweet potatoes.

SWEET POTATOES BRÛLÉE

    2½ cups (1 lb. 1-oz. can) mashed cooked
        sweet potatoes or yams
     2 tablespoons butter or margarine
     3 tablespoons orange juice
    Dash salt
    ⅛ teaspoon cinnamon, if desired
     3 tablespoons chopped pecans or walnuts
    ¼ cup firmly packed brown sugar

In 1-quart casserole, combine potatoes, butter, orange juice, salt and cinnamon; mix well. Arrange evenly in casserole. Sprinkle with pecans and brown sugar. COOK, covered with wax paper, **4 MINUTES** or until hot.

4 to 5 Servings

> **TIPS:** The amount of orange juice needed may vary with potatoes. We used a vacuum pack which does not contain liquid. If using ones with liquid, drain and add only enough orange juice to moisten.
>
> • Try this topping with cooked squash, too.

GLAZED SQUASH

4 cups (2 lb.) cubed hubbard or other winter squash (1-inch cubes)
⅓ cup butter or margarine
⅓ cup honey
1 teaspoon salt
1 tablespoon grated orange peel

In 2-quart casserole, combine all ingredients. COOK, covered, **6 TO 8 MINUTES** or until tender, stirring occasionally.   4 to 5 Servings

Apples — fresh or prepared pie filling — make a great addition to acorn squash halves.

ACORN SQUASH 'N APPLES

2 acorn or butternut squash
Salt
2 medium apples, peeled and sliced
8 tablespoons brown sugar
4 tablespoons butter or margarine
Cinnamon

Leave squash whole and **COOK 8 TO 10 MINUTES** or until they feel soft to the touch. **LET STAND 5 MINUTES.** Cut in half and remove seeds. Place cut-side up in shallow baking dish. Sprinkle with salt. Fill with apples, top each half with 2 tablespoons brown sugar, 1 tablespoon butter and dash of cinnamon. **COOK,** covered with wax paper, **4 TO 5 MINUTES** or until apples are tender.

4 Servings

> **TIPS:** If desired, use the frozen scalloped apples, thawed, or prepared pie filling to spoon into the squash halves. Omit brown sugar and butter and reduce final cooking period to 2 minutes or until hot.
>
> • If desired, add 1 tablespoon raisins with apples to each squash half.

The flavors of onion dip and spinach — a winning combination even for those not fond of spinach.

SPINACH DELISH

1 package (10 oz.) frozen chopped spinach
½ cup sour cream
2 tablespoons dry onion soup mix

In 1-quart casserole, place spinach, icy side up. **COOK,** covered, **6 MINUTES** or until just about tender, stirring once. Stir in sour cream and onion soup mix. **COOK,** covered, **30 SECONDS.** Let stand, covered, a few minutes to finish cooking.   3 to 4 Servings

> **TIP:** For 6 servings, use 1½-quart casserole, double ingredient amounts and use cooking periods of 8 minutes and 1 minute.

This is a good combination for late fall when corn, tomatoes and green pepper are plentiful. Hollowed out tomatoes make good "servers" for many cooked vegetables.

CORN FILLED TOMATOES

6 large or 8 medium tomatoes
Salt
2 tablespoons butter or margarine
1 tablespoon chopped onion or 1 teaspoon instant minced onion
2 tablespoons chopped green pepper
2 cups (16-oz. can) drained whole kernel corn
¼ cup crushed potato chips, crackers or bread crumbs
Grated Parmesan cheese

Cut off tops of tomatoes and hollow out inside (grapefruit knife or spoon works well). (Save inside of tomatoes and add to salad, casserole or other vegetable dishes.) Place hollowed out tomatoes on serving plate; sprinkle with salt. In mixing bowl, combine butter, onion and green pepper. **COOK,** uncovered, **2 MINUTES,** stirring once after butter melts. Stir in corn and crushed chips. Spoon into tomatoes, sprinkle with Parmesan cheese. **COOK,** uncovered, **5 MINUTES** or until heated through.

6 to 8 Servings

Fresh tomatoes are topped with buttery bread crumbs and Parmesan cheese. For another tomato recipe, see Tomatoes with Mayonnaise Topping, page 26.

CHEESY CRUMB TOMATOES

4 tomatoes
⅓ cup bread crumbs
2 tablespoons butter or margarine
2 tablespoons grated Parmesan cheese
½ teaspoon salt
Dash pepper

Cut tomatoes in half crosswise and arrange on serving plate cut side up. In small bowl, combine bread crumbs and butter. **COOK,** uncovered, **3 TO 4 MINUTES** or until golden brown, stirring frequently. Stir in remaining ingredients. Sprinkle crumb mixture over each tomato half. **COOK,** uncovered, **3 TO 4 MINUTES** or until hot.   4 Servings

> **TIPS:** For 2 tomatoes, use half the ingredient amounts and cook 1 minute, 30 seconds.
>
> • For a bacon flavor, cook 2 to 3 slices bacon, use drippings for butter and crumble bacon over top of crumb mixture.

Breads and Salads

You can prepare a variety of breads in your microwave oven although we have found some that work better than others. All kinds of breads rise well in the oven. Best results are obtained when breads are cooked uncovered.

Quick Breads: We have given recipes for a caramel biscuit ring that uses refrigerated dough, a coffee cake made from scratch and another coffee cake that begins with a mix. Most basic coffee cakes need additional color such as fruit toppings or brown sugar glaze. Any batter will rise higher when cooked in a microwave oven so fill the baking dish only half full rather than the customary two thirds. A coffee cake mix tends to overflow a smaller round dish so it is a good idea to use an 8-inch square or a 10 x 6-inch oblong dish. If you feel that your baking dish is too small, you can always put extra batter in custard cups to make muffins. There is also a bran muffin recipe with a batter that can be refrigerated or frozen; you can bake just a few muffins at a time and store the remainder of the batter to use whenever you like.

Yeast Breads: We have included a couple yeast bread recipes for you to try. One has to remember that there will be no browning or hard crust so you may want to try a bread with a dark dough, such as the Casserole Bread or one that is to be toasted later, such as the English Muffin Bread. You can also use your oven to thaw and proof frozen bread dough. Bread baked in the oven is especially good for sandwiches because it does not have a hard crust and it will stay moist for several days. Your oven also can be used to reheat any bread or rolls, giving even slightly stale bread a fresh taste. Reheat bread and rolls on a paper napkin, paper plate or cloth napkin to absorb moisture.

See the Breakfast section (page 13) for reheating pancakes, waffles, and French toast.

To go with bread: Garlic bread will have more flavor if you add the garlic to butter and heat it before buttering the bread.

If you have forgotten to take butter out of the refrigerator before a meal, you can soften it slightly in the oven.

The oven can be used to dry bread thoroughly before putting it into a blender to make bread crumbs.

Pictured, clockwise: Wilted Lettuce Salad, page 131, Banana Bread and Corn Muffins made from mixes, page 128, English Muffin Bread ready for toasting, page 130, and Casserole Bread, page 130.

REHEATING CHART – BREAD ITEMS

Heated bread items will be hotter in the center than the outside because the center contains more moisture than the crust. (Overcooking tends to make bread items tough or rubbery.) Bread should be reheated on a paper napkin, paper plate or cloth napkin to absorb moisture.

		COOKING TIMES	
PRODUCT	AMOUNT	ROOM TEMPERA-TURE	FROZEN
Sweet Rolls	1	15 seconds	20 seconds
	2	20 seconds	30 seconds
	3	25 seconds	40 seconds
	4	30 seconds	50 seconds
Bread Slices	1	5 seconds	15 seconds
	2	10 seconds	25 seconds
	3	15 seconds	35 seconds
	4	20 seconds	45 seconds
	5	25 seconds	55 seconds
Bagels	1	10 seconds	20 seconds
	2	15 seconds	30 seconds
	3	20 seconds	40 seconds
	4	25 seconds	50 seconds
Dinner Rolls	1	10 seconds	20 seconds
	2	15 seconds	25 seconds
	3	20 seconds	30 seconds
	4	25 seconds	35 seconds
	5	30 seconds	40 seconds
	6	35 seconds	45 seconds
	8	45 seconds	55 seconds
Toaster Pastries	1	10 to 15 seconds*	
	2	15 to 20 seconds*	
	3	25 to 30 seconds*	
	4	35 to 40 seconds*	
Plain Donuts	1	10 seconds	25 seconds
	2	15 seconds	35 seconds
	3	20 seconds	45 seconds
	4	25 seconds	55 seconds

*use maximum time for Danish or refrigerated types

You can make these quick breads in a hurry from a mix, following the package directions. There will not be the customary browning but buttered slices on a plate will look very acceptable.

QUICK BREAD MIXES

MIX	SIZE	PAN	TIME	YIELD
Corn Muffins	16-oz. pkg. or two 8½-oz. pkgs.	1½-quart (9x5) loaf dish	6 minutes	1 loaf
	16-oz. pkg. or two 8½-oz. pkgs.	2-quart (8x8) baking dish	3 minutes	9 squares
	8½-oz. pkg. or half 16-oz. pkg.	2-quart (8x8) baking dish	3 minutes	9 squares
	8½-oz. pkg. or half 16-oz. pkg.	5 (5 or 6-oz.) custard cups	1 minute, 30 seconds	10 small muffins
Nut Bread	17 oz.	1½-quart (9x5) loaf	7 minutes	1 loaf
Date Bread	17 oz.	1½-quart (9x5) loaf	8 minutes	1 loaf
Banana Bread	15½ oz.	1½-quart (9x5) loaf	7 minutes	1 loaf

CARAMEL BISCUIT RING-A-ROUND

⅓ cup firmly packed dark brown sugar
3 tablespoons butter or margarine
1 tablespoon water
⅓ cup chopped nuts
1 can (8 oz.) refrigerated biscuits

In shallow 1-quart casserole or 1½-quart (8-inch round) baking dish, combine brown sugar, butter and water. COOK, uncovered, 1 MINUTE, stirring after butter melts. Stir in nuts. Separate can of biscuit dough into 10 biscuits. Cut each into quarters and add to sugar mixture. Stir to coat each piece. Push mixture away from center and set a custard cup or glass in center (this makes a ring mold). COOK, uncovered, 2 MINUTES, 30 SECONDS or until biscuits are firm and no longer doughy. LET STAND 2 MINUTES; remove custard cup and invert onto serving plate. Serve warm by pulling sections apart.   3 to 4 Servings

> **TIP:** We suggest dark brown sugar for best color but the light brown sugar will also give acceptable results.

POPOVERS

Popovers cannot be cooked in the microwave oven because they do not form a crust to hold their shape. The batter puffs up beautifully but they collapse as soon as the door is opened or the oven turned off. Since the conventional oven is often being used for other foods when you would like to serve popovers, it may be convenient to bake them early in the day and let them cool completely. Then just arrange them in a napkin-lined basket and COOK in the microwave oven for about 1 MINUTE to heat to piping hot.

SOUR CREAM COFFEE CAKE

¼ cup butter or margarine
½ cup sugar
1 egg
½ cup sour cream
1 cup unsifted all purpose flour
½ teaspoon soda
¼ teaspoon baking powder
¼ teaspoon salt
½ teaspoon vanilla
Topping
¼ cup firmly packed brown sugar
¼ cup chopped nuts
½ teaspoon cinnamon

In mixing bowl, soften butter (15 sec.). Stir in sugar and egg; beat well. Add remaining ingredients except Topping; stir until well blended. Place a glass or paper cup with 1½ to 2-inch diameter, right-side up, in center of 1½-quart (8-inch round) baking dish or 1½-quart casserole. Combine Topping ingredients and sprinkle ⅓ in bottom of pan around glass. Spoon half of batter over Topping, spreading to edges; sprinkle with ⅓ of Topping. Spoon remaining batter in pan; spread to cover Topping. Spoon remaining Topping over top. (If using paper cup, place a little water in cup to add weight and hold it in place during cooking.) COOK, uncovered, 4 MINUTES, 30 SECONDS or until toothpick comes out clean and no doughy spots remain. Cool 5 minutes; remove glass and invert onto serving plate. If desired, drizzle favorite glaze over warm coffee cake. Serve warm or cool.

4 to 6 Servings

A handy batter to keep on hand in refrigerator or freezer. Hot muffins can be ready in minutes. The recipe can easily be cut in half. If you don't have custard cups, use shallow coffee cups.

BRAN MUFFINS

1 cup water
3 cups all bran cereal
½ cup butter or margarine
1½ cups sugar
2 eggs
2½ cups unsifted all purpose flour
2 teaspoons soda
2 cups buttermilk or sour milk

In 1-cup measure, heat water to boiling (1 min.). Place bran cereal in covered storage container. Stir in water until moistened. Add butter and let set until softened. Stir in sugar and eggs; beat well. Blend in flour, soda and buttermilk. Mix well. Spoon into paper-lined custard cups filling half-full. Store any remaining batter in refrigerator for up to 6 weeks, using from it as desired. Cook muffins, uncovered, until no doughy spots remain:

        6 muffins — 2 minutes, 15 seconds
        4 muffins — 2 minutes
        2 muffins — 1 minute, 45 seconds

When batter is refrigerated, add 15 seconds additional cooking time.   40 to 48 Muffins

> **TIP:** Batter can be spooned into paperlined muffin pans and frozen until firm, about 4 hours. Remove from pans and store in plastic bags in freezer. Cook muffins by placing frozen muffins in custard cups:
>
>   6 muffins — cook 30 seconds; rest
>   1 minute, cook 1 minute, 30 seconds.
>   4 muffins — cook 30 seconds; rest
>   1 minute, cook 1 minute, 15 seconds.
>   2 muffins — cook 30 seconds; rest
>   1 minute, cook 45 seconds.
>   1 muffin — cook 15 seconds; rest
>   1 minute, cook 30 seconds.
>
> The rest period is necessary for even cooking with frozen batter.

GARLIC FRENCH BREAD

1 loaf French bread
⅓ cup butter or margarine
½ teaspoon garlic salt or 1 clove garlic

Cut bread into ½-inch slices, but do not slice all the way through loaf. In small cup or dish, melt butter with garlic (about 30 sec.). Brush mixture on each slice of loaf. Place in oven on paper towels and **COOK**, uncovered, **45 SECONDS TO 1 MINUTE** or until loaf feels warm.   1 Loaf

Peaches make a colorful and attractive topping on this coffee cake that begins with a mix. It can be ready to serve in just 15 minutes.

PEACH GLORY COFFEE CAKE

1 package (14 oz.) butter pecan coffee cake mix
2 tablespoons milk
⅓ cup butter or margarine
2 eggs
1½ cups (1-lb. can) drained sliced peaches (reserve ⅓ cup syrup)

In 4-cup measure, combine topping (from mix) with milk and butter. Stir to combine; **COOK**, uncovered, **2 MINUTES**, stirring once. Set aside. In small mixer bowl, combine coffee cake mix with eggs and the ⅓ cup peach syrup. Blend about 1 minute or 100 strokes. Spread batter in unlined 1½-quart (10 x 6) or 2-quart (8 x 8) baking dish. Pour about ⅓ of Topping over batter. Swirl through batter (save remaining topping). **COOK**, uncovered, **4 MINUTES, 15 SECONDS** or until toothpick comes out clean and top still looks moist. Arrange peach slices over top of cake. Drizzle remaining Topping over cake. Return to oven and **COOK**, uncovered, **1 MINUTE**. Serve warm or cool.
        8 to 9 Servings

Frozen bread dough can be thawed, proofed and cooked in about 1 hour. These same times and procedure will guide you in proofing and cooking other yeast breads in the oven. When bread dough is below optimum proofing temperature, the oven can be used to warm the dough and speed proofing. Touch the dough occasionally to be sure it does not become hot. If you have refrigerated dough to proof, use cooking periods of about 10 seconds; if dough is room temperature, use cooking periods of about 5 seconds.

FROZEN BREAD

Grease a 1-lb. loaf of frozen bread dough and place in greased 1½-quart (8 x 4) loaf dish. To thaw and proof, use **COOKING PERIODS OF 15 SECONDS** with a **3 MINUTE REST** period between each. **REPEAT** this about **12 TO 15 TIMES** or until double in size. To cook bread in microwave oven, **COOK**, uncovered, **5 MINUTES** or until no doughy spots remain.
        1 Loaf

> **TIPS:** An egg timer is handy to quietly time the 3 minute rest periods.
>
> • If you desire a brown crust on the bread, cook bread in microwave oven 3 minutes and then place in a preheated 450° oven for about 8 minutes or until brown and loaf sounds hollow when tapped.

An easy casserole bread that is mixed in the casserole the night before, proofed in the refrigerator and then quickly cooked in just 10 minutes. Try it toasted or for sandwiches.

CASSEROLE BREAD

  1½ **cups cold water**
   ⅓ **cup yellow cornmeal**
    1 **teaspoon salt**
   ⅓ **cup molasses**
    2 **tablespoons butter or margarine**
   ¼ **cup warm water**
    1 **package active dry yeast**
  3¼ **to 3½ cups unsifted all purpose flour**

In 2 or 2½-quart casserole, combine water, cornmeal and salt. **COOK**, uncovered, **4 TO 5 MINUTES** until mixture boils, stirring occasionally. Add molasses and butter; cool to lukewarm. Dissolve yeast in warm water. Stir into lukewarm cornmeal mixture. Mix in flour until well combined. Arrange evenly in casserole. Rub top with oil or softened butter. Cover casserole (allowing space for bread to rise) and refrigerate overnight.

Next day, remove from refrigerator and **COOK**, uncovered, **10 MINUTES** or until no doughy spots remain. Cool 5 minutes in casserole; turn out of pan and cool completely.   1 Loaf

The porous, chewy texture of English Muffins is characteristic of this bread loaf. It stores well in the refrigerator or freezer for ready slicing and toasting.

ENGLISH MUFFIN BREAD

    5 **cups unsifted all purpose flour**
    2 **packages active dry yeast**
    1 **tablespoon sugar**
    2 **teaspoons salt**
  2½ **cups milk**
   ¼ **teaspoon soda**
    1 **tablespoon warm water**

In large mixing bowl, combine 3 cups flour, yeast, sugar and salt. In 4-cup measure, heat milk until warm, about 2 minutes. Add milk to flour mixture. Beat by hand or mixer until smooth. Stir in remaining flour to make a stiff batter. Cover; let rise in warm place until light and doubled in size, about 1 hour.

Dissolve soda in warm water. Stir down yeast batter; blend in soda mixture, mixing until well blended. Divide batter between 2 unlined 1½-quart (8 x 4) loaf dishes. Cover and let rise in warm place until doubled, about 45 minutes. **COOK** each loaf, uncovered, **6 MINUTES** or until no doughy spots remain. Cool 5 minutes; loosen edges and remove from pan. Cool completely. To serve, slice and toast in toaster or under broiler until edges are brown.
2 Loaves

SALADS AND SALAD DRESSING

You can use your oven for a variety of tasks to make salad preparation easier and simpler. Use it to cook bacon or potatoes for a salad, to dissolve gelatin for a mold or to soften cream cheese that has been removed from the foil wrapper. If you wish, the oven can bring refrigerated fruits and vegetables to room temperature before they are combined in a salad.

Salad dressings can be cooked in the same bowl in which the salad is served. Most hot salads can be made ahead and then reheated which allows your meal preparation to be even more relaxed.

When preparing a salad dressing that contains oil and garlic, you can infuse garlic flavor by heating the oil and garlic until the oil bubbles. You can use the same procedure with oil and a lemon peel, too.

This salad is good for picnics or company dinners when you want a salad that is easy to make ahead. In summer, you may like to keep dressing on hand in the refrigerator for quick fruit salads. It should be used within 4 or 5 days.

MAKE AHEAD FRUIT SALAD

    1 **egg, beaten**
    2 **tablespoons sugar**
   ½ **cup fruit syrup (from pineapple or other fruit)**
    2 **tablespoons lemon juice**
    5 **cups fresh fruit (blueberries, melon balls, banana chunks, apple pieces, grapes, pear cubes or orange segments)**
    1 **cup drained pineapple (crushed, chunk or tidbits)**
    2 **cups miniature or cut up large marshmallows**
   ½ **cup whipping cream, whipped, or 1 cup frozen whipped topping, thawed**

In large bowl, combine egg, sugar, fruit syrup and lemon juice. **COOK**, uncovered, **45 SECONDS** or until mixture is slightly thickened, stirring occasionally. Cool. Add fruit, pineapple, marshmallows and whipped cream. Fold together just until well mixed. Cover and refrigerate at least 3 hours before serving.
6 to 8 Servings

TIP: The salad can be made a day ahead, but apples are best if stirred in a few hours before serving; they may turn a little brown when added a day ahead.

Peaches and curry flavor blend well with chicken or turkey in this easy rice salad. The frozen cooked rice can be quickly thawed in the oven.

PEACHY CHICKEN-RICE SALAD

   1 package (12 oz.) frozen rice pilaf
   ¼ cup mayonnaise or salad dressing
   1 tablespoon chopped onion or
      1 teaspoon instant minced onion
   ½ teaspoon curry powder
   1½ cups (1-lb. can) cubed, drained sliced
      peaches
   2 cups cubed cooked chicken
   ½ cup chopped celery
   ¼ cup chopped green pepper

Place frozen pouch of rice in oven. COOK 3 MINUTES, 30 SECONDS or until thawed. Empty into serving bowl and cool. Stir in mayonnaise, onion, curry, peaches and chicken. Chill thoroughly. Just before serving, stir in celery and green pepper. If desired, garnish with toasted almonds.   4 Servings

   TIP: Pineapple chunks can be used for part or all of peaches.

WILTED LETTUCE SALAD

   5 slices bacon
   1 head leaf lettuce, torn into bite-size
      pieces
   2 green onions, sliced
   ¼ cup cider vinegar
   1 tablespoon sugar
   2 tablespoons water
   ½ teaspoon salt
   ¼ teaspoon dry mustard
   ¼ teaspoon pepper

COOK bacon, covered with paper towel, 2¾ to 3¼ MINUTES or until crisp. Reserve 2 tablespoons drippings for dressing. Combine lettuce and onions in salad bowl; refrigerate until ready to serve. In 1-cup measure, measure vinegar. Add bacon drippings, sugar, water, salt, mustard and pepper. COOK, uncovered, 1 MINUTE or until mixture boils; stir to dissolve sugar. Pour over salad greens, tossing to coat. Garnish with crumbled bacon.   6 Servings

   TIP: If desired, add 2 hard-cooked eggs, chopped; 1 tomato, diced or 6 radishes, sliced.

The tangy flavor of warm cooked dressing blends well with potatoes. The dressing is cooked in the same bowl used to combine the salad and cooks while the potatoes cool.

OLD-FASHIONED POTATO SALAD

   3 to 4 medium potatoes
   3 hard-cooked eggs, chopped
   1 small onion, chopped
   2 stalks celery, chopped
   ¼ cup chopped pickle
Dressing
   2 tablespoons flour
   2 tablespoons sugar
   1 teaspoon salt
   1 teaspoon dry mustard
   ¾ cup milk
   1 egg, slightly beaten
   1 tablespoon butter or margarine
   ¼ cup vinegar

Cook potatoes as directed in cooking chart, page 117. Set aside to cool. While potatoes cook, cook eggs conventionally. Prepare Dressing in large mixing bowl (can be dish you'll store or serve salad in) by combining flour, sugar, salt and mustard. Stir in milk and egg, mixing until smooth. COOK, uncovered, 2 MINUTES, 30 SECONDS or until mixture boils, stirring occasionally. Stir to make smooth. Blend in butter and vinegar. Cool slightly.

   Peel potatoes and slice into warm dressing. Add cooked eggs, onion, celery and pickle; mix well. Refrigerate until served.
                              4 to 6 Servings

   TIPS: If you prefer to use mayonnaise or salad dressing, allow the potatoes to cool before mixing with about 1 cup of dressing.

   • When you need just a little more dressing, add mayonnaise or salad dressing.

The mild flavor of this delicate green gelatin salad will go well with many meals.

PINEAPPLE CHEESE SALAD

   1 can (13 oz.) crushed pineapple
   1 package (3 oz.) lime-flavored gelatin
   1 cup (½ pt.) cottage cheese
   1 cup (½ pt.) whipping cream, whipped

Drain pineapple, reserving liquid. Add enough water to liquid to make 1½ cups. In medium mixing bowl, stir together liquid and gelatin. COOK, uncovered, 3 MINUTES or until mixture comes to a boil, stirring once. Chill until thickened, but not set. Beat until foamy. Stir in cottage cheese and pineapple. Fold in whipped cream. Pour into oiled 1½-quart (6 cup) mold and chill until firm. Unmold to serve.   6 to 8 Servings

Rice and Noodles

When cooking rice you are basically rehydrating it so it takes about the same amount of time when cooked in a microwave oven as it does conventionally. You may find it more convenient at times to cook these in a microwave oven, especially since lasagna and spaghetti noodles fit the 12 x 7-dish so well.

You can reheat rice and noodles, covered, until steaming hot, whether they have originally been cooked conventionally or not. If refrigerated, stir during heating.

SEASONED REGULAR RICE MIXES

In 2½-quart casserole, combine rice with additions as directed on package. **COOK,** covered, **18 MINUTES** or until rice is just about tender, stirring occasionally. **LET STAND,** covered, **5 MINUTES** to finish cooking.

SEASONED QUICK-COOKING RICE MIXES

In 1-quart casserole, combine additions as directed on package. **COOK,** covered, **3 MINUTES** or until boiling. Stir in rice. **LET STAND,** covered, as directed on package. Fluff with fork.

RICE PILAF

⅓ cup butter or margarine
1½ cups uncooked long grain rice
½ cup chopped onion or 2 tablespoons instant minced onion
½ cup chopped celery
¼ cup chopped parsley or 2 tablespoons parsley flakes
1 can (10½ oz.) condensed chicken broth
½ teaspoon salt
¼ teaspoon leaf thyme or ⅛ teaspoon powdered thyme
Dash pepper
1¾ cups water

In 2-quart casserole, combine butter, rice, onion and celery. **COOK,** uncovered, **5 MINUTES.** Add remaining ingredients. **COOK,** covered, **16 MINUTES** or until rice is almost tender, stirring occasionally. **LET STAND,** covered, **5 MINUTES** to finish cooking.

6 Servings

TIP: If desired, use 2 chicken bouillon cubes for chicken broth and increase water to 3 cups.

COOKING RICE AND NOODLES

	COOKING DISH	HOT WATER	NOODLES OR RICE	ADDITIONS	COOK WATER	COOK NOODLES OR RICE	STAND
Noodles	3-qt. casserole	Fill half full	4 cups (8 oz.)	1 tsp. salt	5-6 min. (covered)	7-9 min. (uncovered)	5-10 min. (covered)
Lasagna Noodles	2-qt. (12 x 7) baking dish	Fill half full	8 oz.	1 tsp. salt	7-8 min. (uncovered)	7-9 min. (uncovered)	5-10 min. (covered)
Macaroni/ Broken Spaghetti	3-qt. casserole	Fill half full	2 cups (7 oz.)	1 tsp. salt	5-6 min. (covered)	7-9 min. (uncovered)	5-10 min. (covered)
Long Spaghetti	2-qt. (12 x 7) baking dish	Fill half full	2 cups (7 oz.)	1 tsp. salt	5-8 min. (covered)	7-9 min. (uncovered)	5-10 min. (covered)
Quick-Cooking Rice	1-qt. serving dish or casserole	1½ cups	1½ cups	1 tsp. salt	2½-3 min. (covered)	—	5 min. (covered)
Long Grain Rice	3-qt. casserole	2 cups	1 cup	1 tsp. oil or butter	—	12-13 min. (covered)	5 min. (covered)
Wild and White Rice Mix	3-qt. casserole	1¾ cups	6-oz. pkg.	2 tsps. butter	—	15 min. (covered)	5 min. (covered)

Noodles: Place water in cooking dish and bring to boil; add noodles. Cook. Let stand, covered. Drain and Rinse. If necessary, reheat to serving temperature.
Rice, Quick-Cooking: Bring water and salt to boil. Stir in rice. Let stand, covered. Fluff with fork.
Rice, Regular: Combine water, rice, salt and oil. Cook. Let stand, covered. Fluff with fork.

Sauces

Most of these sauces are easy to make ahead before serving with a main course or to keep on hand in the refrigerator for quick reheating. Dessert sauces are found in the Frosting section (page 153). Sauces are exceptionally failproof in a microwave oven, without danger of scorching or burning. You may want to adapt one of your own sauce recipes, using a similar recipe in this chapter as a guide to the timing and method. Sauces that you buy already prepared can also be heated if first transferred to a container that can be used in the oven.

White Sauce is easy to reheat if made ahead or leftover. For cheese and egg sauces, see Tips.

WHITE SAUCE

  2 tablespoons butter or margarine
  2 tablespoons flour
  ½ teaspoon salt
  1 cup milk

In 2-cup measure, melt butter (20 sec.). Blend in flour and salt. Gradually stir in milk. **COOK**, uncovered, **2 MINUTES, 30 SECONDS** or until mixture boils and thickens, stirring occasionally during last half of cooking time.   1 Cup Sauce

  TIPS: For Thick White Sauce, increase butter and flour to 3 tablespoons each.

  • For Thin White Sauce, decrease butter and flour to 1 tablespoon each.

  • For Cheese Sauce, add ¼ teaspoon dry mustard with flour. After cooking, stir in ½ cup shredded cheese until melted.

  • For Creamed Egg Sauce, add ¼ teaspoon dry mustard with flour. After cooking, stir in 2 to 3 chopped or sliced hard-cooked eggs.

Try this spicy, hot tomato sauce over zucchini, green beans or leftover beef roast.

QUICK AND EASY TOMATO SAUCE

  1 cup (8-oz. can) tomato sauce
  ⅓ cup water
  1 teaspoon Worcestershire sauce
  ½ teaspoon salt
  Dash pepper

In 2-cup measure, combine all ingredients; mix well. **COOK**, uncovered, **2 MINUTES, 30 SECONDS** or until hot, stirring occasionally during last half of cooking time.   1 Cup Sauce

Celery soup is the base for this easy dill sauce. The celery and dill flavors go well with green vegetables or fish.

CREAMY DILL SAUCE

  1 can (10½ oz.) condensed cream of celery soup
  2 tablespoons milk
  ¼ teaspoon dill weed

In 2-cup measure, combine all ingredients; mix well. **COOK**, uncovered, **3 MINUTES** or until mixture boils, stirring occasionally during last half of cooking time.   1⅓ Cups Sauce

  TIP: The sauce ingredients can be mixed ahead for easy last minute heating.

Try this spicy, shrimp-flavored cream sauce with cauliflower, broccoli, spinach or fish fillets.

SPEEDY SHRIMP SAUCE

  1 can (10 oz.) frozen shrimp soup
  ½ cup milk
  1 teaspoon instant minced onion
  Dash pepper
  Dash Tabasco sauce

Remove one end of soup can and place in 4-cup measure. Add water to cover ¾ of soup can. **COOK**, uncovered, **2 MINUTES**. Let stand several minutes. Empty partially thawed soup into 4-cup measure and stir in remaining ingredients. **COOK**, uncovered, **3 MINUTES** or until hot, stirring occasionally during last half of cooking time.   1½ Cups Sauce

Hollandaise sauce is easy to make or reheat in the oven for serving with vegetables or fish. If you prefer to use a Hollandaise Sauce mix, see the directions in Ham-Asparagus Hollandaise, page 86.

HOLLANDAISE SAUCE

  ¼ cup butter or margarine
  ¼ cup light cream
  2 egg yolks, beaten
  1 tablespoon lemon juice or vinegar
  ¼ teaspoon salt
  ½ teaspoon dry mustard

In 2-cup measure, melt butter (30 sec.). Add remaining ingredients; mix well. **COOK**, uncovered, **1 MINUTE** or until thickened, stirring every 15 seconds. Remove and beat until light.   ⅔ Cup Sauce

  TIPS: If sauce curdles, it is overcooked.

  • For half a recipe, use half the ingredient amounts, cook in 1-cup measure 25 seconds.

This mild flavored cheese sauce complements flavors of veal, pork and lamb, and vegetables such as broccoli or artichokes.

MORNAY SAUCE

 2 tablespoons butter or margarine
 2 tablespoons flour
 ⅓ cup milk or cream
 1 cup water
 1 cube or teaspoon chicken bouillon
 ¼ cup grated Parmesan cheese
 ¼ cup shredded Swiss cheese

In 2-cup measure, melt butter (20 sec.). Stir in flour. Add milk, water and bouillon; mix well. COOK, uncovered, **2 MINUTES, 30 SECONDS** or until mixture boils, stirring occasionally during last half of cooking time. Stir in cheeses and let stand, covered, until cheeses melt.

1⅔ Cups Sauce

The curry flavor in this sauce goes well with vegetables, seafoods, lamb, veal, pork or poultry.

SOUR CREAM SAUCE

 1 cup sour cream
 ½ teaspoon salt
 ½ teaspoon curry powder
 ⅛ teaspoon pepper
 1 tablespoon lemon juice

In 2-cup measure, combine all ingredients; mix well. COOK, uncovered, **2 MINUTES** or until hot, stirring occasionally during last half of cooking time.

1 Cup Sauce

Try this mushroom sauce over your next barbecued or broiled steak or hamburger.

MUSHROOM SAUCE

 ¼ cup butter or margarine
 1 cup (8 oz. or ½ pt.) sliced fresh
   mushrooms
 4 teaspoons cornstarch
 1 teaspoon salt
 1 teaspoon Worcestershire sauce
 1 cup water

In 1-quart casserole, combine butter and mushrooms. COOK, covered, **2 MINUTES**, stirring occasionally. Stir in remaining ingredients. COOK, uncovered, **3 MINUTES, 30 SECONDS** or until mixture boils, stirring occasionally during last half of cooking time.

2 Cups Sauce

TIPS: Sauce can be prepared ahead; reheat from room temperature, uncovered, 1 minute, 30 seconds or until hot.

● If desired, ½ cup (4-oz. can) drained mushroom stems and pieces can be substituted for fresh mushrooms.

Enhance the flavor of vegetables and meats with this creamy, onion-flavored sauce.

BECHAMEL SAUCE

 1 teaspoon finely chopped onion or
   ¼ teaspoon instant minced onion
 2 tablespoons butter or margarine
 1 tablespoon flour
 ½ cup light cream
 ½ cup water
 1 cube or teaspoon chicken bouillon
 Dash pepper

In 4-cup measure, combine onion and butter. COOK, uncovered, **2 MINUTES**. Stir in flour and remaining ingredients. COOK, uncovered, **3 MINUTES, 30 SECONDS** or until mixture boils and thickens. 1 Cup Sauce

TIP: If desired, prepare sauce ahead and reheat from room temperature, uncovered, 1 minute, 30 seconds or until hot.

A spicy, sweet sauce to serve with ham, pork or turkey.

SPICY RAISIN SAUCE

 ½ cup firmly packed brown sugar
 1 tablespoon cornstarch
 1½ teaspoons dry mustard
 ⅛ teaspoon ground cloves
 1 cup water
 ¼ cup raisins
 2 tablespoons lemon juice
 1 tablespoon butter or margarine

In 4-cup measure, combine all ingredients. COOK, uncovered, **4 MINUTES** or until mixture boils and raisins are plump, stirring occasionally during last half of cooking time.

1½ Cups Sauce

TIP: If desired, prepare sauce ahead and reheat from room temperature, uncovered, 2 minutes, 30 seconds or until hot.

CRANBERRY SAUCE

 1½ cups fresh or frozen cranberries
 ½ cup sugar
 ¼ cup water

In 1-quart casserole, combine cranberries, sugar and water. COOK, covered, **3 TO 5 MINUTES** or until cranberries have popped, stirring once. Let stand, covered, several minutes to finish cooking. Serve warm or cold.

2 Cups Sauce

TIP: For orange flavor, use orange juice for water and add 1 tablespoon grated orange peel.

Fruit

Butterscotch Fondue Sauce

Fruit cooks very quickly in the oven with no problems of scorching. The recipes use fresh, frozen and canned fruit in a variety of manners from cobblers and sauces to crisps and dumplings.

The oven is handy for bringing refrigerated fruit to room temperature in just a few seconds. Also, you can more easily peel some fruits such as peaches if you heat them for a few seconds and then let them stand for several minutes. If you want to get more juice from a cold lemon or lime, heat it for about 30 seconds before squeezing it.

Fruit desserts usually are easy to rewarm if they have cooled between cooking and serving so you can make dessert earlier in the day if it is more convenient for you.

See the Breakfast section (page 16) for Spicy Breakfast Prunes recipe.

Peaches simmered in an orange flavored wine sauce develop an orange liqueur flavor.

PEACHES IN WINE SAUCE

> ½ **cup sugar**
> 2 **tablespoons cornstarch**
> 1 **to 2 tablespoons grated orange peel**
> **or 1 teaspoon dried orange peel**
> ½ **cup sherry or sweet to medium white wine**
> 3½ **cups (1 lb. 13-oz. can) undrained peach slices or halves**

In 2-quart casserole, combine all ingredients. **COOK**, uncovered, **9 MINUTES**, stirring twice during last half of cooking time. Serve warm or cold over ice cream or gingerbread.

5 to 6 Servings

> **TIP:** You can use canned pears for peaches.

A good sauce for fondue, ice cream or spice cakes and puddings. Keeps well in the refrigerator for quick reheating in the jar.

BUTTERSCOTCH FONDUE SAUCE

> ½ **cup evaporated milk or light cream**
> 1½ **cups firmly packed brown sugar**
> 3 **tablespoons butter or margarine**
> 1 **teaspoon vanilla or 2 tablespoons rum**

In 4-cup measure, combine evaporated milk, brown sugar and butter. **COOK**, uncovered, **4 MINUTES**, stirring occasionally. Stir in vanilla; cool slightly. Serve in fondue pot or warmer dish at the table with fruits, cake or cookies to dip into the sauce. 1⅓ Cups Sauce

> **TIP:** For more sauce, use 2-quart casserole, double the ingredients and cook 6 minutes.

A good dessert idea for company. Any leftover sauce can be stored in the refrigerator for serving on ice cream. Use the amount of chocolate according to your taste preference: 2 envelopes for light chocolate, 3 for medium and 4 for deep chocolate.

CHOCOLATE FONDUE SAUCE

    1 cup evaporated milk or light cream
1½ cups sugar
  ½ cup butter or margarine
  ⅛ teaspoon salt
  2 to 4 envelopes premelted chocolate
10 large marshmallows

In 4-cup measure, combine milk, sugar, butter, salt and chocolate. **COOK**, uncovered, **6 MINUTES**, stirring occasionally and watching carefully last couple of minutes to avoid boiling over. Stir in marshmallows and **COOK 30 SECONDS**; stir until marshmallows are melted. Cool slightly and serve in fondue pot or warmer dish at the table with fruits, cake or cookies to dip into the sauce.   **3 Cups Sauce**

> **TIP:** Squares of unsweetened chocolate can be used for the premelted; just stir more often during the first couple minutes to melt and distribute the chocolate.

This combines the flavors of the traditional Peach Melba but is made in a new and easy way.

EASY PEACH MELBA

1¼ cups (10-oz. pkg.) frozen sweetened raspberries
1¼ cups (10-oz. pkg.) frozen sweetened peaches
  1 tablespoon cornstarch
  ½ cup currant jelly
Vanilla ice cream

In 1-quart casserole or medium size bowl, place frozen raspberries and peaches. **COOK**, uncovered, **1 MINUTE, REST 30 SECONDS,** and **COOK 1 MINUTE** or until thawed. Strain juices into 2-cup measure or small bowl. Add cornstarch and currant jelly. **COOK**, uncovered, **4 MINUTES**, stirring twice during last half of cooking time. Pour over fruit in bowl and mix. (This will bring the sauce to a warm temperature for serving.) Spoon sauce over vanilla ice cream.
          6 Servings

> **TIP:** To use 1-lb. can sliced peaches in place of frozen peaches, drain peaches adding ¼ cup of syrup, and increase cornstarch to 2 tablespoons. When thawing raspberries, use cooking periods of 30 seconds.

Wine flavored bananas are good served plain or as topping for ice cream or cake.

GOING BANANAS

3 tablespoons butter or margarine
3 tablespoons brown sugar
⅛ teaspoon ground cloves
Pinch salt
¼ cup lemon juice
½ cup muscatel wine or cream sherry
5 bananas

In shallow baking dish, melt butter (1 min.). Stir in remaining ingredients except bananas. Slice bananas once lengthwise and once crosswise and add to sauce, turning to coat. **COOK**, uncovered, **3 MINUTES** or until friut is softened and hot, rearranging bananas once.
          4 to 6 Servings

A quick, flaming sauce to serve over ice cream. Serve any leftovers cold because reheating would overcook bananas.

BANANAS ROYALE

6 tablespoons butter or margarine
6 tablespoons brown sugar
¼ teaspoon cinnamon
¼ teaspoon nutmeg
¼ cup light cream
4 medium bananas, peeled
¼ cup brandy or 2 teaspoons brandy or rum flavoring

In 9 or 10-inch pie plate or shallow casserole, melt butter (30 sec.). Add brown sugar, cinnamon, nutmeg and cream. Slice bananas once lengthwise and then once crosswise. Add to sugar mixture, turning to coat. **COOK**, uncovered, **2 MINUTES** or until mixture begins to bubble on bananas, rearranging after 1 minute. Stir in brandy. (Or heat brandy 20 seconds, ignite and pour over bananas.) Serve over ice cream.   **6 to 8 Servings**

> **TIPS:** Recipe can be halved; use 8-inch pie plate or shallow casserole; half of ingredient amounts; 1 minute cooking time for bananas and same time for heating brandy.
>
> • When serving as dessert immediately following a meal, you can prepare it in advance through the step of coating the bananas and have ice cream spooned into serving dishes in freezer. Then, while clearing dishes, cook mixture and flame brandy, if desired.

Tangy orange sauce is a good contrast to the mildly flavored bananas. Serve as fruit alone or use as topping over ice cream or cake.

BAKED ORANGE BANANAS

- 3 large bananas, peeled
- 3 tablespoons sugar
- ¼ teaspoon cinnamon
- ¼ teaspoon nutmeg
- Dash ground cloves
- ½ teaspoon grated orange peel
- ¼ cup orange juice
- 1 tablespoon butter or margarine

Cut bananas once crosswise and once lengthwise. Place in 2-quart (12x7) baking dish. In small custard cup, combine sugar, cinnamon, nutmeg and cloves. Add orange peel, orange juice and butter. COOK, uncovered, 1 MINUTE or until sugar dissolves and butter melts. Pour mixture over bananas. COOK, uncovered, 4 MINUTES or until bananas are slightly soft. Serve warm.   4 to 6 Servings

This makes a tasty fruit dessert when only canned fruits are available.

MIXED FRUIT AMBROSIA

- ½ cup flaked coconut (plain or toasted*)
- 2 tablespoons graham cracker crumbs
- 1½ cups (1 lb. 4-oz. can) drained pineapple chunks
- 1½ cups (1-lb. can) drained sliced peaches
- 1 cup ((11-oz. can) drained mandarin oranges
- 6 maraschino cherries, halved

In 2-quart (12 x 7) baking dish, mix all ingredients together. COOK, uncovered, 4 MINUTES or until hot. Serve with whipped cream.   6 to 8 Servings

  TIP: *To toast coconut, spread ½ cup in pie or cake dish. Cook, uncovered, 2 minutes, stirring every 30 seconds for even browning.

RHUBARB SAUCE

- 2 cups sliced rhubarb
- 2 tablespoons water
- ½ cup sugar

In 2-quart casserole, combine rhubarb and water. COOK, covered, 4 MINUTES or until rhubarb is soft, stirring once. Stir in sugar and COOK, covered, 1 MINUTE to dissolve sugar.
          4 Servings

  TIP: For 4 cups rhubarb, use 2 or 3-quart casserole and cook 6 minutes, then 1 minute after adding sugar.

Serve this hot over ice cream. Easy to make if pears are on hand; no other special ingredients are necessary.

PEARS A LA' CRÈME

- 2 tablespoons butter or margarine
- ⅓ cup firmly packed brown sugar
- ½ teaspoon cinnamon
- ¼ teaspoon nutmeg
- ¼ teaspoon ginger
- 2½ cups (1 lb. 13-oz. can) drained pear halves
- Vanilla ice cream

In 2-quart casserole or shallow baking dish, combine butter, brown sugar and spices. COOK, uncovered, 1 MINUTE, 30 SECONDS, stirring once. Add pears and COOK, covered, 4 MINUTES. Serve a hot pear half, cut-side down, over a scoop of ice cream, spooning the glaze over pears.   6 to 8 Servings

You will need a long handled dish for the flaming brandy in this recipe. If you do not have such a dish that can be used in your microwave oven, it would be better to heat the brandy conventionally in a long handled small saucepan.

CHERRIES JUBILEE

- 2 cups (1-lb. can) undrained pitted Bing cherries
- 1 tablespoon cornstarch
- ¼ cup brandy
- Vanilla ice cream

In 1-quart casserole, blend cornstarch with cherries. COOK, uncovered, 4 MINUTES or until thickened, stirring twice. COOK brandy in a long handled dish 20 SECONDS. Ignite brandy and carefully pour over cherries. Serve over vanilla ice cream.   6 to 8 Servings

  TIPS: In June and July when fresh cherries are plentiful, use 2 cups fresh pitted Bing cherries, adding ¼ cup sugar and ½ cup water with cornstarch. Increase cooking time to 5 minutes.

  • To pit cherries, use fork to loosen and remove pit.

APPLESAUCE

- 6 to 8 medium cooking apples, peeled and quartered
- ½ cup water
- ½ to 1 cup sugar

In 2-quart casserole, combine apples and water. COOK, covered, 8 TO 10 MINUTES or until apples are soft, stirring once. Stir in sugar and let stand, covered, a few minutes to dissolve sugar.   6 Servings

APPLE CRISP

**5 to 6 cups sliced and peeled cooking
   apples**
½ cup unsifted all purpose flour
½ cup rolled oats
¾ cup firmly packed brown sugar
1 teaspoon cinnamon or apple pie spice
⅓ cup butter or margarine

In 2-quart (8 x 8) baking dish, arrange apples.
Combine flour, rolled oats, brown sugar and
cinnamon; cut in butter until crumbly. Sprinkle
over top of apples. **COOK,** uncovered,
12 MINUTES or until apples are tender. If
you prefer a more crunchy, brown topping,
place under the broiler a few minutes.

5 to 6 Servings

TIP: In late winter, apples tend to be less
juicy so you may want to add 1 to 2
tablespoons water to apples before adding
topping.

FRUIT CRUNCH

**2 cups (21-oz. can) favorite prepared pie
   filling**
¼ cup butter or margarine
⅓ cup rolled oats
**12 gingersnaps or 10 graham cracker
   squares, crushed (1 cup)**
¼ cup sugar
½ teaspoon cinnamon

Spread pie filling in 2-quart (8 x 8) or
1½-quart (8-inch round) baking dish. In a
small bowl, melt butter (30 sec.). Stir in
remaining ingredients. Sprinkle crumb mixture
over pie filling. **COOK,** uncovered, **6 MINUTES**
or until hot and bubbly. Serve warm.

4 to 6 Servings

*A spicy mincemeat sauce to serve over
ice cream. Try it for a fall or early winter
dinner party.*

MINCED ORANGE DESSERT

**1 can (11 oz.) mandarin oranges,
   undrained**
1 can (21 oz.) mincemeat pie filling
**1 can (1 lb. 4 oz.) pear halves, drained
   Ice cream**

In medium bowl, combine oranges and pie
filling. **COOK,** uncovered, **2 TO 3 MINUTES**
or until hot, stirring once. Spoon mixture over
pear halves filled with ice cream. 6 to 8 Servings

TIPS: If desired, add 2 tablespoons brandy
to sauce before serving or warm brandy
about 15 seconds, flame and add to sauce.

● The sauce is also good served over
ice cream without the pears.

*This homemade type biscuit shortcake cooks
right in the serving dishes in just 3 minutes.
While it is still warm, top with sweetened
strawberries (or other fruit, too) and whipped
cream.*

LAST MINUTE SHORTCAKE

1 cup unsifted all purpose flour
3 tablespoons sugar
1 teaspoon baking powder
¼ teaspoon salt
¼ cup butter or margarine
⅓ cup milk
1 egg

In mixing bowl, combine flour, sugar, baking
powder and salt. Cut in butter. Measure milk
and add egg; mix with fork and stir into flour
mixture just until moistened. Spoon into 4 to 5
dessert dishes (1-cup size). **COOK,** uncovered,
2½ TO 3 MINUTES or until shortcakes are
firm and no longer doughy. Best while warm
or reheat about 30 seconds.

To serve, top with strawberries (10-oz. pkg.
frozen berries, thawed, or 1 pint fresh berries,
sweetened) and whipped cream. 4 to 5 Servings

TIP: If desired, use 1½ cups biscuit mix
adding sugar, milk and egg.

*The old-fashioned goodness of spicy moist
apple dessert with the convenience of mixing
in your baking dish. A good last minute
dessert for a busy fall evening.*

APPLE PUDDING CAKE

3 eggs
**3 cups (3 med.) chopped peeled cooking
   apple**
½ cup unsifted all purpose flour
1 cup rolled oats
1 cup firmly packed brown sugar
1½ teaspoons baking powder
½ teaspoon salt
1 teaspoon cinnamon
¼ teaspoon nutmeg
1 teaspoon vanilla
½ cup chopped nuts

In 2-quart casserole, beat eggs. Stir in
remaining ingredients except nuts, mixing until
well combined. Sprinkle nuts over top.
COOK, uncovered, **10 MINUTES** or until
toothpick comes out clean and apples are
tender. Serve spooned into dishes and topped
with ice cream, whipped cream or Nutmeg
Sauce, page 153. 6 to 8 Servings

TIP: If desired, use 1¼ teaspoons apple
pie spice for cinnamon and nutmeg.

This is a quick way to make family dessert. Try it with other types of berries, cherries or peaches.

BERRIES AND DUMPLINGS

>   4 cups (20 oz.) fresh or frozen
>   blackberries, boysenberries or
>   blueberries
>   ¾ cup sugar
>   ¼ cup water

Dumplings
>   1 cup unsifted all purpose flour
>   2 tablespoons sugar
>   1 teaspoon baking powder
>   ½ teaspoon salt
>   2 tablespoons cooking oil
>   ½ cup milk

In 2-quart casserole, combine berries, ¾ cup sugar and water. COOK, covered, 5 MINUTES or until mixture just begins to bubble. (If berries are frozen, time will be about 7 minutes.) Meanwhile, prepare Dumplings in mixing bowl by combining flour, sugar, baking powder and salt. Add oil and milk; mix just until moistened. Drop by spoonfuls onto hot fruit mixture. COOK, covered, 5 MINUTES or until dumplings are no longer doughy underneath. Serve warm.

5 to 6 Servings

TIP: To prepare with biscuit mix, use 1 cup mix, 2 tablespoons sugar and ½ cup milk.

Refrigerated biscuits make easy dumplings cooked in a caramel sauce under apple slices. The wax paper cover holds in the heat to cook apples quickly.

APPLES 'N DUMPLINGS

>   1 can (8 oz.) refrigerated biscuits
>   4 medium cooking apples, peeled and
>   sliced
>   ½ cup raisins, if desired
>   ½ cup chopped nuts, if desired
>   ½ cup water
>   ½ cup dark corn syrup
>   ½ cup firmly packed brown sugar
>   ¼ cup butter or margarine

Separate biscuits and cut each in half. Arrange in 2-quart (12 x 7) baking dish. Top with apples, raisins and nuts. In 2-cup measure, combine water, corn syrup, brown sugar and butter. COOK, uncovered, 2 MINUTES, 30 SECONDS or until mixture boils. Pour over apples, coating most of apples. COOK, covered with wax paper, 8 TO 9 MINUTES or until apples are tender. Serve warm with cream or ice cream.

6 to 8 Servings

TIPS: This dish freezes well. Thaw and reheat to serve.

An easy cobbler to fix when rhubarb is plentiful.

RUBY BERRY COBBLER

>   ¾ cup sugar
>   3 tablespoons flour
>   1 package (10 oz.) frozen sweetened
>   raspberries or strawberries
>   3 cups cut-up rhubarb

Topping
>   ⅓ cup butter or margarine
>   1 cup rolled oats
>   1 cup unsifted all purpose flour
>   ¾ cup firmly packed brown sugar
>   1 teaspoon cinnamon
>   ⅓ cup chopped nuts, if desired

In 2-quart (8 x 8) baking dish, combine sugar and flour. Add frozen berries. COOK, uncovered, 4 MINUTES, stirring once to mix in thawed berries. Stir in rhubarb. Prepare Topping by melting butter (30 sec.) in mixing bowl. Stir in remaining ingredients until crumbly. Sprinkle evenly over fruit mixture. COOK, uncovered, 8 MINUTES or until mixture is bubbly toward center. For crisper topping, place under broiler a few minutes. Serve warm with cream or ice cream.

5 to 6 Servings

An easy and tasty dessert using cake and frosting mix in combination with prepared pie filling. About 15 minutes to mix and bake.

CHERRY CRUMBLE SQUARES

>   2 tablespoons butter or margarine
>   ½ package (2¼ cups) yellow cake mix
>   1 egg
>   2 cups (21-oz. can) prepared cherry pie
>   filling
>   2 tablespoons butter or margarine
>   ½ package (1 cup) coconut pecan or
>   almond frosting mix

In large mixing bowl, melt 2 tablespoons butter (20 sec.). By hand, stir in dry cake mix and egg until mix is moist. Pat into 2-quart (12 x 7) baking dish. Spoon pie filling over mixture, spreading to cover. In same mixing bowl, melt 2 tablespoons butter (20 sec.). Stir in frosting mix. Sprinkle over cherries. COOK, uncovered, 9 MINUTES or until mixture is bubbly. Serve warm or cool, cut into squares and topped with whipped cream or ice cream.

6 to 8 Servings

TIP: With some brands of cake mix the mixture will be more moist and will be spread rather than patted. The baked dessert should still be very good.

Puddings and Custards

A microwave oven eliminates the possibility of scorched puddings and custards because the cooking occurs from all sides, rather than only the bottom. And, for real convenience, you can measure, mix and cook puddings right in a 4-cup measure. A glass pitcher is also handy for preparing puddings.

Custards can be cooked in individual custard cups and are great make aheads for dessert or a busy morning's breakfast (see Breakfast section page 14). The oven also can be used to cook custard mixtures that are the beginning step of desserts such as Custard Bavarian Creme, Vanilla Custard Ice Cream or the Frozen Lemon Dessert that is in the Dinner section page 35.

CHOCOLATE MOUSSE

2 squares semi-sweet chocolate
⅓ cup sugar
1 tablespoon (1 envelope) unflavored gelatin
3 eggs, separated
⅛ teaspoon salt
1 cup milk
1 teaspoon vanilla
⅓ cup sugar
1 cup whipping cream

In 4-cup measure, melt chocolate (2 min.). Blend in ⅓ cup sugar and gelatin. Beat in egg yolks and salt. Stir in milk. **COOK,** uncovered, **4 MINUTES** or until slightly thickened, stirring occasionally. Add vanilla and cool. In mixing bowl, beat egg whites until foamy. Gradually add ⅓ cup sugar and beat until stiff. Fold beaten egg whites into cooled chocolate mixture. In large bowl, whip cream. Fold chocolate mixture into whipped cream. Spoon mixture into 6 to 8 sherbet dishes, 12 Chocolate Cups or one 8 or 9-inch Chocolate Cookie Crumb Crust. Chill 2 to 3 hours.   6 Servings

These cups are made conveniently one at a time; while you are forming one cup, the next one can be cooking.

CHOCOLATE CUPS

Place paper cupcake liner in 5 or 6 oz. custard cup. Add one heaping tablespoon of semi-sweet chocolate pieces. **COOK,** uncovered, **1 MINUTE** or until chocolate is soft. With a table knife, spread chocolate evenly in liner. Chill and fill with Chocolate Mousse, ice cream or other chilled dessert fillings. Peel off paper liner for serving.

Egg whites are beaten and folded into this easy pudding to give it a light, airy texture.

TAPIOCA PUDDING

2 cups milk
¼ cup sugar
2½ tablespoons quick-cooking tapioca
¼ teaspoon salt
2 eggs, separated
2 tablespoons sugar
1 teaspoon vanilla

In 4-cup measure, combine milk, sugar, tapioca and salt. Separate eggs, placing whites in large mixing bowl and adding yolks to milk mixture. Beat until well combined. **COOK,** uncovered, **5 MINUTES, 30 SECONDS** or until mixture boils, stirring occasionally during last half of cooking time. Beat egg whites until frothy. Gradually beat in 2 tablespoons sugar, continuing to beat until mixture holds soft peaks. Fold in pudding mixture and vanilla. Serve warm or cold.
                                                    6 Servings

> **TIP:** If desired, fold in ½ cup finely chopped dates, peaches, apricots, strawberries, raspberries or other desired fruit.

Pudding or custard mix makes this stirred bread pudding very simple to prepare. It cooks in just 6 minutes.

EASY BREAD PUDDING

1 package (3¼ oz.) vanilla pudding and pie filling mix
2 cups milk
½ cup raisins
1 cup cubed white bread (2 slices)

In 4-cup measure or 1-quart casserole, combine all ingredients. **COOK,** uncovered, **6 MINUTES** or until mixture boils, stirring occasionally during last half of cooking. Serve warm or cool.
                                                    4 to 6 Servings

> **TIPS:** A 3-oz. package custard mix can be used for pudding mix. Prepare and cook as directed. Mixture will need to cool before it sets up.
>
> • Leftover white or yellow cake, sweet rolls or coffee cake may be used for bread.

Cherry pie filling cooks under a thin layer of custard and bread, making a colorful and tasty sauce to go with the bread pudding.

SAUCY CHERRY BREAD PUDDING

    1 can (21 oz.) prepared cherry pie filling
    3 slices bread, cut into ½-inch cubes
    2 eggs
    ⅓ cup sugar
    ¾ cup milk
    1 teaspoon vanilla

In 1½-quart (8-inch round) baking dish, spread pie filling. Top with cubes of bread. Combine remaining ingredients and beat until well mixed. Pour over bread cubes, pushing cubes into custard mixture if necessary. **COOK**, uncovered, **6 MINUTES, 30 SECONDS** or until center is set. Serve warm or cold.   5 to 6 Servings

> **TIPS:** Try pudding with other favorite flavors of prepared pie filling.
>
> • This is a good way to use leftover cake, too. Cut into cubes and use about 3 cups in place of bread. Since there is more sugar in cake than in bread, reduce the sugar to 2 tablespoons.

This fudgy cake that cooks with a sauce underneath is sure to be a favorite served warm from the oven. Prepare and cook in about 15 minutes.

CHOCOLATE PUDDING CAKE

    2 cups water
    1 cup unsifted all purpose flour
    ¾ cup sugar
    ½ cup chopped nuts
    2 tablespoons unsweetened cocoa
    1 teaspoon baking powder
    ½ teaspoon salt
    1 teaspoon vanilla
    2 tablespoons oil
    ½ cup milk
    ¾ cup sugar
    ¼ cup unsweetened cocoa

Measure water in 4-cup measure and place in oven to boil (about 4 minutes). In 2½-quart casserole, combine flour, sugar, nuts, cocoa, baking powder and salt. Add vanilla, oil and milk; mix until well combined. Spread evenly in dish. Combine sugar and cocoa; sprinkle over top of cake. Pour boiling water over all. **COOK**, uncovered, **9 MINUTES** or until cake is no longer doughy. Serve with ice cream or whipped cream.   5 to 6 Servings

Pudding does not scorch in the oven because it cooks evenly from all sides. This recipe gives basic directions for cooking pudding as well as a way to dress it up for company.

CRUNCHY PUDDING SQUARES

    2 cups milk
    1 package (4-serving size) butterscotch or
      vanilla pudding and pie filling mix
    3 tablespoons butter or margarine
    1¼ cups (20 squares) graham cracker
      crumbs or pre-packaged crumbs
    ¼ cup sugar
    ¼ cup peanut butter

In 4-cup measure, combine milk and pudding mix. **COOK**, uncovered, **5 MINUTES** or until mixture boils, stirring occasionally during last half of cooking time. Set aside. In mixing bowl, soften butter (10 sec.). Stir in cracker crumbs, sugar and peanut butter, mixing until crumbly. Press ¾ of mixture on bottom of 1½-quart (10 x 6) or 2-quart (8 x 8) baking dish. Top with pudding, spreading evenly. Sprinkle remaining crumbs over top. Refrigerate several hours or until chilled. To serve, cut into squares and top with whipped cream.   5 to 6 Servings

> **TIP:** Try with other pudding flavors and cookie crumbs such as gingersnaps, vanilla wafers or chocolate creme-filled cookies.

This traditional cake-like dessert is mixed in the casserole dish and then cooks in 7½ minutes. The dessert is cooked, covered, to achieve a steaming effect.

STEAMED CHRISTMAS PUDDING

    2 cups unsifted all purpose flour
    ⅓ cup firmly packed brown sugar
    1 teaspoon baking powder
    ½ teaspoon salt
    1 teaspoon cinnamon
    ¼ teaspoon nutmeg
    ¼ teaspoon ground ginger
    ⅛ teaspoon ground cloves
    1 cup (4 oz.) ground or grated suet or
      ⅓ cup cooking oil
    1 cup raisins or chopped dates
    ½ cup chopped nuts
    1 cup milk
    ⅓ cup molasses

In 2-quart casserole, combine all ingredients and mix until moistened. **COOK**, covered, **7 MINUTES, 30 SECONDS** or until toothpick comes out clean. **LET STAND**, covered, **2 MINUTES** before inverting onto serving plate. Serve warm or cold with Nutmeg Sauce, page 153 or whipped cream.   10 to 12 Servings

A make ahead soufflé that looks like a soufflé and has a light airy texture but is served cold. The gelatin custard is easily cooked in the oven.

CHILLED LEMON SOUFFLÉ

- ½ cup sugar
- 1 tablespoons (1 envelope) unflavored gelatin
- ¼ teaspoon salt
- 1 cup water
- 3 eggs, separated
- 1 tablespoon grated lemon peel
- 3 to 4 tablespoons lemon juice
- ⅓ cup sugar
- 1 cup whipping cream, whipped, or 2 cups (4½-oz. pkg.) frozen whipped topping, thawed

Prepare a 3 to 4-cup soufflé dish by forming a collar of wax paper around top of dish that extends about 3 inches above dish. (Greasing inside upper edge of dish holds paper in place.) In 4-cup measure, combine ½ cup sugar, gelatin, salt and water. Separate eggs, placing whites in small mixer bowl and adding yolks to gelatin mixture. Beat in yolks until well mixed. COOK, uncovered, **3 MINUTES, 15 SECONDS** or until mixture just begins to boil, stirring occasionally during last half of cooking time. Stir in lemon peel and juice. Cool until mixture is thickened, but not set. Beat egg whites until frothy. Beat in ⅓ cup sugar until mixture forms stiff peaks. Fold in lemon mixture and whipped cream. Pour into prepared dish. Refrigerate 6 hours or until served. Remove wax paper before serving from soufflé dish. Spoon into individual serving dishes and if desired, top with whipped cream.   5 to 6 Servings

TIP: For a large group, double recipe and use a 7 to 8-cup soufflé dish. Cook about 5 minutes.

GLORIFIED ORANGE RICE

- 1 can (8¾ oz.) crushed pineapple
- 1 can (11 oz.) mandarin oranges
- 1 cup quick-cooking rice
- ¼ cup sugar
- ½ cup flaked coconut
- ½ cup whipping cream, whipped, or 1 cup frozen whipped topping, thawed

Drain pineapple and oranges, reserving syrup. Add enough water to syrup to make 1¼ cups liquid. Pour into 1½-quart casserole and COOK, covered, **2 TO 3 MINUTES** or until mixture boils. Stir in rice and sugar. Let stand, covered, to cool to room temperature. Fold in pineapple, mandarin oranges and coconut. Chill thoroughly. Before serving, whip cream until stiff and fold into rice mixture.   6 Servings

Milk and whole eggs reduce the cost and calories of this Crème Brûlée. The method and times would also apply to the more traditional recipe using cream and egg yolks of the same total volume.

CRÈME BRÛLÉE

- ¼ cup sugar
- 1 tablespoon cornstarch
- ¼ teaspoon salt
- 2 cups milk
- 3 eggs
- 1 teaspoon vanilla
- 3 tablespoons brown sugar

In 4-cup measure, combine sugar, cornstarch and salt. Stir in milk; COOK, uncovered, **5 MINUTES** or until mixture boils, stirring occasionally during last half of cooking time. Beat eggs; stir into hot mixture, beating well. COOK, uncovered, **30 SECONDS** or until mixture just begins to cook around edges, stirring once. Stir in vanilla and pour into 1-quart casserole dish. Cool and refrigerate 6 to 12 hours. Just before serving sift brown sugar over top of soft custard. Place under broiler 2 to 5 minutes or until brown sugar is bubbly. Serve over fresh fruit or cake.   5 to 6 Servings

TIP: If broiler is not convenient, sprinkle sugar on soft custard 30 minutes before serving. The moisture from the sauce will cause the sugar to become syrupy.

Chilled Lemon Soufflé

This delicate molded dessert should be made at least 4 hours before serving to have time to chill. Serve with sweetened fresh fruit.

CUSTARD BAVARIAN CRÈME

- **1 tablespoon (1 envelope) unflavored gelatin**
- **⅔ cup sugar**
- **⅛ teaspoon salt**
- **2 cups milk**
- **4 eggs**
- **2 teaspoons vanilla or 2 tablespoons orange flavored liquer**
- **2 cups whipping cream, whipped, or, 4 cups (9-oz. pkg.) frozen whipped topping, thawed**

In 2-quart casserole, combine gelatin, sugar, salt, milk and eggs; beat until well mixed. COOK, uncovered, **6 MINUTES** or until mixture bubbles around edges, stirring occasionally during last half of cooking time. Cool until mixture thickens. Add vanilla and fold in whipped cream. Pour into 8-cup mold or 8 individual molds. Refrigerate 4 hours or until set. Unmold and serve.   8 Servings

> **TIPS:** Overcooking will result in separation of milk and egg mixture; cook only until mixture bubbles. If it does separate, beat with rotary beater to make smooth.
>
> • The mold should be no more than 2 to 3 inches high. If you are using a high mold like a Turk's head mold, add ½ tablespoon (½ envelope) more gelatin to assure it holding its shape when unmolded.

This recipe is for old fashioned ice cream frozen in an ice cream freezer. The timing of the custard mixture will be a guide if you are using your own favorite recipe. If convenient, prepare the custard early so it can cool and chill before using; the freezing will be faster when custard is chilled.

VANILLA CUSTARD ICE CREAM

- **2 eggs, beaten**
- **2 cups milk**
- **¾ cup sugar**
- **⅛ teaspoon salt**
- **1 tablespoon vanilla**
- **2 cups light cream**

Prepare freezer according to manufacturer's directions. In 2-quart casserole, combine eggs, milk, sugar and salt. COOK, uncovered, **6 MINUTES, 30 SECONDS** or until mixture begins to bubble, stirring occasionally during last half of cooking time. Cool. Add vanilla and cream. Pour into freezer can. Freeze as directed.   2 Quarts

> **TIPS:** For Chocolate Custard Ice Cream, increase sugar to 1 cup. Add 2 squares (1 oz. each) unsweetened chocolate or 2 envelopes premelted chocolate before cooking. Before adding cream, beat with rotary beater until smooth.
>
> • For Strawberry Ice Cream, wash, hull and crush 2 cups (1 pt.) fresh strawberries. Stir in ¼ cup sugar. Add with cream and omit vanilla.

A delightfully tasty and pretty combination: fresh strawberries (or other fresh fruit), creamy custard sauce and a topping of fluffy meringue. The meringues can be briefly cooked just before serving because glass or crystal dishes can be used in the oven.

SNOW-CAPPED CUSTARD

- **2 eggs, separated**
- **¼ cup sugar**
- **1 teaspoon cornstarch**
- **1½ cups milk**
- **½ teaspoon vanilla**
- **3 tablespoons sugar**
- **½ teaspoon vanilla**
- **2 cups (1 pt.) fresh whole strawberries or other fruit**

Separate eggs, placing whites in small mixer bowl and yolks in 4-cup measure. To yolks, add ¼ cup sugar and cornstarch, mixing well. Stir in milk. COOK, uncovered, **4 MINUTES** or until mixture just about boils, stirring occasionally during last half of cooking time (mixture will be thin). Stir in ½ teaspoon vanilla; cool until ready to serve.

Just before serving, beat egg whites until frothy. Gradually beat in 3 tablespoons sugar, beating until mixture forms soft peaks. Beat in ½ teaspoon vanilla. Divide strawberries among 4 or 5 dessert dishes. Pour cooled custard over berries; top each with mound of beaten egg white. Place desserts in oven and COOK, uncovered, **45 SECONDS** to set meringue. Serve within a few hours.   4 to 5 Servings

> **TIP:** The desserts can stand longer than a few hours, but there will be some wateriness from the juice in the fruit and meringue.

Cookies and Candies

COOKIES: Bar cookies will normally save the greatest amount of time when you are preparing cookies in your microwave oven. When cooking a large number of individual cookies, you may use your conventional oven more frequently to save time and also because the texture of individual cookies is often different when cooked with microwaves. The next time you bake individual cookies conventionally, test a couple of them in your microwave oven to see how well that particular recipe works. Use the Sugar Cookie recipe as a guide to timing on individual cookies.

It is usually easiest to obtain a thoroughly cooked center of bars if you use an oblong dish. The cookies that have been found to be successful in a square dish have been noted in the recipes. If cookies are overbaked, brown spots will appear in the interior. You may grease the pan or not as you wish. However, do not add flour because it will combine with the grease to form a layer on the bottom of the cookies.

To recapture that "just baked" flavor of a cookie, reheat it on a napkin (about 15 seconds if room temperature, 30 seconds if frozen) and taste the amazing freshness.

CANDY: Making candy in your microwave oven takes the worry out of scorching because the cooking occurs on all sides, rather than only the bottom. The stirring in candy recipes equalizes the heat that is beginning from all sides of the dish. As with conventional candy making, the cooking dish should be two to three times as large as the volume of the candy mixture to allow sufficient boiling space.

If you are using a candy thermometer, be certain to *carefully* remove the cooking container from the oven before testing the temperature. Never use a thermometer while the oven is on because microwave energy will ruin the thermometer by causing the mercury in it to separate. You may find it more convenient to use the soft ball test: dip a clean spoon into the boiling syrup and then let a small amount of the syrup drip into a cup of very cold water. Test with your fingers if it has reached the right consistency.

If you have stored candy in the refrigerator or freezer, you can use the oven to bring it to room temperature before serving.

Pictured: Brownies from mix, page 145, with chocolate frosting, Sugar Cookies, above, with multi-colored sugars, Surprise Teacakes, page 147, and No-Fail Fudge, page 145.

Many cookie recipes spread and flatten when cooked in the microwave oven but we found that this recipe holds its shape nicely during cooking.

SUGAR COOKIES

- **1 cup butter or margarine**
- **1 cup sugar**
- **2 eggs**
- **3 cups unsifted all purpose flour**
- **1 teaspoon cream of tartar**
- **½ teaspoon soda**
- **½ teaspoon salt**
- **1 teaspoon almond extract**

In large mixer bowl, soften butter (25 sec.). Cream butter until fluffy. Add sugar and eggs, beating until well blended. Add remaining ingredients and mix well; chill. Form into 1-inch balls and place on wax paper. Flatten with a glass dipped in sugar. Cook chilled cookies until there are no doughy spots:

> 3 cookies — 45 seconds
> 6 cookies — 1¼ to 1½ minutes
> 9 cookies — 2¼ to 2½ minutes

Allow cookies to cool on wax paper to become firm before removing them.   48 to 54 Cookies

TIPS: If desired, use 2 teaspoons anise seed or 1 teaspoon anise extract for almond extract.

• Cookie dough can be formed into two rolls, 2 inches in diameter and frozen. Slice ¼ inch thick and cook 9 cookies at a time, 1 minute, 15 seconds.

You can make these bar mixes in a hurry, following package directions. Although customary browning does not occur, you will still find these satisfactory.

COOKIES AND BARS

MIX	SIZE	PAN	TIME	YIELD
Brownies	15½ or 17¼ oz.	2-quart (8x8) baking dish	6 minutes	12 brownies
Vienna Dream Bars	12½ oz.	1½-quart (10x6) baking dish	Crust — 2 minutes; Remainder — 3 minutes	10 to 12 bars
Date Bars	14 oz.	2-quart (8x8) baking dish	Dates — 1½ minutes; Remainder — 6 minutes	10 to 12 bars

COCOA BUTTER COOKIES

¾ cup butter or margarine
¾ cup sugar
1 egg
1¾ cups unsifted all purpose flour
1 teaspoon baking powder
½ teaspoon salt
2 tablespoons unsweetened cocoa
½ teaspoon vanilla
⅓ cup chopped nuts
Sugar

In large mixing bowl, soften butter (20 sec.). Blend in sugar and egg, beating until light and fluffy. Add flour, baking powder, salt, cocoa, vanilla and nuts; mix until blended. If necessary, chill dough for easier handling. Shape rounded teaspoons of dough into 1-inch balls, roll in sugar and place at least 1-inch apart on wax paper. Flatten slightly, using bottom of glass or cup. Cook, uncovered, until cookie has puffed and no doughy spots remain:

> 12 cookies — 3 minutes, 30 seconds
> 6 cookies — 1 minute, 45 seconds
> 4 cookies — 1 minute, 15 seconds
> 2 cookies — 1 minute

Leave cookies on wax paper to cool. Peel off wax paper and store in tightly covered container.

About 24 Cookies

TIP: Dough can be stored in refrigerator for up to 3 days; then, just cook fresh cookies as you need them.

ROCKY ROAD CANDY

¼ cup butter or margarine
1 cup (6-oz. pkg.) semi-sweet chocolate pieces
3 to 4 cups miniature marshmallows
½ cup chopped nuts

In large mixing bowl, combine butter and chocolate pieces. **COOK,** uncovered, **1 MINUTE** or until chocolate is soft. Stir to combine butter and chocolate. Stir in marshmallows and nuts until coated with chocolate. Spoon onto wax paper or into greased shallow baking pan. Refrigerate until set, about 30 minutes. To serve, remove from wax paper or cut into squares.

24 Pieces

PEANUT BUTTER BARS

1 package (9½ oz.) pie crust mix or
2 pie crust sticks
1 cup firmly packed brown sugar
½ cup peanut butter
3 tablespoons water
½ to 1 cup chocolate pieces

In large mixing bowl, combine all ingredients except chocolate; mix well. Press into unlined 1½-quart (10 x 6) or 2-quart (8 x 8) baking dish. **COOK,** uncovered, **4 MINUTES, 30 SECONDS** or until mixture is puffy. Sprinkle with chocolate; **COOK,** uncovered, **30 SECONDS** to soften chocolate. With back of spoon, carefully spread chocolate to frost bars. Cool. Cut into bars.

42 to 48 Bars

TIP: For Peanut Butter Cookies, form dough into 1-inch balls. Place up to 8 at a time on wax paper. Flatten with fork. Slide into oven and cook until cookies are puffed and no longer look doughy:

> 4 cookies — 1 minute, 15 seconds
> 6 cookies — 1 minute, 30 seconds
> 8 cookies — 1 minute, 45 seconds

Cool on wax paper before removing and storing in covered container. Make 4 dozen cookies.

This sure-to-please fudge takes about 10 minutes plus cooling time.

NO-FAIL FUDGE

3 cups sugar
¾ cup butter or margarine
⅔ cup (5-oz. can) evaporated milk
2 cups (12-oz. pkg.) semi-sweet chocolate pieces
2 cups (7-oz. jar) marshmallow creme
1 cup chopped nuts
1 teaspoon vanilla

In large mixing bowl, combine sugar, butter and evaporated milk. **COOK,** uncovered, **8 MINUTES,** stirring occasionally. Stir in chocolate until melted. Add marshmallow creme, nuts and vanilla; mix well. Pour into greased 13 x 9-inch pan. Cool; cut into squares.

90 to 96 Squares

POPCORN BALLS

⅓ cup light corn syrup
⅓ cup water
1 cup sugar
1 teaspoon salt
¼ cup butter or margarine
1 teaspoon vanilla
Food coloring, if desired
7 cups popped corn

Measure syrup and water in 4-cup measure. Add sugar, salt and butter. **COOK**, uncovered, **11 MINUTES** or to 250° (hardball stage), stirring once. Add vanilla and food coloring. Pour in a thin stream over popped corn in a large buttered bowl; mix well. With buttered hands, shape popcorn into balls.

10 to 12 Balls

TIPS: This mixture can be molded into many interesting shapes for holiday time: angels, Christmas trees, snowmen, bells, etc.

• For best results, pop corn conventionally.

• Do not use thermometer in oven during cooking.

A candy with the built-in nutrition of rolled oats and peanut butter.

PEANUT BUTTER FUDGE CANDY

½ cup butter or margarine
2 cups sugar
½ cup unsweetened cocoa
⅛ teaspoon salt
½ cup milk
3 cups quick-cooking rolled oats
½ cup shredded or flaked coconut
½ cup chopped peanuts or other nuts
½ cup peanut butter
2 teaspoons vanilla

In mixing bowl, melt butter (45 sec.). Add sugar, cocoa, salt and milk; blend well. **COOK**, uncovered, **5 MINUTES**, stirring once. Stir in remaining ingredients. Pour into greased 12 x 7 or 13 x 9-inch pan. Cool several hours at room temperature or in refrigerator. Cut into squares.

54 to 60 Squares

TIPS: To make individual candies, drop by teaspoon onto wax paper.

• This candy freezes well. To thaw quickly, arrange several pieces on plate and heat about 15 seconds.

SIX LAYER BARS

½ cup butter or margarine
1½ cups (18 squares) graham cracker crumbs
1 cup chopped nuts
1 cup (6-oz. pkg.) semi-sweet chocolate pieces
1⅓ cups (3½-oz. can) flaked coconut
1⅓ cups (15-oz. can) sweetened condensed milk

In 2-quart (12 x 7) baking dish, melt butter (45 sec.). Add the next five ingredients, layer by layer. **COOK**, uncovered, **8 MINUTES** or until mixture just begins to show brown areas. Cool. Cut into bars.

48 to 54 Bars

These popular treats can be quickly prepared in the oven without fear of scorching the marshmallows.

KRISPIE MARSHMALLOW TREATS

¼ cup butter or margarine
5 cups miniature or 40 large marshmallows
5 cups rice crispy cereal

In large mixing bowl, melt butter (30 sec.). Stir in marshmallows to coat with butter. **COOK**, uncovered, **30 SECONDS**; stir well and **COOK 15 SECONDS** (30 sec. for large marshmallows). Stir until smooth. Add cereal; mix well. With wet or buttered fingers press into greased 13 x 9-inch pan. Cool and cut into squares.

24 to 30 Squares

Graham cracker squares add an interesting texture and flavor to these candy pieces. The oven makes cooking the butter and brown sugar quick and scorchless.

TOFFEE PIECES

½ cup butter or margarine
¾ cup firmly packed brown sugar
¼ cup chopped nuts
11 graham cracker squares
1 cup (6-oz. pkg.) semi-sweet chocolate pieces

In 4-cup measure, combine butter and brown sugar. **COOK**, uncovered, **2 MINUTES**, stirring 4 times. Add nuts. Place graham cracker squares in buttered 2-quart (12 x 7) baking dish. Pour syrup over crackers. **COOK**, uncovered, **1 MINUTE, 30 SECONDS**; sprinkle with chocolate pieces and **COOK**, uncovered, **30 SECONDS** or until chocolate is soft. With a spatula, spread chocolate evenly over top. Cool; refrigerate 30 minutes. Break apart into pieces or cut into squares and serve.

22 to 24 Pieces

Brownies are quick and easy with either a mix or this "from scratch" recipe. Make extras to keep in the freezer.

BROWNIES

2 squares or envelopes unsweetened chocolate
⅓ cup butter or margarine
1 cup sugar
2 eggs
1 cup unsifted all purpose flour
¼ teaspoon baking powder
¼ teaspoon salt
½ teaspoon vanilla
½ cup chopped nuts

In large mixing bowl, melt chocolate and butter (squares — 2 min.; envelopes — 30 sec.). Stir in sugar; add eggs and beat well. Stir in flour, baking powder, salt, vanilla and nuts until moistened. Spread in unlined 1½-quart (10 x 6) or 2-quart (8 x 8) baking dish. **COOK,** uncovered, **5 MINUTES** or until brownie is puffed and most of top is dry. Cool. Cut into bars.   16 to 24 Bars

> **TIPS:** If nuts are omitted, reduce baking time to 4 minutes.
>
> • When using premelted chocolate, place unopened envelopes in oven when melting butter. The chocolate heats enough to easily squeeze from the plastic envelopes.
>
> • Turn brownies into an easy dessert by topping warm squares with ice cream and chocolate sauce.

Six Layer Bars, page 146, Krispie Marshmallow Treats, page 146.

This traditional "rolled in powdered sugar" butter cookie has a surprise center. Because powdered sugar looks best without browning, these cookies are ideal for the microwave oven. If you have extras, freeze some of them after cooking.

SURPRISE TEACAKES

1 cup butter or margarine
1 egg
1 teaspoon vanilla
½ cup powdered sugar
2⅓ cups unsifted all purpose flour
1 cup finely chopped nuts
2 packages (5¾ oz. each) milk chocolate kisses
Powdered sugar to sprinkle

In mixing bowl, soften butter (20 sec.). Add egg, vanilla and powdered sugar, beating until light and fluffy. Blend in flour and nuts. Shape dough (about size of walnut) around each chocolate kiss. Place 12 at a time on paper towel and **COOK,** uncovered, about **1 MINUTE, 45 SECONDS** or until surface no longer looks doughy. Sprinkle warm cookies with powdered sugar.   45 to 48 Cookies

> **TIPS:** Try other surprise fillings:
>   Candied cherries — same cooking time
>   Halved dates — 1 minute, 30 seconds
>
> • If dough has been refrigerated, increase times 30 seconds.
>
> • Without fillings, cook 12 cookies for 2 minutes, 30 seconds; cook 6 cookies for 2 minutes. Makes 38 to 42 cookies.

OATMEAL CARMELITAS

¾ cup butter or margarine
¾ cup firmly packed brown sugar
½ teaspoon soda
¼ teaspoon salt
1 cup unsifted all purpose flour
1 cup quick-cooking rolled oats
Topping
1 cup (6-oz. pkg.) semi-sweet chocolate pieces
½ cup chopped nuts
¾ cup caramel ice cream topping
3 tablespoons flour

In 2-quart (12 x 7) baking dish, melt butter (1 min.). Add brown sugar, soda and salt. Mix well. Blend in flour and rolled oats. Pat evenly in baking dish. **COOK,** uncovered, **2 MINUTES** (will look slightly doughy). Sprinkle chocolate pieces and nuts over crust. Combine caramel topping and flour; pour over crust. **COOK,** uncovered, **6 MINUTES.** Cool and chill 1 to 2 hours. Cut into bars. Store in refrigerator.
                                    48 to 54 Bars

Cakes

Cakes come in creative shapes from your microwave oven. You can cook cake shaped in individual dessert dishes or in a mixing bowl . . . even cook cake in ice cream cones!

If you use a cake mix that calls for a 13 x 9-inch pan, you will have extra batter for the 12 x 7-inch dish that fits in the oven. Whatever size you use, fill only half full instead of the customary two thirds because cake rises higher in your microwave oven. Cook the remaining batter in any shape that suits your fancy . . . maybe even in a glass measuring cup. A whole box of cake mix, however, will fit into a mixing bowl so you can mix and cook in the same container.

Layered cake is easier to frost if the layers are first refrigerated. Broiled-on toppings also work well on some cakes. Upside down cakes are especially great from your oven. You may want to frost white or light colored cakes because there will be no browning and the surface may be somewhat uneven.

Cake batter can be refrigerated or even frozen ahead of time; you may want to cook one layer and keep another layer in the freezer for unexpected company. We have included some quick, last-minute desserts that adapt well to preparing small amounts. If you want to warm a piece of cake such as gingerbread or freshen leftover cake, just put it into the oven for about 15 seconds.

Cake from your microwave oven is a good make ahead dessert because it often improves after standing. If you adapt one of your own recipes from scratch and notice a leavening taste, try reducing the amount of leavening by about 25% the next time you make it. Use wax paper if you are planning to remove the whole cake from the baking dish before serving; otherwise it is unecessary. Some people find it convenient to cut several cake rounds of wax paper at one time. You don't grease and flour the dish because it tends to form a layer on the bottom of the cake.

CUPCAKES

Fill paper-lined custard cups or shallow coffee cups half full (about 2½ tablespoons batter for each cupcake). Cook, uncovered, until toothpick comes out clean:

    1 cupcake — 15 seconds
    2 cupcakes — 30 seconds
    3 cupcakes — 45 seconds
    4 cupcakes — 1 minute
    5 cupcakes — 1 minute, 15 seconds
    6 cupcakes — 1 minute, 30 seconds

TIPS: For refrigerated batter, increase cooking time 5 seconds; for frozen batter, increase cooking time 15 seconds.

• For a surprise center, push a marshmallow into cupcake batter until covered. Cook as directed.

Pictured: Cake mix ideas — Cake Cones, page 149, topped with ice cream, Cupcakes, above, frosted with Marshmallow Frosting, page 153, and decorated with toasted coconut, page 137 and decorettes, and Cake Mix Cooked in Bowl, see Cake Mix Tips, page 149, frosted with Creamy Whipped Frosting, page 153.

With cake mix, you will usually have leftover batter for cupcakes. The batter rises higher than with conventional cooking so the pans are filled only half full. We found some brands of cake mix cooked with a smoother top surface than others. There is no browning so you may prefer to use a dark colored cake flavor. However, when using a light frosting, the lack of browning eliminates dark cake crumbs showing in the frosting. Chilling the cooked cake in the refrigerator will make frosting the cake easier, especially with layers. Cakes made with cake mixes become more moist on standing.

CAKE MIXES

Prepare cake batter as directed on package. Line baking dishes with wax paper when planning to remove the cake as a whole from baking dish; leave unlined when planning to remove cake in pieces from baking dish. Fill baking dishes half full, using leftover batter for cupcakes. Cook one dish at a time, uncovered, until toothpick inserted in center comes out clean (top may still look moist):

1½-quart (8-inch round)	— 5 minutes
2-quart (8 x 8)	— 7 minutes
2-quart (12 x 7)	— 8 minutes

Cool layers 5 minutes before removing from pans.

> **TIPS:** Cake mix can be cooked in the mixing bowl (if glass) by pressing a tall glass, right side up, down through batter to form a tube shape. Cook, uncovered, 8 to 9 minutes or until toothpick inserted in center comes out clean and batter around glass no longer looks doughy. Let cool 30 minutes. Remove glass by twisting lightly and invert cake onto serving plate.
>
> • Cake mixes that need butter added do not rise as high, so the baking dishes can be filled ⅔ full. Increase cooking time 1 to 2 minutes.
>
> • Cake batter can be refrigerated for 2 to 3 days or frozen up to 2 weeks. For refrigerated batter, increase cooking time 1 to 2 minutes. For frozen batter, cook 3 minutes; rest 5 minutes and then cook 5 to 6 minutes.

GINGERBREAD

Prepare as directed on mix package. Pour into unlined 2-quart (8 x 8) or 1½ quart (10 x 6) baking dish. **COOK**, uncovered, **7 to 8 MINUTES** or until toothpick comes out clean.

Flat bottom ice cream cones become holders for cooking cake batter. Frost the cooked cones or top with whipped cream, ice cream or frozen pudding for a quick children's snack.

CAKE CONES

Spoon 2 tablespoons cake batter into each cone, filling cone half full. Cook, uncovered, until toothpick comes out clean:

1 cone	— 15 seconds
2 cones	— 25 seconds
3 cones	— 40 seconds
4 cones	— 50 seconds
5 cones	— 1 minute
6 cones	— 1 minute, 10 seconds

This is a good recipe to keep in mind when you have extra egg whites. It looks like angel food, but has more body with a moist, chewy texture. It has a candy bar taste when topped with frosting, chocolate and nuts.

ANGEL SQUARES

4 egg whites (⅔ cup)
¼ teaspoon cream of tartar
½ cup sugar
1 cup unsifted all purpose flour
½ cup sugar
1 teaspoon baking powder
½ teaspoon salt
½ cup milk
½ teaspoon vanilla

In mixer bowl, beat egg whites with cream of tartar until soft mounds form. Gradually add ½ cup sugar, beating until stiff peaks form; set aside. In another mixing bowl, combine flour, ½ cup sugar, baking powder and salt. Measure milk in 1-cup measure and heat by cooking, uncovered, 45 seconds or until hot. Add milk and vanilla to flour mixture. Beat until smooth. Pour over egg white mixture and by hand, fold in until well combined. Pour into 2-quart (8 x 8) baking dish. **COOK**, uncovered, **7 MINUTES** or until toothpick comes out clean and mixture has pulled away from sides of dish. Cool. If desired, frost with favorite butter frosting. Top with chopped cashew nuts and shaved chocolate. 9 Servings

> **TIPS:** When you have a few extra egg whites, store them in a small container in the freezer until you have enough to make a recipe like this. They can be quickly thawed in the oven by using cooking periods of 15 seconds with rest periods of 1 minute.
>
> • The firm texture and lack of brown crumbs with this cake would make it a good base for petit fours.

Frosting cooks along with the cake in this recipe. When cooking frozen batter, the rest period allows the temperature to equalize for even cooking of edges and center.

ONE-STEP GERMAN CHOCOLATE CAKE

   ½ cup butter or margarine
   ⅔ cup milk
   1 package (9.9 oz.) coconut almond or pecan frosting mix
   1 package (17.5 oz.) German chocolate cake mix
   2 eggs
   1½ cups water

Melt ¼ cup butter in each of two 1½-quart (8-inch round) baking dishes. Stir ⅓ cup milk and half of frosting mix (1 cup) into each. Set aside. Prepare and beat cake mix with eggs and water as directed on package. Remove 1 cup of batter for cupcakes. Pour half of remaining batter into each prepared pan. **COOK,** one layer at a time*, uncovered, **6 MINUTES** or until toothpick comes out clean. Cool 5 minutes. Loosen edges and invert to cool. If some of frosting sticks in pan, just remove with spatula and spread on cake. When cool enough to handle, stack layers.   8-inch Layer Cake

> **TIPS:** *If desired, freeze batter for other layer for up to 4 weeks. Cook frozen layer 3 minutes, rest 5 minutes, and then cook 6 more minutes.
>
> • Cook 4 cupcakes 1½ to 2 minutes or until toothpick comes out clean.

This cheesecake recipe cooks very well in the oven. Because of the straight-sided pan, the first piece may be slightly difficult to remove.

CHERRY CHEESECAKE

Crust
   ¼ cup butter or margarine
   12 graham cracker squares, crushed (⅔ cup crumbs)
   2 tablespoons flour
   2 tablespoons sugar
   ¼ teaspoon cinnamon
Filling
   1 package (8 oz.) cream cheese
   ⅓ cup sugar
   1 egg
   1 teaspoon lemon extract
Topping
   1 cup sour cream
   3 tablespoons sugar
   ½ teaspoon almond extract (or vanilla)
   1 can (21 oz.) prepared cherry pie filling

Melt butter in 1½-quart (8-inch round) baking dish (30 sec.). Mix in remaining Crust ingredients and press mixture on bottom and halfway up sides of dish. Soften cream cheese (30 sec.) and beat with rest of Filling ingredients, using mixer. Pour over crust and **COOK,** uncovered, **5 MINUTES.** Combine sour cream, sugar and extract for Topping. Spread over filling and **COOK,** uncovered, **2 MINUTES.** Cool slightly. Spoon cherry pie filling on top. Chill several hours or overnight.

6 to 8 Servings

A traditional favorite made easy and delicious in the oven.

GERMAN CHOCOLATE CAKE

    ½ cup hot water
    1 bar (4 oz.) German sweet chocolate
    1 cup butter or margarine
    2 cups sugar
    4 eggs
 2¼ cups unsifted all purpose flour
    1 teaspoon soda
    ½ teaspoon salt
    1 teaspoon vanilla
    1 cup buttermilk or sour milk

In mixer bowl, combine hot water and chocolate. **COOK**, uncovered, **1 MINUTE;** stir until blended. Add butter and let mixture stand a few minutes to cool chocolate and soften butter. Add sugar and beat with mixer until light. Beat in eggs, one at a time, beating well after each. Add flour, soda, salt, vanilla and buttermilk. Mix at low speed just until well combined. Line three 1½-quart (8-inch round) baking dishes* with wax paper. Pour about 2 cups batter into each. **COOK EACH LAYER**, uncovered, **5 MINUTES** or unitl toothpick comes out clean (top may still look a little moist). Cool 5 minutes; loosen edge and turn out of pan. Cool completely and frost between layers and top with Coconut Pecan Frosting.

8-inch Layer Cake

TIP: *The same baking dish can be used each time; just remove paper and loose crumbs, then line with new wax paper. Cake may take about 30 seconds less time if pan is warm.

COCONUT PECAN FROSTING

    1 cup evaporated milk
    3 eggs
    1 cup sugar
    ½ cup butter or margarine
    1 teaspoon vanilla
 1⅓ cups flaked coconut
    1 cup chopped pecans or almonds

In 4-cup measure, measure milk. Beat in eggs until well combined. Stir in sugar and add butter. **COOK**, uncovered, **4 MINUTES, 30 SECONDS,** stirring occasionally until mixture thickens and boils. Stir in vanilla, coconut and pecans. If necessary, cool slightly until of spreading consistency. Use to frost 3 layers of German Chocolate Cake.

Pictured, clockwise: Streusel Rhubarb Cake, page 152, Angel Squares, page 149, topped with fresh peaches, Cherry Cheesecake, page 150, and One-Step German Chocolate Cake, page 150.

CHOCO-SWIRL CAKE

    ½ cup butter or margarine
    1 package (18.5 oz.) yellow batter
       cake mix*
 1⅓ cups water
    3 eggs
    1 package (9.9 oz.) coconut pecan or
       almond frosting mix
    1 envelope premelted chocolate

In large mixer bowl, soften butter (10 sec.). Add cake mix, water and eggs. Blend and beat as directed on package. Place 2 cups of batter in another large mixing bowl. To this batter add 1 cup of dry frosting mix and chocolate; mix well. Spoon this mixture over top of batter in original bowl. Swirl slightly to marble. Place a tall glass in center, right-side up, and press down through batter. (This will form a tube center.) **COOK**, uncovered, **12 MINUTES,** turning cake ¼ turn at 3-minute intervals. Cake should no longer look doughy along glass. Cool in pan 15 minutes. Remove glass by twisting slightly. Loosen edges and invert cake onto serving plate. Cool completely before serving.

1 Large Tube Cake

TIP: *Since we did not find equally good results with all brands of cake mix, we recommend using the batter mix.

An easy fruit-type dessert that uses cake and frosting mixes. A good last minute dessert for guests.

DUTCH APPLE CAKE

    ¼ cup butter or margarine
    ½ package (2⅓ cups) lemon cake mix
    1 egg
 1¼ cups (half of 1 lb. 4-oz. can) drained pie
       sliced apples
    2 tablespoons butter or margarine
    ½ package (1 cup) coconut pecan or
       coconut almond frosting mix

In large mixing bowl, melt ¼ cup butter (30 sec.). By hand, stir in dry cake mix and egg until mix is moistened. Pat into 1½-quart (8-inch round) baking dish. Top with drained apples. In same mxing bowl, melt 2 tablespoons butter (20 sec.). Stir in frosting mix; sprinkle over apples. **COOK**, uncovered, **7 MINUTES** or until toothpick comes out clean. Serve warm or cold with whipped cream or ice cream.

6 Servings

TIPS: We found some brands of cake mix made into more moist mixtures that needed spreading rather than patting. The cooked cakes were still very good.

● If desired, use 1½ cups sliced fresh cooking apples for canned.

This makes a quick dessert for a small number of people. For Pineapple Upside Down Cake, see page 31.

PINEAPPLE CAKETTES

2 tablespoons butter or margarine
2 tablespoons brown sugar
4 tablespoons undrained crushed
pineapple

Cake
½ cup unsifted all purpose flour
⅓ cup sugar
½ teaspoon baking powder
⅛ teaspoon salt
½ teaspoon vanilla
2 tablespoons oil
¼ cup milk
1 egg

Prepare four 6-oz. custard cups by melting ½ tablespoon butter in each cup (30 sec.). Stir ½ tablespoon brown sugar and 1 tablespoon pineapple into each cup. Prepare Cake batter in small mixing bowl by combining all ingredients and mixing until well combined. Spoon onto pineapple mixture, filling cups about half full. **COOK**, uncovered, **3 MINUTES, 30 SECONDS** or until toothpick comes out clean. Loosen edges and invert onto serving plates. Serve warm, topped with whipped cream.   4 Servings

> **TIPS:** For 8 cupcakes, double amounts and cook in 2 batches.
>
> • If desired, use one tablespoon favorite flavor prepared pie filling for pineapple mixture in each cup.

An easy "make yourself" cake that is finished with a broiled topping. It's a moist, light cake for company or family.

EASY COMPANY CAKE

¼ cup butter or margarine
¼ cup milk
¼ teaspoon almond extract
2 eggs
¾ cup sugar
¾ cup unsifted all purpose flour
½ teaspoon baking powder
½ teaspoon salt

Topping
¼ cup sugar
1 tablespoon flour
1 tablespoon milk
¼ cup butter or margarine
⅓ cup slivered almonds or flaked coconut

In 1-cup measure, melt butter with milk (1 min.). Add almond extract; set aside. In medium mixing bowl, beat eggs until light. Gradually beat in sugar until eggs are light and thickened, about 2 minutes. By hand, stir in flour, baking powder, salt and milk mixture until well combined. Pour into unlined 2-quart (8 x 8) or 1½-quart (10 x 6) baking dish. **COOK**, uncovered, **4 MINUTES, 30 SECONDS** until toothpick inserted in center comes out clean (cake should still look moist on top).

While cake is cooking, combine sugar, flour, milk and butter in 2-cup measure for Topping. After cake has cooked, **COOK** Topping, uncovered, **1 MINUTE** or until mixture boils, stirring once. Sprinkle almonds over top of cake; drizzle topping mixture over cake to cover almonds. Place under broiler until bubbly and light golden brown, 2 to 3 minutes.

8-inch Square Cake

A colorful cake that adapts especially well to microwave cooking.

STREUSEL RHUBARB CAKE

2 cups unsifted all purpose flour
½ cup sugar
1½ teaspoons baking powder
1 teaspoon salt
1 cup milk
¼ cup cooking oil
1 egg
4 cups cut-up rhubarb
3 tablespoons (half of 3-oz. pkg.)
strawberry or raspberry-flavored gelatin

Topping
½ cup unsifted all purpose flour
¾ cup sugar
½ cup rolled oats
½ teaspoon cinnamon
¼ cup butter or margarine

In mixing bowl, combine flour, sugar, baking powder, salt, milk, oil and egg. Mix until smooth. Pour into unlined 2-quart (12 x 7) baking dish. Top with rhubarb; sprinkle evenly with gelatin. Combine Topping ingredients and cut in butter. Sprinkle over gelatin. **COOK**, uncovered, **15 TO 17 MINUTES** or until cake is no longer doughy under rhubarb. Serve warm or cool.   12 x 7-inch Cake

> **TIPS:** For 8-inch round cake, use half of ingredients except use 1 egg. Cook, uncovered, in 1½-quart (8-inch round) baking dish, 7 minutes or until rhubarb is tender and cake no longer doughy.
>
> • For apple cake, use 4 cups (4 med.) sliced, peeled or unpeeled apple for rhubarb. Cook 12 x 7-inch cake 10 minutes.

Frostings,Fillings,Sauces

We have given some recipes that can be used as a guide to most frostings, fillings and sauces that have a cooking preparation step. The sauces will need a large enough container to hold the boiling mixture. If you prepare a sauce in a large enough glass jar, you can also store and reheat it in the same jar.

See the Dinner section (page 26) for a Grand Marnier Sauce recipe.

This fluffy egg white frosting with a marshmallow texture is especially easy to make with hot corn syrup.

MARSHMALLOW FROSTING

   1 egg white
⅛ teaspoon salt
   2 tablespoons sugar
   6 tablespoons light corn syrup
¾ teaspoon vanilla
Food coloring, if desired

In small mixer bowl, beat egg white until foamy. Add salt and sugar, beating until soft peaks form. Measure syrup in 1-cup measure. **COOK,** uncovered, **1 MINUTE** or until mixture boils. Pour over egg white, continuing to beat until frosting is stiff. Beat in vanilla and desired food coloring. Spread on cooled cake.

Frosts 8 or 9-inch Square or Layer Cake

> **TIP:** This recipe can be doubled for a two-layer cake or a 12 x 7-inch cake. Cook ¾ cup syrup (12 T.) about 2 minutes, 30 seconds. When using a filling in a layer cake, you may have leftover frosting for cupcakes.

An easy chocolate syrup to use over ice cream, pudding or cake.

FRENCH CHOCOLATE SYRUP

½ cup light corn syrup
¼ cup water
   3 squares (3 oz.) semi-sweet chocolate squares
   1 teaspoon vanilla

Measure corn syrup and water into 4-cup measure. Add chocolate squares. **COOK,** uncovered, **3 MINUTES** or until chocolate melts, stirring once. Blend until smooth. Stir in vanilla and cool.   ⅔ Cup Syrup

> **TIP:** If you prefer a buttery chocolate sauce, add 2 tablespoons butter or margarine.

NUTMEG SAUCE

½ cup sugar
   1 tablespoon cornstarch
½ teaspoon nutmeg
   1 cup water
¼ cup butter or margarine
   2 tablespoons rum or brandy;
     or 1 teaspoon vanilla

In 2-cup measure, combine sugar, cornstarch and nutmeg; stir in water and butter. **COOK,** uncovered, **3 MINUTES** or until mixture boils and thickens, stirring occasionally. Stir in flavoring. Serve warm.   1½ Cups Sauce

LEMON FILLING

½ cup sugar
   2 tablespoons cornstarch
Dash salt
   1 egg yolk
1½ teaspoons grated lemon peel or
   ¾ teaspoon dried lemon peel
   2 tablespoons lemon juice
   1 tablespoon butter or margarine
⅔ cup water
Yellow food coloring, if desired

Combine all ingredients in 4-cup measure. **COOK,** uncovered, **2 MINUTES, 30 SECONDS** or until mixture boils and thickens, stirring twice during last half of cooking time. Cool. Spread on cake. Fills 8 or 9-inch Layer Cake

A not-too-sweet creamy frosting that tastes like pudding and spreads like frosting. Start the frosting when cooking a cake, then let the frosting chill while cake cools.

CREAMY WHIPPED FROSTING

¾ cup sugar
¼ cup flour
¾ cup milk
½ cup butter or margarine
   1 teaspoon vanilla

In small mixer bowl, combine sugar and flour. Stir in milk. **COOK,** uncovered, **3 MINUTES** or until mixture thickens and boils, stirring occasionally. Place butter on top to soften. Refrigerate about 1 hour or until cool. Add vanilla and beat with mixer at high speed until light and fluffy.

Frosts 12 x 7-inch Cake or 8-inch Layer Cake

> **TIP:** For chocolate flavor, add 1 additional tablespoon flour and 1 envelope premelted chocolate before cooking.

Pies

Lemon Cloud Pie, page 156 (pastry shell as cooked in oven).

This section includes recipes for two crust pies, pies with the filling and pastry shell cooked separately and then combined, and also pies with the filling cooked in a precooked pastry shell.

Although crusts do not brown in a microwave oven, they do become exceptionally flaky. You can use pie crust sticks, mix or home recipe that has some yellow food coloring added to it. A cookie based crust cooks the same as it does in conventional cooking; the heat simply fuses together the cookie crumbs and other ingredients.

A two crust pie combines conventional and microwave cooking. The pie is first cooked rapidly in your microwave oven and then finished in a conventional oven to brown the crust.

Most recipes in this section are for pies with the filling and pastry shell cooked separately and then combined.

If a filling is to be cooked in a pastry shell, the shell needs to be precooked. Stirring a custard-like filling such as pumpkin pie will prevent the outside edges cooking too rapidly.

Don't forget that you can rewarm an individual slice of pie to recapture that just from the oven taste: 1 slice, 15 sec.; 2 slices, 25 sec.; 3 slices, 40 sec.; 4 slices, 1 minute.

Cookie crumb crusts hold their shape and have a crunchier texture if cooked a few minutes before adding a filling.

COOKIE CRUMB CRUSTS

TYPE	AMOUNT	SUGAR	BUTTER OR MARGARINE	COOKING TIME
Graham Cracker	1½ cups (18 to 20 squares)	¼ cup	⅓ cup	1 minute, 45 seconds
Vanilla Wafer	1½ cups (36 wafers)	Omit	¼ cup	2 minutes
Gingersnap	1½ cups (30 cookies)	Omit	⅓ cup	2 minutes
Chocolate Creme-Filled Cookies	1½ cups (15 to 20 cookies)	Omit	3 tablespoons	2 minutes
Flaked or Shredded Coconut	2 cups	Omit	¼ cup	2 minutes

In 9-inch pie plate, melt butter (30 sec.). Stir in cookie crumbs and sugar; press into bottom and up sides of dish. Cook as directed or until brown spots just begin to appear.　　9-inch Cookie Crust

The pie crust sticks and mix have a yellow color that cooks nicely in the oven. You don't get as much browning as in the conventional oven, but the crust is exceptionally flaky. Making the pastry shell in the microwave oven is especially convenient on a warm summer day.

BAKED PASTRY SHELL

Prepare pie crust stick or enough mix for 1 crust pie as directed on package. Roll out and fit into 9-inch pie plate. Flute edge and prick bottom and sides with fork. **COOK**, uncovered, **4 MINUTES**, watching carefully last minute to remove just when brown spots begin to appear in crust. If you leave crust in too long, these spots will burn. Cool.

9-inch Baked Pastry Shell

TIP: We also had good results with home recipe pastry when about 4 drops of yellow food color were added to the water.

A thin layer of cheesecake cooks atop cherry pie filling in this easy pie.

CHEESECAKE CHERRY PIE

9-inch Baked Pastry Shell
2 cups (21-oz. can) prepared cherry pie filling
2 packages (3 oz. each) cream cheese
1 egg
⅓ cup sugar
½ teaspoon vanilla or almond extract

Prepare and cook pastry shell as directed to left. Pour cherry pie filling into crust, spreading evenly. Prepare cheesecake topping by softening cream cheese in mixing bowl (30 sec.). Stir in remaining ingredients, mixing well. Pour over pie filling. **COOK**, uncovered, **5 MINUTES, 30 SECONDS** or until topping is set. Cool and refrigerate 2 hours before serving.

9-inch Pie

Grasshopper Pie (example of plate with metal trim not to be used in oven).

In this recipe the oven is used to cook the crust and melt the marshmallows.

GRASSHOPPER PIE

9-inch Chocolate Cookie Crust
30 large or 3 cups miniature marshmallows
½ cup milk
2 to 3 tablespoons creme de cocoa
2 to 3 tablespoons green creme de menthe
1 cup whipping cream, whipped, or 2 cups (4½ oz. pkg.) frozen whipped topping, thawed

Prepare and cook chocolate cookie crust as directed on page 154. Cool. In large mixing bowl, combine marshmallows and milk. **COOK**, uncovered, **2 MINUTES** or until marshmallows begin to puff. Stir to blend together. (If marshmallows are not completely melted, cook a few seconds more.) Stir in creme de cocoa and menthe. Cool until mixture is thickened, but not set, about 30 minutes. Fold in whipped cream. Pour into crust. Refrigerate 4 hours or until served. If desired, garnish with whipped cream and chocolate curls.

9-inch Pie

TIP: If you have white crème de menthe, add 4 to 5 drops green food coloring.

Fresh Fruit Pie, below, with rhubarb-strawberry filling (combination of microwave and conventional cooking).

Two crust pies need a combination of microwave and conventional cooking. With only microwave cooking, the crust would not become brown and crisp. Since the filling cooks very quickly, the bottom crust stays crisp and flaky, even the second day. Try this method for cherry, rhubarb, peach, apple or combination fruit pies.

FRESH FRUIT PIE

Prepare favorite recipe for 2-crust 9-inch fresh fruit pie. Preheat conventional oven to 450°. **COOK** pie, uncovered, in microwave oven **7 TO 8 MINUTES** until fruit is just about tender or juices start bubbling through slits in crust. Transfer to preheated oven and **COOK 10 TO 15 MINUTES** or until golden brown. 9-inch Pie

> **TIPS:** For an attractive "golden" crust, use the pie crust sticks or mix that has a yellow color, or add 7 to 8 drops yellow food color to the water for pastry.
>
> • To cook a frozen uncooked fruit pie, transfer pie from foil pan to glass. Cook in microwave oven, uncovered, 15 minutes to thaw and cook fruit; then transfer to conventional oven and cook as directed above.
>
> • Crumb-topped fruit pies can be cooked this way but omit ingredients with a high fat content such as nuts or coconut as they tend to scorch.
>
> • For 8-inch pie, decrease cooking in microwave oven to 6 to 7 minutes; for 10-inch pie, increase time to 8 to 9 minutes.

Here is a way to cook lemon meringue pie in the microwave oven. Since meringue on top of a pie does not cook well in the oven, fold it into the filling to make a light, creamy texture.

LEMON CLOUD PIE

  9-inch Baked Pastry Shell
¾ cup sugar
  3 tablespoons cornstarch
  1 cup water
  1 teaspoon grated lemon peel
¼ to ⅓ cup lemon juice
  2 eggs, separated
  1 package (3 oz.) cream cheese
¼ cup sugar

Prepare and cook pastry shell as directed on page 155 and set aside to cool. In mixing bowl, combine ¾ cup sugar with cornstarch. Stir in water, lemon peel and juice. Separate eggs, placing whites in small mixer bowl and yolks in measuring cup or small bowl. Beat egg yolks slightly and add to lemon mixture, stirring to combine. **COOK,** uncovered, **4 MINUTES** or until mixture starts to bubble, stirring occasionally during last half of cooking time. Add cream cheese and allow to soften; mix well. Cool mixture until it begins to thicken. Beat egg whites until foamy. Gradually beat in ¼ cup sugar, beating until mixture forms stiff peaks. Fold into lemon mixture. Pour into pastry shell. Refrigerate at least 2 hours or until served.
9-inch Pie

Pumpkin pie filling cooks before it has a chance to soak into the crust, which sometimes happens in conventional cooking. Stirring after partial cooking allows the filling to cook evenly. Since the crust is already cooked and some shrinking may have taken place, there will be leftover filling to make into pumpkin custards.

PUMPKIN PIE

   9-inch Baked Pastry Shell
   2 eggs
  ½ cup sugar
  ½ cup firmly packed brown sugar
   1 tablespoon flour
  ½ teaspoon salt
   2 to 3 teaspoons pumpkin pie spice
   2 cups (1-lb. can) cooked pumpkin
 1⅔ cups (14½-oz. can) evaporated milk

Prepare and cook pastry shell as directed on page 155. In mixing bowl or blender, combine remaining ingredients, beating until well mixed. Pour into pastry shell. (Any remaining filling can be poured into custard cups and cooked after cooking pie.) **COOK, uncovered, 4 MINUTES** or until edges just begin to set. Carefully stir to move cooked portion from edge to center. **COOK, uncovered, 6 MINUTES** or until knife inserted near center comes out clean. Cool.

                               9-inch Pie

> **TIPS:** Individual spices can be used for pumpkin pie spice. Use 1 teaspoon cinnamon and ¼ teaspoon each nutmeg, ginger and allspice.
>
> • Cook 3 to 4 individual custards, covered, 3 to 4 minutes or until knife inserted near center comes out clean.

A refreshing pie for a summer day. By using the oven for both the crust and filling, you can keep your kitchen cool.

KEY LIME PIE

   9-inch Baked Pastry Shell
  ½ cup water
  ⅓ cup lime juice (2 limes)
  ¾ cup sugar
   1 tablespoon (1 envelope) unflavored gelatin
   2 eggs, separated
   4 to 5 drops green food coloring
   1 teaspoon grated lime peel, if desired
   2 tablespoons sugar
   1 cup whipping cream or 2 cups (4½-oz. pkg.) frozen whipped topping, thawed

Prepare and cook pastry shell as directed on page 155. While pastry shell cools, prepare filling by combining in 4-cup measure, water, lime juice, sugar, gelatin and beaten egg yolks. **COOK, uncovered, 3 MINUTES** or until mixture is steaming hot and just begins to bubble, stirring occasionally during last half of cooking time. (If it boils, the mixture may curdle; if so, just beat with beater until smooth.) Stir in food coloring and lime peel. Cool until mixture is thickened, but not set. Beat egg whites until frothy. Gradually beat in 2 tablespoons sugar, beating until mixture holds stiff peaks. Using same beater and a bowl that is large enough to combine all filling ingredients, beat cream until thickened. Fold cooled gelatin mixture and egg white mixture into cream. Pour into pastry shell. Refrigerate at least 4 hours or until served.

                               9-inch Pie

> **TIPS:** A crumb crust or coconut crust can also be used for pie.
>
> • If you need a little extra lime juice, just use the bottled juice or add lemon juice.

Pumpkin Pie (pastry shell as cooked in oven).

Convenience Foods Guide

Convenience foods are part of our daily lives. Many have been used as ingredients in the recipes throughout the entire cook book. We have gathered here some of the more frequently used foods as a handy reference guide. The chart is organized into the same food categories as the rest of the book. If you have a similar type of food, be it take out, canned, frozen, dry mix or leftover, refer to the guide to determine the timing, container and method for the same amount of food. If a convenience food, such as pudding, is accompanied by additional directions elsewhere in the book, there is a page reference in the chart.

PRODUCT	WEIGHT	COOKING CONTAINER	DIRECTIONS	STIR OR REARRANGE	COOK TIME	DONE-NESS	COMMENTS
APPETIZERS AND BEVERAGES Frozen cooked appetizers that need reheating can be heated in oven, but will not have crisp crusts. Frozen unbaked appetizers should be prepared conventionally for a crisp brown crust. See page 42 for chart on heating times for beverages.							
Frozen Crab Puffs (Batter dipped and fried crab snacks)	7 oz.	Paper plate	Arrange in circle on plate	None	1 min.	Hot	
Frozen Pizza Rolls	6 oz.	Paper plate (uncovered)	Arrange in circle on plate	None	2 min.	Hot	If you prefer a crisp crust, cook conventionally.
Cocoa Mix	1 cup	Cup or mug (uncovered)	Fill cup with milk. Heat. Stir in cocoa mix.	After heating	1¼ min.	Hot	See page 11 for additional directions.
Instant Coffee or Tea	1 cup	Cup or mug (uncovered)	Fill cup with cold water. Heat. Stir in coffee.	After heating	2¼-2½ min.	Boiling	See page 12 for additional directions.
Frozen Non-Dairy Creamer	1 pt. carton	Carton		Shake each rest period	45 sec.; rest; 45 sec.; rest; 45 sec.; rest; 45 sec.	Thawed	Use about 1 minute rest times.
Frozen Juices	6-oz. can	Juice can, then pitcher	Remove top. Heat to loosen. Empty into pitcher. Heat to soften.	None	15 sec. in can; 15 sec. in pitcher	Thawed	See page 17 for additional directions.

MAIN COURSES

PRODUCT	WEIGHT	COOKING CONTAINER	DIRECTIONS	STIR OR REARRANGE	COOK TIME	DONE-NESS	COMMENTS
TV Dinners Entrées (meat and potato)	9-9½ oz.	Foil tray*	Remove foil cover from tray and return tray to paper carton or cover with wax paper.	None	6-7 min.	Hot	
2-course Dinner	15-16 oz.	Foil tray*	″ ″	None	7 min.	Hot	
Foreign Dinners	16 oz.	Foil tray*	″ ″	None	6 min.	Hot	
Low Calorie Dinners	16 oz.	Foil tray*	″ ″	None	8 min.	Hot	
3-course Dinner	15-16 oz.	Foil tray*	″ ″	None	8 min.	Hot	

Soup spills easily without the cover, so you may prefer to heat in a small bowl first (2 min.) then heat dinner same as 2-course dinner.

PRODUCT	WEIGHT	COOKING CONTAINER	DIRECTIONS	STIR OR REARRANGE	COOK TIME	DONE-NESS	COMMENTS
Breakfasts	4½ oz.	Foil tray*	″ ″	None	2½-3 min.	Hot	

Use minimum time with French toast or Pancake breakfasts; maximum time with eggs and potato breakfasts.

*If food is removed from foil tray reduce time for breakfasts 15 seconds; for dinners reduce times 1 minute.

PRODUCT	WEIGHT	COOKING CONTAINER	DIRECTIONS	STIR OR REARRANGE	COOK TIME	DONE-NESS	COMMENTS
Canned Casserole Mixtures	8-oz. can (1 cup)	Dinner plate	Cover with over-turned bowl.	None	1½-2 min.	Hot	
	15-16-oz. can (2 cups)	1-quart casserole or serving dish (covered)	Empty into casserole.	Once	2½ min.	Hot	
	1½ lbs. or 24 oz. (3 cups)	1½-quart casserole (covered)	Empty into casserole.	Once	4 min.	Hot	
	2 lbs. 8 oz. or 40 oz. (5 cups)	2-quart casserole (covered) or serving dish	Empty into casserole.	Once	7 min.	Hot	

PRODUCT	WEIGHT	COOKING CONTAINER	DIRECTIONS	STIR OR REARRANGE	COOK TIME	DONE-NESS	COMMENTS
MAIN COURSES—Continued							
Casserole Mixes (with freeze-dried meats)	About 6½ oz.	1½-quart (covered)	Combine mix with additions on package directions.	Occasionally	12-14 min. let stand 5 min.	Noodles about tender	
Casserole Mixes (you add ground beef)	About 3½ oz.	1½-quart (covered)	Crumble ground beef and sprinkle with seasoning packet from mix. Cook. Add remaining ingredients and additions on package directions, reducing liquid by about ½ cup.	Occasionally	½ lb. meat — 3 min. 1 lb. meat — 5 min. Casserole 7-10 min.	Done	If mixture is too thick, add additional liquid and heat.
Skillet Casserole Mixes — (you add ground beef)	12-18 oz.	2-quart (covered)	" " reducing liquid by about ¼ cup.	Occasionally	1 lb. meat — 5 min. Casserole 7 min.	Done	If mixture is too thick, add additional liquid and heat.
FISH AND SEAFOOD							
Frozen precooked and breaded Fish Sticks	8 oz.	Paper plate (uncovered)	Arrange spoke fashion.	None	Cook 1 min.; rest; cook 2 min.	Hot	See recipe for Fishwiches, page 113.
Frozen precooked and breaded Scallops, Fish or Shrimp	7 oz.	Paper plate or towel	Arrange in circle.	None	1½ min.	Hot	
Frozen Fish with Sauce	11 oz.	Shallow foil packing tray with cooking film cover	Remove from paper carton; leave in foil tray with cooking film cover.	Once	8 min.	Done	If removed from foil, cook covered, about 6 minutes.
MEATS AND POULTRY							
Frozen meat loaf	1½ lbs.	1½-quart (8x4) loaf dish	Remove from foil pan; cover with wax paper.	None	Cook 8 min.; rest 5 min.; cook 5 min.; stand 5 min.	Done	To make your own, see Meat Loaf directions on page 73.
Frozen cooked barbecued ribs	2 lbs.	Plastic container, then serving platter	When edges are softened, transfer to serving platter. Cover with wax paper.	Twice	1 min. transfer 6 min.	Hot	
Frozen stuffed cabbage rolls	14 oz.	1-quart casserole (covered)	Remove from foil container.	Once	8 min.	Hot	
Frozen shortribs of beef	11½ oz.	1½-quart (covered)	Remove from foil container.	Twice	9-10 min.	Hot	Used in Shortribs of Beef Italienne, page 82.
Frozen macaroni, beef and tomatoes	11½ oz.	1-quart (covered)	Remove from foil container.	Twice	7-8 min.	Hot	Used in Pizza Casserole, page 75.
Frozen Sloppy Joe Sauce with Beef	26 oz.	2-quart (covered)	Remove from foil container.	Twice	9-10 min.	Hot	Used in Simple Stuffed Green Peppers, page 73.
Take Out Meats	4 servings (1-1½ lbs.)	Serving plates (uncovered; with sauce, covered)	Place larger pieces toward outside of plate.	None	5-6 min.	Hot	
	1 serving	Serving plate (uncovered; with sauce, covered)		None	45 sec. to 1 min.	Hot	
Vienna Sausages	5-oz. can	Plate (uncovered)	Arrange on plate.	None	45 sec.	Hot	
Frozen battered and cooked chicken	17¼ oz.	Plate (uncovered)	Remove from foil pan and arrange on plate with larger sides toward outside.	Once	6 min.	Hot	

PRODUCT	WEIGHT	COOKING CONTAINER	DIRECTIONS	STIR OR REARRANGE	COOK TIME	DONE-NESS	COMMENTS
MEATS AND POULTRY—Continued							
Frozen creamed chicken	6½ oz.	2-cup casserole (covered)	Remove from foil.	Twice	5-6 min.	Hot	
EGGS AND CHEESE							
Frozen Cheese Ravioli in Tomato Sauce	12½ oz.	1-quart casserole (covered)	Remove from foil container.	Once	5 min.	Hot	
Macaroni and Cheese Sauce Mix	7¼ oz.	2-quart (covered)	Combine all ingredients as directed on package.	Occasionally	10 min.; stand 5 min.	Macaroni tender	Used in Tomato Macaroni and Cheese, page 104.
Frozen Macaroni and Cheese	12 oz.	1-quart (covered)	Remove from foil.	Twice	7-8 min.	Hot	
Frozen Welsh Rarebit	10 oz.	1-quart casserole (covered)	Remove from foil container.	Twice	7-8 min.	Hot	Stir or beat until smooth before serving.
SOUP							
Canned soups	10½ oz.	2 or 3 soup bowls (covered)	Divide soup among bowls adding water as directed on can.	None	3-4 min.	Hot	For other amounts see page 20.
Dehydrated soup mix	1 envelope	4-cup measure (uncovered)	Combine with liquid as directed on package.	Twice	2-3 min.; stand 5 min.	Boils	For more information, see page 108.
Frozen soups	10 oz.		Add liquid as directed on can.	Occasionally	5-6 min.	Heated through	See Speedy Shrimp Sauce, page 133, for directions on removing frozen soup from can.
SANDWICHES							
Frozen English muffin halves with Ham and Cheese topping	10 oz. (4 halves)	Paper plate (uncovered)	Arrange on plates.	None	4 halves — 3½ to 4 min.	Hot	
Frozen Corn Dogs (batter dipped and fried wieners)	12½ oz. (5 hot dogs)	Paper plate (uncovered)	Arrange on plates.		1 — 1 min. 2 — 1½ min. 4 — 2 min. 5 — 2¼ min.	Hot	
Frozen Reuben Sandwiches	9 oz. (2 sandwiches)	Paper plates	Remove plastic covering. Place on 2 plates.	None	2½ min.	Hot	Filling for frozen sandwiches should be thinly sliced to heat filling without overcooking bread.
MEAL ACCOMPANIMENTS **VEGETABLES** — See pages 114-125, for cooking fresh and frozen vegetables other than these.							
Canned vegetables	8-oz. can (1 cup)	Serving plate or dish	Cover with overturned bowl.	None	1½-2 min.		
	12-oz. can (1½ cups)	2 or 3-cup bowl (covered)	Drain part of liquid. If desired, add seasonings before heating.	Once	2 min.	Hot	
	15-oz. can (2 cups)	1-quart bowl (covered)	″ ″	Once	2½ min.	Hot	
Mashed Potato Flakes	1½ cups	1½-quart (covered)	Follow package directions, heating water, butter and salt in oven.	None	2-3 min.	Boils	See Savory Potatoes, page 124.
Scalloped Potatoes Mix	5⅛ oz.	3-quart (covered)	Combine ingredients on package directions.	Occasionally	14-16 min.	Potatoes tender	Large casserole needed to prevent boiling over.

PRODUCT	WEIGHT	COOKING CONTAINER	DIRECTIONS	STIR OR REARRANGE	COOK TIME	DONE-NESS	COMMENTS
VEGETABLES — Continued							
Frozen Tater Tots or Tri Taters	16 oz.	Paper plate or paper towel lined plate (uncovered)	Place on paper plate.	None	5-6 min.	Hot	
	8 oz.	"	Place on paper plate.	None	2-3 min.	Hot	
Frozen French fries or Shoestring potatoes	16 oz.	Paper plate or paper towel lined plate	Place on paper plate.	None	5-6 min.	Hot	If you prefer crisp potatoes, prepare conventionally.
Frozen Baked Stuffed Potatoes	6 oz. (2 halves)	Shallow baking dish	Cover with wax paper.	None	7 min.	Hot	To make your own, see page 123.
Frozen Batter fried Onion Rings	16 oz. (30-32 rings)	Paper plate (uncovered)	Place on paper plate.	None	2 min. for 8 rings	Hot	For crisp onion rings, prepare conventionally.

BREADS — See page 127 for reheating and thawing baked breads, page 128 for cooking quick bread mixes and page 129 for thawing and cooking frozen bread dough.

PRODUCT	WEIGHT	COOKING CONTAINER	DIRECTIONS	STIR OR REARRANGE	COOK TIME	DONE-NESS	COMMENTS
Thawing Frozen Coffee Cake	11 oz.	Serving plate (uncovered)	Remove from foil container.		45 sec.; rest; 1 min.	Warm	Use about 30 sec. rest period.
Thawing Baked Frozen Bread	4 slices	Paper towel (uncovered)	Arrange in single layer.	None	10 sec.; rest 15 sec.; 10 sec.	Thawed	Remaining bread can be left frozen.

RICE AND NOODLES — See page 132 for other basic cooking methods and times.

PRODUCT	WEIGHT	COOKING CONTAINER	DIRECTIONS	STIR OR REARRANGE	COOK TIME	DONE-NESS	COMMENTS
Noodles Romanoff Mix	6¼ oz.	2-quart (covered)	Combine mix with 1½ cups water and ½ cup milk.	Occasionally	10 min.	Noodles tender	See Ham Romanoff recipe, page 83.
Frozen Cooked Rice	10 oz.	Pouch	Make small slit in top of bag.	Move toward outside edge of pouch	5 min.	Hot	

SAUCES

PRODUCT	WEIGHT	COOKING CONTAINER	DIRECTIONS	STIR OR REARRANGE	COOK TIME	DONE-NESS	COMMENTS
Frozen Sauces	8 oz.	1½-cup bowl or pitcher	Remove from foil pouch. Cover if convenient.	Twice	2½-3 min.	Hot	
Canned Sauces	8 oz. can (1 cup)	1½-cup bowl or pitcher	Cover if convenient.	Once	1¾ min.	Hot	
Gravy Mix	⅝ oz.	2-cup measure (uncovered)	Additions as directed on package.	Occasionally	2 min.	Boils	Used in Turkey Buns, page 109
Hollandaise Sauce Mix	⅝ oz.	2-cup measure (uncovered)	Additions as directed on package.	3 times	2½ min.	Boils	Used in Ham-Asparagus Hollandaise recipe, page 86

OTHER

PRODUCT	WEIGHT	COOKING CONTAINER	DIRECTIONS	STIR OR REARRANGE	COOK TIME	DONE-NESS	COMMENTS
Flavored Gelatin	3 oz.	1-quart bowl (uncovered)	Combine gelatin and 1 cup water. Cook. Add 1 cup cold water.	Occasionally	2 min.	Dissolve	See Pineapple Cheese Salad, page 131.
Butter, Melting	1-4 tbsp. ¼-½ cup ½-1 cup				15 sec. 30 sec. 45 sec.	Melted Melted Melted	
Butter Softening	½ cup				5 sec.; rest; 5 sec.; rest; 5 sec.	Softened	See page 13 for more directions.

DESSERTS
Fruits, Sauces and Topping

PRODUCT	WEIGHT	COOKING CONTAINER	DIRECTIONS	STIR OR REARRANGE	COOK TIME	DONE-NESS	COMMENTS
Frozen Fruit	10 oz. carton	Carton and serving dish	Remove one end if metal. Heat to loosen. Empty into serving dish, breaking apart fruit. Heat to thaw.	After each cook period	30 sec. in carton 30 sec. in bowl	Thawed	See page 16 for more directions and other types of containers.

PRODUCT	WEIGHT	COOKING CONTAINER	DIRECTIONS	STIR OR REARRANGE	COOK TIME	DONE-NESS	COMMENTS
Fruits, Sauces and Topping — Continued							
Ice Cream Topping		Jar if less than half full; otherwise 2-cup measure or pitcher (uncovered)	Remove metal lid.	After heating	45 sec.	Bubbles	If full jar is heated, it will boil over.
Frozen Whipped Topping	4½ oz. carton	Plastic carton	Remove cover so you can see if it starts to melt.	Twice	5 sec.; stir; 5 sec.; stir	Thawed	Watch times carefully as it is easy to melt.
PUDDINGS AND CUSTARDS							
Custard Mix and Pudding Mix	3 oz.	4-cup measure (uncovered)	Package additions and directions.	Occasionally	5 min.	Boils	See page 23 for more directions.
Frozen Pudding	17½ oz.	Plastic carton with cover		Twice	1 min.; stir; ½ min.; stir	Thawed	
Frozen Individual Puddings	17½ oz. (4 containers)	Plastic package (uncovered)	Remove foil cover; cook; stir to distribute heat.	After heating	1 container — 15 sec. 2 containers — 30 sec.	Thawed Thawed	
Danish Dessert	4 oz.	4-cup measure	Add 2 cups water.	Occasionally	5 min.	Boil 1 minute	
COOKIES AND CANDIES — See page 145 for cooking bar mixes.							
Frozen Brownies (Frosted)	13 oz.	Serving plate (uncovered)	Remove from foil container.	None	10 sec.; rest; 10 sec.; rest; 10 sec.	Thawed	Use about 1 minute rest periods.
Frozen Cookies or Brownies	1 cookie or unfrosted brownie	Paper napkin	Place on napkin.	None	30 sec.	Warm	More directions, page 36.
Warm Cookies	1 cookie	Paper napkin	Place on napkin.	None	10 sec.	Warm	See page 22 for other amounts.
CAKE See page 149 for cooking cake and gingerbread mixes.							
Warm Cake Squares (without frosting)	1 square	Paper napkin	Place on napkin.	None	15 sec.	Warm	See page 22 for other amounts.
Frozen Cake (without frosting)	1 square	Paper napkin or plate	Place on napkin.		15 sec.	Thawed	For warm cake squares, see page 36.
Frozen Layer Cake with Frosting	17 oz.	Styrofoam tray (uncovered)	Remove from paper container.	None	10 sec.; rest 15 sec.; 5 sec.	Thawed	Be careful with frosted cakes as the frosting heats first and will slide off the cake as it starts to melt.
	1 serving	Plate	Remainder can be returned to freezer.	None	5 sec.; rest 15 sec.; 5 sec.	Thawed	
Frozen Cheesecake	17 oz.	Serving plate (uncovered)	Remove from foil container.	None	15 sec.; rest; 15 sec.; rest; 15 sec.; rest.; 15 sec.	Thawed	
	1 serving	Plate	Remainder can be returned to freezer.	None	20 sec.; rest 10 sec.	Thawed	
PIES — See page 156 for cooking frozen uncooked fruit pies.							
Frozen Cream Pies	8 or 9-inch pie	Glass pie plate (uncovered)	Remove from foil pan.	None	10 sec.; rest; 10 sec.	Thawed	
Warm Pie Slice	1 serving	Plate	Place on serving plate.	None	15 sec.	Warm	For other amounts, see page 154.
Frozen Cooked Fruit Pies	9-inch pie	Glass pie plate	Remove from foil pan.	None	5 min.; rest; 3 min.	Warm	For a crisp crust, place in 450° oven for last 3 minutes.

More Ideas

Now that you have become more familiar with your microwave oven and how it can help your meal preparation, here are some suggestions for other uses of your oven. Let your imagination and needs be a guide to using the oven in your own life.

MORE IDEAS FOR USING YOUR OVEN

- Warming a baby's bottle or jar of baby food for about 15-20 seconds (without the jar top).
- Heating a damp cloth for a hot compress (15-20 seconds).
- Warming lotion or baby oil (10-15 seconds).
- Dry bread cubes for stuffing (stirring occasionally).
- Curl false eyelashes . . . wet and wrap around pencil, wrap with tissue and heat (20-30 seconds).
- Dry flowers for a pot pourri (in cycles).
- Warm oil to clean and condition boots, guns . . . (15-20 seconds).
- Heat damp cloth beneath postage stamp for steam removal (20-30 seconds).
- Remove coffee or tea stains by boiling stain remover and water in coffee cup.
- Pre-shrink about a yard of material.
- Dry a wet newspaper (15-30 seconds).

When canning fruits, the mixture inside the jar needs to reach a near boiling temperature. This can easily be done in the microwave oven. Because of the amount of food, the metal lids and bands can be on the jars during cooking. Low-acid foods like vegetables are not recommended for canning in the microwave oven because they need to reach a higher temperature that is possible only with pressure cooking. The times may vary slightly with the type and size of fruit, but the bubbling of the syrup should be a good guide for canning any type of fruit or tomato. The rest period is necessary to assure getting the fruit hot enough without the syrup boiling out.

CANNING FRUIT

If you are not familiar with conventionally recommended methods of home canning, please read a reliable booklet before proceeding with microwave canning. The only foods recommended in microwave are those ordinarily using the boiling water bath method. Do not attempt to can foods that require a pressure cooker.

Pint jars work best in the oven and you can cook from 1 to 6 jars at a time. Follow basic canning procedures for preparing fruits. To prepare the syrup, place ¼ cup sugar and ⅓ cup hot water in each pint jar. Place in oven and cook, uncovered, until mixture boils (about 45 seconds for each jar); stir, fill jars with fruit to 1-inch from top. Syrup should come to 1-inch from top; if additional syrup is needed, add hot water. Clean top of jar. Top with metal vacuum lid and metal screw band. Place in oven and cook until syrup just begins to bubble (see Timing Guide below). Turn off oven and let stand 1 minute. Cook until syrup again bubbles (it may be necessary to remove some jars before others, but syrup in each jar should bubble). Remove jars and place out of draft to cool. After 12 hours, remove metal bands, clean jars and store in a cool, dark place. Jars are sealed when vacuum lid is depressed in center.

TIMING GUIDE:

1 pint — cook 1 minute, 15 seconds; let stand 1 minute; cook 20 seconds

3 pints — cook 4 minutes; let stand 1 minute; cook 1 minute

6 pints — cook 8 minutes; let stand 1 minute; cook 1½ minutes

Index